THE INSTITUTIONAL APPROACH TO LABOUR AND DEVELOPMENT

T0330939

EADI BOOK SERIES 17

The Institutional Approach to Labour and Development

edited by

GERRY RODGERS, KLÁRÁ FÓTI
and
LAURIDS LAURIDSEN

FRANK CASS • LONDON

in association with

EADI The European Association of Development Research
and Training Institutes (EADI), Geneva

First published in 1996 in Great Britain by
FRANK CASS & CO. LTD.
Newbury House, 900 Eastern Avenue,
London IG2 7HH

and in the United States of America by
FRANK CASS
c/o ISBS
5602 N.E. Hassalo Street
Portland, Oregon 97213-3644

Transferred to Digital Printing 2004

Copyright © 1996 EADI and authors

British Library Cataloguing in Publication Data
A catalogue record for this book
is available from the British Library

ISBN 0 7146 4242 8 (paperback)

Library of Congress Cataloging-in-Publication Data
The institutional approach to labour and development / edited by Gerry
Rodgers, Klárá Fóti and Laurids Lauridsen.
p. cm. — (EADI-book series : 17)
"Published in collaboration with the European Association of
Development Research and Training Institutes (EADI), Geneva."
Includes bibliographical references.
ISBN 0-7146-4242-8 (pbk.)
1. Labor—Developing countries—Congresses. I. Rodgers, Gerry.
II. Fóti, Klárá. III. Lauridsen, Laurids S. IV. European
Association of Development Research and Training Institutes.
V. Series.
HD8943.I54 1995
331'.09172'4 to B&E; se10'subj 10-18-95; se03 10—dc20   95-44532
                                                            CIP

Typeset by Regent Typesetting, London

Contents

Preface

After the 1990 General Conference of the European Association of Development Research and Training Institutes (EADI) in Oslo, it was decided to set up a Working Group on Labour, Employment and Development. Over the period 1990–93, around fifty researchers from different European institutions have been associated with its work at one time or another. The editors of the present volume were convenor (Rodgers) and co-convenors (Lauridsen and Fóti) of the group.

The group met first in Geneva in November 1991, with support from the International Institute for Labour Studies, and decided to concentrate its attention on the relationships between institutional change on the one hand, and the mobilization and exclusion of labour in development on the other. There are major transformations in progress in both political and economic systems in many parts of the world. These transformations involve institutional changes with considerable implications for labour and employment, implications which are not always adequately perceived or understood. Work under three headings was thought to be important:

The nature of the institutional transformations in progress

Much institutional transformation is related to economic liberalization, which may take the form of a shift from state to market (privatization, deregulation, reduced reliance on central planning or on bureaucratic central control), changes in the relationship with the world economy, new forms of industrial organization at national and international level (informalization, globalization), a restructuring of labour relations and of labour organization. Less visible changes in underlying social institutions may also be important. The aim of the group was to identify and understand those aspects of institutional change of most importance for labour.

Processes of labour mobilization and exclusion and how they underlie development patterns

This includes in particular, the mechanisms leading to unemployment and other forms of labour underutilization and inadequate job access; the different forms of labour and the ways they contribute to or are created by processes of mobilization and development; mechanisms for the creation and use (or non-use) of skill; patterns of labour mobility. The aim was to better understand the mechanisms determining labour utilization and unemployment, stressing the ways they interact with patterns and institutional frameworks of development.

The nature of the linkage between institutional transformation and labour mobilization

One such linkage relates to the way economic restructuring is associated with significant changes in labour market institutions such that certain groups of workers are excluded, creating open unemployment. Another linkage would be the informalization of production relationships affecting the way labour is mobilized. These are examples of the effects of institutional transformation on labour. At the same time, patterns of labour use create or transform institutional structures. Labour market outcomes affect the system of labour organization (trade unionism or other forms), or labour underutilization may be associated with particular social and cultural institutions for the sharing of income or the controlling of job access. It was considered that both conceptual and empirical work were required to better understand these relationships.

These issues were addressed in a workshop on "Institutional Change and the Mobilization or Exclusion of Labour in Development", held in Göttingen at the Georg-August University in November 1992, with support from the Volkswagen Foundation and the International Institute for Labour Studies. Twelve papers were presented and discussed. Revised versions of most of these papers, along with several new papers, were then discussed in a Working Group meeting held during the EADI General Conference in Berlin in September 1993.

The present publication is one outcome of this work. It does not cover all the ground explored by the Working Group; in particular, the group paid considerable attention to the issue of labour in transformation in Eastern Europe, a topic which would merit more in-depth investigation from an institutionalist perspective, and where further empirical research would be desirable. The present volume is a selection, from the material presented to the meetings of the group, of articles which are representative of the institutional approach in development research, showing its relevance to the analysis of labour issues, indicating what sorts of institutions are important and why, and offering important pointers to priorities for future work in this area. Responsibility for views and opinions expressed in these articles remains, of course, with their authors.

The editors would like to thank the EADI, and particularly Claude Auroi and Janine Rodgers of the EADI secretariat, and Meine Pieter van Dijk of the Publications Committee, for providing the institutional framework which made it possible to undertake this work. We would like to particularly thank Jutta Hebel for hosting and organizing the workshop in Göttingen. We would also like to thank a number of anonymous referees for comments on earlier drafts of the chapters of this book. And we would like to thank all those who have participated in the meetings of the Working Group and contributed to its endeavours.

Gerry Rodgers, Laurids Lauridsen, Klárá Fóti
Geneva, August 1994

Introduction

GERRY RODGERS, LAURIDS LAURIDSEN
and KLÁRÁ FÓTI[1]

This book is about social institutions, and about how the analysis of institutions contributes to an understanding of development. While institutions are ubiquitous, their effects on labour are particularly obvious. Labour markets, labour relations and employment patterns respond to institutional forces, and thereby shape development paths and determine how different groups benefit from economic growth.

But institutions are also diverse. Their nature and their effects depend on economic, social and historical context. Because so many institutions are specific to particular situations, it is hard, and perhaps undesirable, to isolate general rules or broader conclusions. But the opposite risk is one of description without explanation. Even if general models are a chimera, it is important to understand the ways in which institutions emerge and change in interaction with other aspects of economic and social transformation.

This book takes up the challenge. By juxtaposing theory and empirical evidence from a variety of sources, it attempts to demonstrate that institutions are important, that their role needs to be analysed if we are to understand social and economic patterns, and that it is possible to explore these issues empirically. A collective effort, it brings together the work of economists and sociologists in research programmes in a number of European institutions concerned with development, in Germany, the UK, Switzerland, Hungary and Denmark. Most of the research reported here is based on work in Asia, but the intention is not a systematic analysis of Asian labour institutions. Rather the aim is to contribute to a broader debate on institutions in development on the basis of Asian experiences.

The first chapter, by Rodgers, reviews some of the methodological and theoretical issues raised by an institutional approach. The paper evaluates alternative ways in which institutions can be defined, and critically assesses some of the schools of thought which have developed around institutional analysis. It then suggests a number of research priorities: the interactions of institutions with macro-economic growth patterns, the institutions for mobilizing labour within enterprises and on urban and rural labour markets, the roles of different actors.

There follow two chapters, by Fleming and Wangel and by Lauridsen, which present and discuss institutional approaches, especially with respect to the position of labour, in two East Asian countries at different levels of development. Both contributions adopt historical-structural versions of the new institutionalism, i.e. take an approach which uses the collective as the unit of analysis, considers theory as place- and time-specific and aims to offer theoretically-informed explanations that illuminate the observed social and economic patterns.

Daniel Fleming and Arne Wangel's chapter on 'Models of management-labour relations and labour institutions in Malaysia' studies a broad spectrum of institutionalized forms of regulation of management-labour relations. They demonstrate how the model of management-labour relations found in Nordic transnational companies differs from the ones found in Japanese, American and other European TNCs, and how there is a mismatch between the Nordic state-capital-labour model and the configuration of the Malaysian national development model. Laurids Lauridsen's contribution, 'Labour institutions and flexible capitalism in Taiwan', applies the workplace regime concept developed by Burawoy and Deyo in order to demonstrate how particular labour institutions have formed a central part of Taiwan's successful flexible niche industrial strategy. Moreover, he explores the possible links between the role of labour and the two ongoing processes of capital accumulation and political democratization.

The next three chapters look at labour market arrangements in India. Arjan de Haan's contribution, 'Labour recruitment in an Indian industry – Historical roots of a labour surplus', is concerned with understanding the institutions underlying the mobilization of labour for industrial development. He shows how these institutions have had both expected and unforeseen effects, and especially how their functioning has become transformed as the urban economy shifted from labour shortage to surplus. The behaviour of inter-mediaries in the labour recruitment process was as important as the formal institutions, while the nature of the rules providing formal protection was such as to exclude large groups of the population, notably women, from labour market access. Ben Rogaly, 'Explaining diverse labour arrangements in rural South Asia', extends the story to rural India. He shows that neither neo-classical nor Marxian models provide an adequate explanation of the institutional structures of rural labour markets, and in particular their diversity. To explain the latter, one important factor is the advantage to employers of fragmented labour markets; more generally, he argues, institutional analysis has to be grounded in detailed local contexts, rather than attempting to support some general theory. The following chapter, 'Eastward Ho! Leap-frogging and seasonal migration in Eastern India', by the authors of the two preceding papers, applies these ideas to a particular labour phenomenon: labour

2

migration. Different streams of migration intersect in Eastern India, and to explain them it is necessary to fall back on a broader understanding of institutional mechanisms, the interests they serve, and the mechanisms by which they are controlled.

The transformation of labour institutions in the specific circumstances of transition from a planned to a market economy is considered in the last three chapters, which examine the situation in China, alone or in a comparative framework. Two of these contributions offer insights into recent developments within the Chinese labour system. In her chapter, 'Institutional change in an enterprise-based society and its impact on labour. The case of the People's Republic of China', Jutta Hebel focuses on current changes in enterprises or work units called *danwei* which are characteristic of urban society, whereas Flemming Christiansen's contribution, 'Chinese labour in transition 1978–92', gives a more general overview of the impacts of recent reforms on labour. The former contribution suggests that as a result of reform measures so far, the role of the State has changed to a considerable extent and the concept of an enterprise-based society has lost its meaning. Christiansen's chapter warns against premature conclusions from these and other recent developments, arguing that they have not resulted in a capitalistic labour market as yet. A final chapter by Flemming Christiansen and Klárá Fóti, 'Transitions from the public to the private: Different strategies for the labour market in the transforming Chinese and Hungarian economies', emphasizes the major differences between countries in transition. Through a comparison of changes in labour institutions in China and in Hungary, the authors can point to divergent outcomes of policy measures which are superficially seen as comparable. The similarities of institutional change in different cultural and economic situations are sometimes striking, but the ways in which institutional, economic and social mechanisms interact can vary enormously, and so also the economic and social outcomes.

NOTE

1. Respectively International Institute for Labour Studies, Geneva; International Development Studies, Roskilde University, Denmark; and Institute for World Economics, Budapest.

3

1

Labour Institutions and Economic Development: Issues and Methods

GERRY RODGERS[1]

INTRODUCTION

Development economics, as it emerged as a branch in its own right in the 1950s and 1960s, was very much concerned with institutional transformation. The classic development literature – Arthur Lewis or Gunnar Myrdal, for instance – is rich in institutional detail. Development was seen as a process of institutional change, as 'traditional' institutions were supplanted by modern, each with their own complement of economic and social mechanisms. The co-existence of differing systems of economic and social organization, each with its own rules for the creation and distribution of value, gave rise to models of dualistic development which implied the presence of powerful institutional forces. The diversity of systems of social organization demonstrated that exchange could occur within a variety of alternative institutional frameworks. Given the normative approach of much of the development literature, the question was which system was most likely to induce economic development. Promoting development implied promoting the institutions to support development. Institutions then came to be viewed in a very concrete way: banks to extend rural credit, local planning infrastructures, markets, community organizations, agricultural extension services. A telling example is the entry for 'institutional development' in the index of an influential World Bank publication on rural development from the mid 1970s (Lele 1975); it reads, 'see Program administration'.

But alongside this positivist approach, much of the development literature has been built around a different concept of institutions, involving questions of the underlying economic and social rules and structures, implying an interest in differences across societies in goals and patterns of behaviour; less by economists than by other social scientists, of course, but much work has also been done in a multi-disciplinary framework. Sometimes the interpretation is that such institutions are obstacles to development – e.g. that culture and traditions inhibit commitment to wage work; alternatively, many authors reach the conclusion it is the definition of development in terms of economic goals that needs to be reconceptualised. But the point for this paper is that they imply a view of social institutions as part of the framework which determines social and economic behaviour. Understanding development implies understanding institutions, both in the sense that institutions determine the nature and pace of development, and in a more fundamental sense that institutions and institutional change are embedded in the very concept of development.

The institution-oriented approach to development economics seems to have become less influential in the 1980s. Perhaps a certain disillusionment set in, because of the economic failures of alternative development models. The political hegemony of mainstream, hands-off, institution-free economics also played a role, and as a result the identity of development economics within the broader discipline became less distinct. Development was increasingly seen as the outcome of general economic laws, the global replication of the market relationships thought to prevail in the industrialized North. The failure of central planning reinforced this trend. Not that it was truly believed that the economies of industrialized countries were institution-free; rather that they had a specific, minimal set of institutions which facilitated market exchange – the physical facilities of markets and the legal framework which permitted them to operate efficiently. The failure of development was due to a failure to adopt such institutions, or to a failure to sweep away social structures and behaviour patterns which interfered with the free operation of markets.

But while this message was being spread to the Third World and to the reforming countries of Eastern Europe, a renewed concern with institutions was manifesting itself within the economics discipline. The problem was that institutions did persist, they affected economic outcomes, and treating them in the traditional way as imperfections causing failure to reach market equilibrium was found unsatisfactory by many economists. There is an increasing credibility gap between the mainstream neoclassical economic literature, concerned with efficient exchange between rational, utility maximizing individuals, and the real world problems, central to development, of unemployment, poverty, economic dynamism, entrepreneurship, of motivation and participation.

INSTITUTIONS

There are many ways and levels at which one can consider institutions. One definition is that 'institutions are the humanly devised constraints that structure political, economic and social interaction' (North 1991). Others refer to 'rules of a society or of organizations that facilitate co-ordination among people by helping them form expectations which each person can reasonably hold in dealing with others' (Ruttan and Hayami); or 'complexes of norms of behaviour that persist over time, by serving collectively valued purposes'

5

(Uphoff) (both cited in Nabli and Nugent 1989b, p. 7). All of these seem to imply some purpose or function. Veblen's more neutral definition, 'settled habits of thought common to the generality of men' (1909, cited in Hodgson 1992a), makes regularities in behaviour the starting point for understanding institutions. Upon these regularities may be built organizations – social organizations such as firms, associations and administrations – but it is the regularities themselves which are the building blocks. They may be formalized in written rules, or merely, as Veblen puts it, reflect habits. Some may be quite deliberate, a social mechanism deliberately designed for a social purpose reflected a particular set of interests and a particular pattern of cognition; others may be – apparently – accidental outcomes of the aggregation of individual behaviour or even exogenous.

The way labour is used and remunerated is a crucial aspect of institutional economics, and institutions of many sorts are correspondingly important in the labour market. The purchase of labour time is usually part of a much more complex system of relationships, involving not just the payment of a wage in return for a number of hours worked, but also levels of commitment and motivation, work intensity, a continuing relation over time (since most work occurs in continuing jobs), control over the pace and content of work, a working environment, a social position, an income level and a set of consumption standards, etc. These relationships are controlled or affected by institutions at various levels. The legal or contractual framework determines rights and obligations; Veblen's 'habits of thought' are clearly crucial, in determining whether workers accept industrial discipline, but also in determining employers' attitudes to labour and whether negotiation or dialogue form part of the accepted mode of behaviour; organizations at different levels – firms, unions, labour inspectorates, pension funds – all play an important role. Underlying social rules and behaviour patterns will also determine who obtains access to what sorts of jobs, and social hierarchies will affect the ranking of jobs and the levels of income which they generate. All of these I am calling labour institutions, i.e. the social institutions which affect or derive from the incorporation of labour in production, the remuneration and working conditions of labour, and associated social and income guarantees.

These labour institutions can be conveniently visualized in five categories: 1) organizations, 2) formal labour market institutions, 3) informal labour market institutions, 4) underlying formal social rules, and 5) underlying informal social rules.

1. Organizations

These are social bodies based on a co-ordinated set of rules, having a separate existence and usually an explicit purpose. Labour institutions under this heading include trade unions and other organizations of labour, and similarly organizations of employers; firms; State bodies aimed at labour processes (e.g. the labour inspectorate, employment exchanges); training organizations; etc.

2. Formal labour market institutions

These are structured, usually written rules controlling labour use, generally with formal sanctions or methods of enforceability. The most basic such institution is the employment contract which defines the nature of jobs, the conditions under which they are done and the rights and obligations attached to them. Not all such contracts are explicit and formal, of course, and they never cover all aspects of the work situation. Labour legislation more generally (some of which applies to employment contracts) falls under the heading of formal labour market institutions, but so do voluntarily agreed collective bargaining systems, rules for wage determination, rules for job hierarchies and career progression within firms, rules for access to jobs (e.g. educational qualifications).

3. Informal labour market institutions

We may not be able to understand the operation of formal labour market institutions if we do not understand the underlying informal institutions. These include aspects of employment contracts which are implicit, based upon social deference or control, or on the internalization by workers and employers of habits, procedures and patterns of behaviour in the workplace. Informal mechanisms limit access to jobs and income opportunities to particular population groups, for instance discriminating against women. Informal networks of information may be important in controlling access to jobs. The transmission of skills and their recognition by employers also rely heavily on informal learning processes. Informal institutions, again based heavily on the control of information and skills, are important in determining the extent of self-employment and the conditions under which it is performed. This is notably true of dependent self-employed workers such as sharecroppers, subcontractors and homeworkers. The linkage between different markets (credit, land and labour) equally involves an indirect and informal control over labour. Formal and informal institutions may co-exist and either complement or compete with each other. Assaad's (1991) investigation of formal and informal institutions in the Egyptian labour market shows written employment contracts alongside casual labour relationships, formal training alongside traditional apprenticeship, and trade unions alongside coffee houses; in each case the informal institution was in practice more important.

4. Underlying formal social rules

Behind the labour market institutions there are sets of other formal social institutions which have a direct bearing on the nature of employment relationships. The most basic concerns the system of rights within society, including property rights and the rules for the ownership and operation of firms; State-defined rights of individuals to income, to public goods, to subsistence; rights of expression, of association, of political activity. All of these determine the ways in which labour market institutions function. Property rights are obviously rather basic to the way productive organizations and hence jobs are created – indeed, jobs may be regarded as forms of property in some systems, and permanent jobs generally have some of the attributes of property. The formal entitlements of members of society to income, goods or services clearly affects their dependence on the labour market. Broader political, ethical and moral rights, and the system of justice by which they are enforced, affect both the recognition of authority and the ability of different groups to defend their interests.

5. Underlying informal social rules

The informal underlying rules are as important as the formal, encompassing values and norms, culture and ideology. They affect the roles and perceptions of particular social groups in the labour market (women; particular ethnic groups), affect the 'work ethic' and the social valuation of leisure, affect perceived needs for consumption. Household, kinship and community systems generate patterns of exchange and reciprocity, and affect the way labour is supplied. Religious precepts may serve as a way of strengthening commitment to labour, supporting a division of labour, or restricting benefits to a particular elite. These underlying social rules are the means by which patterns of behaviour are internalized, hierarchical relationships legitimized, social divisions of labour determined – all crucial if the labour market institutions and organizations are to function effectively.

Of course, labour institutions do not fall neatly into these five categories. Employment contracts involve elements from all five, even if they mainly fall under the second. The functioning of organizations depends on the formal and informal underlying rules on which they are based. Training and educational systems provide a useful illustration. At one level these are *organizations* – schools, or the school system as a whole, or training bodies – which directly affect employment and labour productivity. At a second level, the qualifications which educational systems provide (or at least the interpretation of those qualifications) are important *formal labour market institutions*, because they determine who has access to what sort of job according to well defined and often written rules. But the educational requirements for job access also change over time as those controlling particular segments of the job market defend their territory, implying that *informal labour market institutions* are also involved. And because education affects attitudes and perceptions, it also modifies the structure of labour supply through other institutional mechanisms (e.g. the widespread tendency for high levels of female education to be associated with high levels of female labour force participation). Education therefore plays a role through its effects on the *underlying informal social rules* as well. So intersecting taxonomies are involved. An annex to this chapter gives a list of labour institutions broken down in a different way, in terms of subject and function rather than analytical category.[2]

LABOUR INSTITUTIONS AND DEVELOPMENT: THEORETICAL OPTIONS

There is today a resurgence of interest in institutional economics. For instance, Veblen's pioneering work is receiving increasing attention again, and is particularly relevant for the analysis of labour institutions in development, notably his work on institutions within firms.[3] Veblen saw institutions as providing stabilization to economic systems in the short term, but also a mechanism for evolution; social change arose out of the conflict between new forms of production and social institutions representing the existing power relationship. Instead of a tendency towards equilibrium, there was an open-ended process of cumulative causation in institutional change, so that economic relationships had to be analysed in their historical context. But economic forces were important in determining which institutions emerged. An example, from Papola (1992), is the role of the 'jobber' in recruitment to organized industry in India. The jobber, an intermediary who supplied and managed labour, emerged because of a particular historical – colonial – context, but the success of this institution can be understood in terms of its contribution to efficiency once it had emerged. It then survived until new institutions emerged, as a result of changes in the economic and social environment, which successfully took over its functions. This illustrates the idea that the process of institutional change is not smooth, but can rather be characterized as 'punctuated equilibria' (Gould; see the discussion in Hodgson 1992a).

The question of the efficiency of institutions also underlies the recent development of the 'new institutional economics' (NIE) or 'neoinstitu-tionalist' school[4], built upon the importance of transactions costs in economic exchange (Coase 1960). Transactions costs include the costs of information and of enforcement of contracts. If information is perfect and all exchange is free of cost, under the assumptions of neo-classical economics economic systems would move rapidly to optimal equilibrium. But as soon as knowledge is incomplete and asymmetrical, agreements have to be arranged, monitored and enforced. To enter into agreements, agents have to have rights over economic resources, and these rights also have to be agreed and enforced. These mechanisms give rise to a range of formal and informal institutions. It is important to realize that while alternative institutional arrangements are possible, no economic exchange is institution-free; as a result, one should not compare outcomes under particular institutional conditions with the theoretical cost-free equilibrium (the Nirvana fallacy), but only with alternative institutional conditions. The primary logic of neoinstitutionalist economics is that there will be a tendency for more efficient institutions, in the sense of institutions which reduce transactions costs, to drive out less efficient institutions, through the effects of competition – rational, utility maximizing economic agents will seek new contractual forms which reduce transactions costs. This approach to institutional economics attempts not to replace mainstream neo-classical economics, but to 'modify or broaden the mainstream toolkit and then to use this broadened analytical framework to explain phenomena that had previously seemed impenetrable' (Nabli and Nugent 1989b, p. 10).

This basic idea gives rise to a rich set of theoretical propositions. In particular, it suggests a variety of ways in which institutions may interact with economic development. In societies where transactions take place at a personal level, the possibilities for cheating are limited so transactions costs are low, but production costs are high because of the small scale of operations. In contrast, under impersonal exchange production costs are reduced as a result of specialization, but transactions costs may be important (North 1989). In order to reduce such costs, third party enforcement becomes important, and this is used as a starting point for a theory of the state (Eggertsson 1990). Institutions which constrain participants to a determined pattern of behaviour may reduce transactions and information costs, as the need to seek information and monitor one's counterpart's behaviour is substantially reduced. This is true, for instance, of property rights, and of legal restrictions on contracts. But it is equally true of norms, values, ideology and custom which may generate solidarity, trust and co-operation. These relationships are seen as fundamental in development: 'Third World countries are poor because the institutional constraints define a set of payoffs to political/economic activity that do not encourage productive activity' (North 1990, p. 110).

A quite different institutionalist vision of development is represented by the 'Régulation' school, which also considers the interplay of multiple institutions in regulating the economic system. Here institutions are not only concerned with efficiency but also with control. Growth paths are necessarily based on particular forms of social control, notably in terms of the incorporation of labour in production, and particular patterns of accumulation, which again requires a framework for social action and co-ordination. This is institutionalist in the Veblen sense, in that development is open-ended; at any point of time, alternative sets of institutions can be envisaged, which may stabilize economic systems at different levels of economic activity, with different growth rates and with different patterns of distribution; see for instance typologies developed by Boyer (reported in Boyer 1994). There is a strong historical strand in this approach – institutional frameworks and their effects need to be studied in historical context, and outcomes are path-dependent, in the sense that history limits the range of choices. For instance, Dore's comparison of industrial relations systems in Japan, Sri Lanka, Mexico and Senegal (Dore 1979) shows how the choice of institutions was conditioned by the models which dominated at the international level at the time the systems were crystallizing at the national level.

The 'Régulation' school might be classified as macro-institutionalist, and the neoinstitutionalist school as micro-institutionalist, since the starting point of the Régulationists is societal and that of the neoinstitutionalists the individual. The difference is fundamental, but in practice it is difficult to maintain a clear distinction in these terms, for the macro-institutional picture depends on micro-level workplace relationships, while the micro-institutionalists require a theory of the state and North at least applies the model to broad historical patterns. Perhaps the crucial institution for both lies rather uncomfortably between the micro and the macro: the market. In a neo-institutionalist perspective, the market can be understood as a device to minimize transactions costs, and the institutional framework of the market – the rules, formal and informal, which govern its operation – are ultimately determined by efficiency in these terms. In a régulationist perspective, the function of the market in distributing power and in controlling economic processes is equally crucial. When market processes 'shape the capacities, values and desires of the exchanging parties' (Bowles 1991), and when they influence the definition and distribution of property rights, they modify the rules of the game in ways which need a macro-social framework for their analysis. Efficiency in a neoinstitutionalist sense will not do because the very meaning of efficiency depends on the way the market operates within society.

Another important difference is that a neo-institutionalist approach will tend to study the efficiency of specific institutions in partial isolation – the wage-fixing mechanism, property rights – whereas the Régulation approach looks at combinations and sets of institutions which underpin particular economic structures or particular patterns of development. Thus the Fordist model of development in industrialized countries is described as a combination of elements (involving particular types of organization of the firm, particular types of employment contracts, particular ways of regulating them, particular forms of social guarantee and of training, particular consumption norms, etc.) and not just in terms of the characteristics of the production line. 'Modern' sector production in many developing countries would be regarded as co-ordinated by a similar set of interlinked institutions. Of course, this implies that it is much less easy to advance simple, testable hypotheses under a Régulation model.

Labour institutions are important in all these approaches to institutional theory. For Veblen, workplace institutions were crucial; the organization of labour and of working arrangements within firms are common subjects for neo-institutionalist analysis; while in the Régulation approach, the 'wage labour nexus' is at the centre of the institutional structure of production. Labour issues lend themselves naturally to institutional analysis – witness the size of the industrial relations literature. Theories of dualism and of labour market segmentation may also be cast in institutional terms, as labour institutions vary in strength or nature across different parts of the production system and of the labour force, and this determines inequality in the quality and availability of jobs. The resulting structures (e.g. a particular stratification of the labour market in terms of contractual status) may themselves in turn be regarded as derived labour institutions. Segmentation may also make it possible to cheapen labour overall, by rewarding and co-opting those with market or political power, but discouraging solidarity between this group and the mass of workers. State regulation of labour conditions and institutionalized labour relations may apply to only a fraction of jobs (Portes 1990); labour markets may be fragmented, with very different sets of institutions governing jobs of different types (Harriss, Kannan and Rodgers 1990).

LABOUR INSTITUTIONS AND DEVELOPMENT: RESEARCH PRIORITIES

Addressing these issues opens up a substantial research agenda. In this section we consider some of the questions which arise at macro, meso and micro levels.

1. Labour institutions in the macro-economics of development

To understand the link between labour institutions on the one hand, and patterns of growth and distribution on the other, requires an analysis of how the system of institutions as a whole interacts with the macro-economy. Certain sets of institutions may be mutually complementary and may taken together define a 'growth regime', which encompasses a growth path and a pattern of distribution; this is the basic method adopted by the régulation school. Only certain combinations of institutions will be stable, but there may be several stable options for a given economy at a particular historical point. The challenge is to understand the emergence and evolution of systems of labour institutions and how they function in particular social, economic and historical contexts, and thence develop models of the growth paths which such institutional frameworks imply.

Methodologically there are several options. One is to attempt to distinguish growth regimes in the historical or regional experience of development in a single country; perhaps more fruitfully, to undertake in-depth paired comparisons of countries with similar experiences (in terms of institutional structures, political economies and external environments). Institutional interactions with development usually work themselves out over long periods of time, so historical analysis is required. The analysis has to take into account the broader political economy, such as the role of repression (especially of labour movements), or of alternative forms of democracy, or the nature of patronage relations (especially involving the state, and some groupings within industry and labour), since these clearly underlie many of the important labour institutions.

More general multi-country comparisons may permit the development of taxonomies of growth regimes, based on regularities and sets of relationships which recur in different environments. The latter would involve classifying countries or production systems in terms of major macro-economic variables – production, wage and profit shares, economic structure – as well as in terms of the dominant labour institutions, and no doubt also bringing in other major social and political institutions which interact strongly with labour institutions. Such an approach could provide a basis around which country experiences can be differentiated in a comparative framework.

These aggregate relationships between economic and institutional change may ultimately dominate the many more detailed ways in which particular labour institutions and particular aspects of development interact. Nevertheless, macro-level patterns depend on meso-level relationships which also need to be explored. The meso level refers to the study of the functioning of institutions at a sectoral or intermediate level. There are several possible priorities here, including labour market structure, institutions for the mobilization of labour, wage setting institutions and the interaction between agrarian systems and labour institutions.

2. Labour market structure

A priority at the meso-level is to try to understand how labour market heterogeneity interacts with productivity and growth. Labour markets in developing countries (and in industrialized countries too) are widely segmented, but the nature and strength of the underlying institutions vary. Among these, first, there is the formal structure of labour market regulation by the state or collective agreement. Second, there is the question of how large a fraction of the workforce is effectively covered by this formal structure of regulation. Third, the structuring of the labour market is linked to the diversification of contractual relations in employment, involving a range of labour statuses which can be classified in terms of their protection and permanence, their regularity, and their independence. Fourth, recruitment patterns and job access for different population groups are related to the way labour markets and the income flows that they generate are controlled. Such labour market institutions, and the ways they are changing (e.g. growth of regulation and protection of jobs, or inversely casualisation or informalisation), are widely believed to be important for growth and development, but little convincing empirical research can be found showing the specific impact either directly on growth, or on factors underlying growth such as investment, technological change, the organization of production, productivity or competitivity. On the other hand, the implications for inequality are fairly obvious.

The links between labour market structures and development are very diverse. Take for example the labour market structures observed in rural India. In relatively stagnant, backward situations one could observe a frequent use of *jajmani* systems of specialized labour in which payment is related to a social position rather than to work actually done, the prevalence of payment in kind, the tying of labour to landowners, tenancy systems related to labour obligations, and other linkages between land, credit and labour markets. Many of these institutions can be interpreted in transactions costs terms – means for the control and enforcement of contracts, ways of generating increased labour intensity, mechanisms for assuring landowners of guaranteed labour supply at peak agricultural periods, and the like, and hence as institutions designed to maximize or at least increase the rental incomes of landowners. Most, but not all of these institutions are informal in nature, and reinforced by norms and conceptions of status. Such institutions, though, tend to discourage mobility and innovation, and support hierarchies unrelated to productivity, so that they are unlikely to be consistent with rapid agricultural output growth; more dynamic rural production systems seem to generate different forms of labour contract, often less personalized as far as casual labour is concerned, with a decline in tenancy, cash wages and – where the political institutions permit – more effective labour organizations. In practice, different systems seem to co-exist in geographical proximity, giving rise to a different type of labour market heterogeneity, although this may be a transitional phenomenon.

3. The mobilization of labour

Among the economic interpretations of specific labour institutions, one important one is the mobilization of the labour force. This applies to institutions promoting say the use of female labour, or the absorption of migrants (or the prevention of out-migration). An interesting case concerns intermediaries in the labour market – labour contractors, temporary work agencies and the like – which may be important in mobilizing specific sorts of labour and thereby promoting the development of particular labour market structures. Systems of skill development and recognition also involves elements of mobilization: productivity growth is closely linked to human capital, so that the latter may be one of the most important links between labour institutions and economic development. But institutions concerned with education, training and skills also play an important role in determining the distribution of the gains from growth.

The inverse of mobilization is exclusion. This may arise if economic restructuring modifies labour market institutions such as to exclude certain groups of workers, creating open unemployment. Another process of this type might be found in the informalization of production relationships, affecting the way labour is mobilized and organized. These are examples of the effects on labour of the institutional framework. At the same time, patterns of labour use create or transform institutional structures. Labour market outcomes may affect the system of labour organization (strengthening or weakening trade unionism, for example), or labour underutilization may be associated with particular social and cultural institutions for the sharing of income or controlling job access. Both conceptual and empirical work is required to better understand these relationships.

4. Wage-setting institutions.

The ways in which wage setting institutions interact with productivity and technical change are potentially important for both growth and distribution, especially the extent to which intervention in wage fixing contributes to economic dynamism – either intervention to keep wages low which might contribute to competitiveness and accumulation, or intervention to raise low wages in order to trigger technological change or increase motivation. Wage-setting institutions evolve over time in response to changes in the economic environment, as well as affecting sectoral and aggregate economic performance.[5] Attempts to build up taxonomies of such institutions have been made (Banuri and Amadeo 1991), and this could provide an important input to taxonomic exercises at the macro-level. A variety of more specific comparative studies is also possible. A second level of analysis might be to look at specific institutional interventions in wage-setting designed to raise or lower wages, and attempt to understand the developmental consequences. Examples would include minimum wages and various wage-related benefits, or state intervention on one side or another in collective bargaining (repression of trade unions or, on the contrary, support for workers' demands). Conventional economic theory suggests some clear hypotheses (basically that wages above or below market clearing levels are sub-optimal) but it would be important to also explore the relationships between wage-fixing institutions and productivity and technical change, as well as the consequences for wage and profit shares, perceived 'fairness' and labour commitment, and the stability of industrial relations.

5. Agrarian systems and rural labour institutions

The development of labour markets in rural areas is an important aspect of the interaction between labour institutions and development, with ramifications (e.g. in terms of workforce diversification) which go far beyond agriculture (Bhalla 1992). The process of agricultural development under alternative institutional frameworks has in fact been studied more intensively than the corresponding processes in industry, presumably because the institutional alternatives are more obvious. But there is scope for research with a more explicit focus on the labour institutions – in terms of the extent of wage labour, the nature of contractual arrangements, patterns of organization of labour, systems of land control and use and returns to labour – and how they respond to and interact with innovation and productivity growth in agriculture. The comments on rural labour markets under the 'labour market structure' heading above is a case in point. This should also extend to the interaction with urban and rural non-agricultural labour institutions. One important area for study concerns transitions in countries with large agricultural sectors (who makes the transition to a non-agricultural job, what institutional factors are involved in control over access to jobs and segmentation, do particular sets of rural institutions promote industrialization?). Again, an international comparative perspective should provide insights, although there may be difficulties in establishing general comparisons because of institutional diversity.

6. Labour institutions and development at the micro level

At the micro-level, the most obvious focus of attention is the factors determining productivity in the workplace. Employment contracts are incomplete even when formally specified in detail, and a wide range of institutional mechanisms are brought to bear on workers, involving effects on motivation and commitment, on work intensity and productivity, on adaptation and mobility. Work situations entail a combination of formal and informal obligations and rights, protection through law or through agreement, mechanisms for supervision and control, incentives and penalties. Worker resistance and organization generates further institutional mechanisms. Issues of work culture, of labour discipline and of participation are also relevant. All of these factors have direct or indirect implications for productivity or innovation, as well as for the pattern of income distribution. Their analysis involves the study of work organization and industrial relations at the enterprise level. Other factors, however, such as attitudes to hierarchy or to collective action, may have cultural roots which need to be analysed within a broader societal context.

16

The importance of such mechanisms for the aggregate relationships between labour institutions and economic development probably lies less in their effects on allocative efficiency (although there may be implications for competitiveness in international markets) than in their impact on the dynamics: the effects on innovation and adaptation, the implications for investment and technical change. Certainly there seems to be a widespread belief that the dynamism of the Japanese economy has its roots in the labour institutions within Japanese enterprises, where 'cultural' factors in work relationships are often considered important determinants of the efficient use of capital and a commitment to quality and productivity growth; but how far is culture an independent and how far a dependent variable?

In empirical analysis of these issues at the enterprise level, both subjective (attitudes) and objective (behaviour patterns) responses of workers within alternative institutional environments might be explored. It may also be interesting to test the validity of specific economic concepts, such as efficiency wage models or implicit contracts, within a neoinstitutionalist theoretical framework. Whatever the approach, work at this level is important because it can help understand the proximate determinants of productivity. The ways in which skills are acquired and used by individuals or firms might also be included in analysis of this type. One possibility for comparative research would be to take firms of different national origins – e.g. with US, Japanese, Korean and domestic capital – operating in, say, Indonesia or Thailand, and to try to understand the micro-level determinants of pro- ductivity and of productivity growth in their differing institutional frame- works. Such research would compare work organization and industrial relations across these different categories of firm, and search for the factors generating commitment and motivation.[6] The study of similar firms operating in different national environments is another promising basis for comparative research; multi-country comparisons might be particularly interesting.

At all three levels – macro, meso and micro – identified in the foregoing there are alternative approaches and theoretical frameworks which merit investiga- tion. The advantage of a neoinstitutionalist model, looking at the contributions of institutions to efficiency in a transactions costs, collective action or infor- mation cost sense, is that there is a clear theoretical framework and a growing literature. On the other hand, narrow economistic assumptions underlie such models. A second approach is to explore the evolution and effects of clusters of institutions, trying to build models of how they function in a more descrip- tive or historical mode, which also takes into account social and political economy concerns. While less limited in scope than a neoinstitutionalist approach, this is by the same token likely to be theoretically less rigorous. A third is to choose specific labour institutions which are policy manipulable, and investigate the developmental effects of policy intervention – looking at controlled policy experiments, or comparing situations subject to different policy regimes, or comparing situations before and after policy intervention, so as either to assess the direct effects of specific institutions which are modified through policy changes, or to isolate the institutional conditions which permit successful policy intervention. Comparative analysis is likely to be an effective method in all three approaches, although not the only one.

Since all of these routes seem to offer at least some promise, but they may be theoretically inconsistent, it does not seem reasonable to attempt to work within a unified theoretical frame at present. Perhaps ultimately elements of a theoretical synthesis may emerge. On a rather different plane, more conceptual work needs to be done on identifying, categorizing and measuring labour institutions of different types, and this would be an important input to research at all three levels. This is particularly important as far as the informal institutions are concerned. Work to date has concentrated on formal institutions and organizations such as trade unions, minimum wages and employment contracts. This is natural, partly because the formal is more visible and measurable, partly because such issues have received most attention in the literature. But it is also vital to work out what informal institutions are important and how they can be investigated. For instance, among informal labour institutions, those which restrict job access to particular groups, creating insiders and outsiders, may have considerable implications for the capacity of economic systems to adjust to changing competitive conditions and technology.

ACTORS AND INSTITUTIONS

A variety of social actors are involved in these relationships, sometimes constrained by or responding to social institutions, sometimes consciously trying to shape them. Which actors are the most important varies across situations and over time. Traditionally, of course, it is the actors of the industrial relations system – essentially organizations of workers and of employers – which have attracted the most attention in the literature on labour institutions. The industrial relations literature is voluminous, but relatively little of it is directly concerned with growth and development. Nevertheless, the stress on wage determination and on labour allocation in this literature provides a framework for exploring the consistency between the specific interests of the actors concerned and broader economic development objectives. A neo-institutionalist view would perhaps start by treating industrial relations in terms of game theory. A simple negotiation between employer and worker may be represented as a prisoner's dilemma game, in which both employer and worker are better off with a consensual, high wage-high work input solution, but in which the incentive structure generates a low wage-low work input outcome. Starting from a conflictual situation, if workers take a more consensual approach employers may take advantage of this to reduce wages; if employers become more accommodating, workers may reduce work input. The problem is then one of the institutions which may permit workers and employers to reach the high equilibrium, since the economic incentives trap the system at the low level. Such institutions may include legal instruments, independent arbitration bodies, or less formal elements such as social norms, ideology or personal interdependence through kin or community networks which help to generate trust and co-operation.

This model needs to be extended if broader aspects of development are to be addressed. The linkage between industrial relations and development, for instance, depends crucially on how organizations of workers and employers respond to macro-economic considerations. It is, for example, commonly argued that by successfully defending the real income levels of their members unions indirectly help to create unemployment (because by raising wage costs they encourage capital-labour substitution or reduce competitivity), but among groups not represented in the union. Insider-outsider issues are therefore important here – under what circumstances do unions represent the interests of workers as a whole and when they do not, does the interplay of trade union and employer strategies tend to lead to inequality and exclusion? These are issues on which strong views are encountered distinctly more frequently than hard evidence.

In most countries the most important single actor in the field of labour institutions is the state. The state plays an active role in structuring labour use, most obviously under centralized planning, but to a varying extent also in countries which subscribe to a free market model; this can be clearly seen in rapidly growing market economies such as Singapore or the Republic of Korea, where there has been extensive state intervention in wage fixing and in controlling trade union activity. There is a close relationship between the political institutions underlying the state and labour institutions: democratic institutions render the suppression of trade unions difficult, for instance, which in turn affects the way the labour market functions and hence also the economy. In some countries the whole process of labour market functioning and organization is highly regulated, through a complex system of rules and regulations, enforced either through the state or through a system of control over the organization or labour or of production. These rules may largely serve to protect subgroups of workers or industrial sectors, they may serve to maintain the work force fragmented and to keep wage costs low, or they may reflect broader social goals of the state, and provide a legitimation for its development strategy. In other countries, state legislative intervention may be mainly symbolic because the means of enforcement are absent. But even when the rules are effectively enforced, such systems of regulation are rarely global, and alongside them there usually exists a substantial unregulated sector – unregulated, that is, by the state, for less visible forms of regulation may substitute for legal and administrative structures. The relative importance of these explicit and implicit forms of regulation is often poorly understood, simply because formal regulation is visible to the outside observer and so dominates perception.

The political economy of the state is important for understanding the functioning of labour institutions, in terms of the nature of its popular or class support and the way this support is rewarded. The state as producer also plays a considerable role in structuring labour institutions, and in so doing usually reinforces the power of particular groups with which it becomes allied both politically and economically. These of course will often include parts of the labour movement, where privilege may accumulate in favoured segments. The links between these patterns of state intervention in labour, the nature of the political processes with which they are connected, and the pace and character of development, is an area of both controversy and importance. It underlies, for instance, much of the current debate about the desirability of privatization of state enterprises. It is also central in controversy over the social implications of rapid growth in East Asia; it is argued by Deyo (1987) that in several East Asian countries state intervention has aimed at the 'economic inclusion' of an increasing proportion of workers, but at the cost of their political exclusion. The neoinstitutionalist vision of the state is rather more restrictive (see in particular Eggertsson 1990), but it plays no less important a role in development – as an umpire, an enforcer of the rules, a guarantor of property rights, an institution which by providing social services reduces the costs of private transactions. These different roles of the state, and the compatibility and contradictions between them, appear to be key elements in the analysis of the relationships between institutions and development.

CONCLUSIONS

The pattern of development depends on sets of institutions which permit exchange, determine who has rights to what sorts of entitlements (and property) and the values attached to them, control the terms of agreements and provide for their enforcement. The institutions underlying growth are closely bound up with the institutions underlying distribution – particularly through labour institutions, which are crucial for both production and distribution. Both formal and informal institutions are involved; the formal institutions, on which attention is usually focused because they are more visible, can only be understood when placed in a broader social context. These institutions are to a large degree endogenous – their evolution interacts with the development path, and economic forces determine to a greater or lesser extent which institutions survive – but through processes which are complex, historically specific and involve social and political as well as economic factors.

How then can one understand institutional change? Neoinstitutionalist economics offers one option. Institutions which are less efficient in reducing transactions costs are replaced by others which are more efficient. But a cursory overview of the list of labour institutions presented above suggests that most of them are concerned with distribution: institutions reflect the power of particular groups to control the end use of production, rather than responding to competitive pressure to increase efficiency. Although economic growth might well be promoted by more egalitarian institutions, there is no automatic mechanism for institutional change in the direction of such institutions, indeed a stability of inegalitarian systems because those who benefit are likely to be in a position to obstruct institutional change. In short, the political economy of labour institutions may well provide us with better models of their emergence and persistence than the cost-minimizing approach; while labour institutions which are promoted by both efficiency considerations and the reinforcement of privilege are likely to be particularly stable.

Among other important points about institutional change, one which bears repeating is the inertia of institutions in comparison with economic variables – Banuri refers to this as hysteresis, by analogy with the literature on persistent high unemployment. Part of the reason for inertia, no doubt, lies in the mutual reinforcement of institutions of different types. Rapid institutional shifts do of course occur; but probably there is a tendency to underestimate the persistence of 'old' institutions in 'new' situations. In other words, path dependency is important, because there is a historical process of cumulative change. An this in turn reinforces the desirability of a holistic approach. Partial analysis of specific institutions may be misleading if it does not take into account the broader institutional framework of production and distribution.

The empirical analysis of these issues is not easy. Although it is possible to separate out limited hypotheses which can be rigorously tested, this route leads to excessive simplification, and may be misleading if the dominant institutional relationships are missing from the model. This is the most obvious criticism of the neoinstitutionalist approach. But teasing out coherent patterns from a mass of institutional data, without a well defined theoretical framework, is not only a daunting task, but also one in which the risks of subjectivity are evident. There is no simple answer here, other than the need for continuous iteration between theory and empirical research. The real challenge lies in tracking down the crucial relationships between institutions and development; and the argument here is that the relationships between labour institutions, as we have defined them in this paper, and the pattern of economic growth, are among those where the returns to further research would be highest.

NOTES

1. International Institute for Labour Studies, Geneva. This paper is part of a continuing research project on labour institutions and economic development. Views expressed here are personal and imply no responsibility on the part of the IILS.
2. This annex and the fivefold classification of labour institutions are taken from Rodgers (1994). That article overlaps in content with the present chapter, but explores some of the theoretical issues in more depth. The book of which it is a part also includes other theoretical contributions, and macro-level analyses of labour institutions in development paths in the Republic of Korea, Thailand and the Philipppines.
3. See Hodgson (1992a) for discussion.
4. Eggertsson (1990) distinguishes between 'neoinstitutionalist' economics, based on utility maximization, and the 'new institutional economics' which may incorporate non-maximizing behavioural assumptions such as satisficing. In practice, however, both schools are concerned with similar issues and I refer to them both under the neoinstitutionalist heading.
5. For an analysis of this in Japan, see Tsuru (1993).
6. See Papola (1994) and Park (1994) for examples of empirical work which examines these issues.

REFERENCES

Assaad, Ragui, 1991. 'Formal and informal institutions in the labour market: The case of the construction sector in Egypt'. Minneapolis, Humphrey Institute of Public Affairs, mimeo.

Banuri, Tariq and Edward J. Amadeo, 1991. 'Worlds within the Third World: Labour market institutions in Asia and Latin America', in Tariq Banuri (ed.), *Economic liberalisation: No panacea*. Oxford, Clarendon Press.

Bhalla, Sheila, 1992. 'The formation of rural labour markets in India', in T. S. Papola and Gerry Rodgers (eds.), *Labour institutions and economic development in India*, Research Series No. 97. Geneva, International Institute for Labour Studies.

Boyer, Robert, 1994. 'Do labour institutions matter for economic development: A 'régulation' approach for the OECD and Latin America, with an extension to Asia', in Gerry Rodgers (ed.), *Workers, institutions and economic growth in Asia*. Geneva, International Institute for Labour Studies.

Bowles, Samuel, 1991. 'What markets can – and cannot – do', in *Challenge*, July–August.

Coase, Ronald, 1960. 'The problem of social cost', in *Journal of Law and Economics*, vol. 3, pp. 1–44.

Deyo, Frederic C., 1987. 'State and labor: Modes of political exclusion in East Asian development', in Frederic C. Deyo (ed.), *The political economy of the new Asian industrialism*. Ithaca, Cornell University Press.

Dore, Ronald P., 1979. 'Industrial relations in Japan and elsewhere', in A. M. Craig (ed.), *Japan: A comparative review*. Princeton, New Jersey, Princeton University Press.

Eggertsson, Thrainn, 1990. *Economic behaviour and institutions*. Cambridge, Cambridge University Press.

Fallon, Peter; Lucas, Robert, 1991. 'The impact of changes in job security regulations in India and Zimbabwe', in *World Bank Economic Review*, vol. 5, no. 3.

Harriss, John, Kannan, K.P. and Rodgers, Gerry, 1990. *Urban labour market structure and job access in India: A study of Coimbatore*. Research Series 92. Geneva, International Institute for Labour Studies.

Hodgson, Geoffrey M., 1992a. 'Thorstein Veblen and post-Darwinian economics', in *Cambridge Journal of Economics*, vol. 16, no. 3, Sept.

——, 1992b. 'Institutional economics: Legacy and new directions', in Ulf Himmelstrand (ed.), *Interfaces in economic and social analysis*. London, Routledge.

Lele, Uma, 1975. *The design of rural development: Lessons from Africa*. Baltimore, Johns Hopkins for the World Bank.

Marglin, Stephen and Schor, Juliet (eds.), 1990. *The golden age of capitalism.* Oxford, Clarendon Press.

Matthews, R.C.O., 1986. 'The economics of institutions and the sources of growth', in *Economic Journal*, vol. 96, Dec.

Nabli, Mustapha K. and Nugent, Jeffrey B., 1989a. 'The New Institutional Economics and its applicability to development', in *World Development*, vol. 17, no. 9, pp. 1333–1347.

Nabli, Mustapha K. and Nugent, Jeffrey B., 1989b. *The New Institutional Economics and development.* Amsterdam, North-Holland.

North, Douglass C., 1989. 'Institutions and economic growth: An historical introduction', in *World Development*, vol. 17, no. 9, Sept.

North, Douglass C., 1990. *Institutions, institutional change and economic performance.* Cambridge, Cambridge University Press.

North, Douglass C., 1991. 'Institutions', in *Journal of Economic Perspectives*, vol. 5, no. 1, Winter.

Olsen, Mancur, 1965. *The logic of collective action: Public goods and the theory of groups.* Cambridge, Mass., Harvard University Press.

Papola, T. S., 1992. 'Labour institutions and economic development: The case of Indian industrialization', in T. S. Papola and Gerry Rodgers (eds.), *Labour institutions and economic development in India*, Research Series No. 97. Geneva, International Institute for Labour Studies.

Papola, T. S., 1994. *Labour institutions and productivity: A study based on enterprise level investigations in India.* Discussion paper no. 68. Geneva, International Institute for Labour Studies.

Park, Young-bum, 1994. *Labour institutions and economic development in Asia: Exploratory micro-level research on labour institutions and productivity in the Korean automotive and garment industries.* Discussion paper no. 67. Geneva, International Institute for Labour Studies.

Portes, Alejandro, 1990. 'When more can be less: Labour standards, development and the informal economy', in Herzenberg, Stephen and Jorge F. Perez-Lopez (eds.), *Labor standards and development in the global economy.* Washington, U.S. Department of Labor.

Rodgers, Gerry, 1986. 'Labour markets, labour processes and economic development', in *Labour and Society*, vol. 11, no. 2, May.

Rodgers, Gerry, 1994. 'Institutional economics, development economics and labour economics', in Gerry Rodgers (ed.), *Workers, institutions and economic growth in Asia.* Geneva, International Institute for Labour Studies.

Solow, Robert, 1990. *The labour market as a social institution.* London, Blackwell

Street, J., 1987. 'The institutionalist theory of economic development', in *Journal of Economic Issues*, vol. XXI, no.4.

Thévenot, Laurent, 1985. 'Les investissements de forme', dans Centre d'Etudes de l'Emploi, *Conventions économiques.* Paris, Presses Universitaires de France.

Tsuru, Tsuyoshi, 1993. 'Shunto: The spillover effect and the wage-setting institution in Japan', in *Wage-setting institutions in Japan and the Republic of Korea*, Discussion Paper No. 51. Geneva, International Institute for Labour Studies.

Van Arkadie, Brian, 1990. 'The role of institutions in development', in World Bank, *Proceedings of the World Bank Annual Conference on Development Economics 1989.* Washington, DC.

Veblen, Thorstein B., 1909. 'The limitations of marginal utility', in *Journal of Political Economy*, vol. 17.

ANNEX. LABOUR INSTITUTIONS

1. The nature of employment contracts – the rules, both formal and informal, which govern hiring of workers, firing, working conditions, the length of the working day; the duration of such contracts, the nature of control over work which they imply; the extent of protection and of security. More generally, this fundamental labour institution refers to the nature of jobs, as socially defined entities involving rights, obligations, and social position.

2. The mechanisms for controlling and regulating employment contracts – state regulation (administrative or legal) or collective negotiation, or sets of values or norms held by the parties concerned. The nature of the machinery for enforcement and adjudication (such as the labour inspectorate, labour tribunals). This may also include social forms of control, e.g. through indebtedness or the threat of force.

3. The organization and representation of labour: trades unions, trade or craft associations, etc., and the areas over which they have control or influence, the ways they are organized and function. This may include whether they are unitary or fragmented, their linkage with other (e.g. political) institutions, the range of their activities.

4. The organization and representation of employers: employers' associations, business or enterprise associations and the areas over which they have control or influence, the ways they are organized and function.

5. The institutions of the labour market itself – the dominant procedures for job search and rules for access to jobs of different types, the systems for information – hiring halls, employment exchanges, newspaper advertisements, or alternatively particularistic networks of contacts and intermediaries. Discrimination, screening and selection procedures and institutional constraints on mobility may come in here.

6. The methods by which wages are paid (in cash and in kind, directly or as fringe benefits, piece or time rate, the frequency and reliability of payment, regulated by contract or discretionary).

7. The process of wage fixing: regulatory bodies, procedures, rules to be followed; negotiation and conciliation procedures; reference points and minima, their levels and the processes by which they are determined.

8. Training and skill institutions – the mechanisms for the acquisition of skills and credentials for labour market access; thus the formal and informal education and apprenticeship systems. The recognition of skills and qualifications – their acceptability as credentials for job access; and the systems for learning on the job.

9. The organization of jobs within the firm – the nature of occupational hierarchies and job progression within internal labour markets, criteria for promotion or for dismissal, the operation of work groups and the division of labour; systems for motivation and the operation of 'corporate culture'; the ways different types of firm organize labour use (small and large, formal and informal, ...).

10. The structure of ownership and control over production, and in particular the rules governing the spheres of influence of workers and owners of capital or land: joint decision-making procedures, co-operative or worker-managed organizations, tenancy and the rules governing its functioning.

11. The social and state regulation of self-employment – the rules governing conditions of work, access to the means of production and to markets; the prevalence of indirect or hidden wage relationships in self-employment, e.g. in homeworking and other forms of subcontracting (to which the elements of item 1 above may

apply). Property institutions are important here, particularly (but not exclusively) in agriculture.

12. Social security and income guarantee systems, the institutions for social insurance (health, unemployment ...), the 'social wage' – provided by the state, by the enterprise, through institutionalized private systems, through informal private community or semi-feudal networks; the conditions imposed for access to benefits. The nature of family or community obligations to support the sick or unemployed.

13. The conventional standard of life: norms and values which determine consumption standards and targets, and the social valuation of leisure, of saving and of work. Such values underlie work inputs both directly – through an internalized work ethic – and indirectly, through the pressure they put on individuals to conform to socially valued living standards.

14. The organization of labour supply: (a) within the household: the relative social and economic obligations and constraints on different family members and the way they affect labour market activity (e.g. sexual and age divisions of labour); (b) outside the household: labour gangs, labour pools...

Models of Management-Labour Relations and Labour Institutions in Malaysia: A Comparison of Nordic and other Transnational Companies

DANIEL FLEMING and ARNE WANGEL[1]

Twenty years of export-oriented industrialization has made Malaysia a second tier Newly Industrializing Country (NIC) in Asia; the recently announced development plan 'Vision 2020' sets the official target for achieving the status of industrialized nation. During the two decades from 1970 to 1990, the average annual growth in Malaysia's GDP amounted to 6.7 per cent. In 1992, GDP grew at a rate of 8.5 per cent, a modest decline from the 8.8 per cent in 1991, and the manufacturing sector alone grew by 13 per cent. Manufacturing contributes 29 per cent to total GDP and provides 20 per cent of total employment.

In 1992, the major part of foreign investment, totalling RM 17,055 million, came from Japan (21.7 per cent), Taiwan (21.2 per cent), Indonesia (17.3 per cent), South Korea (10.7 per cent) and the US (10.5 per cent). However, Nordic manufacturing companies are also present in Malaysia. The following study of management-labour relations in Nordic subsidiaries concludes that there is a mismatch between a Nordic model of state-capital-labour relations and the configuration of Malaysia's national development model. While the implementation of Nordic values in management-labour relations is negligible, the managerial models practised in Japanese and American subsidiaries seem to be more successful, with a stronger impact on labour-management relations in Malaysia.

The study compares the performance of foreign multinational companies in Malaysia and relates the findings to a discussion on the prospects of a Nordic model of management-labour relations. In this effort, the study elaborates the 'interface' with the Malaysian context in terms of political regime, labour institutions and cultural differences, as experienced by expatriate managers and through company policies.

INTRODUCTION

When Nordic and other international companies operate abroad, to what extent do they build on their parent company traditions and experiences in organizing work, industrial relations, and human resource development? Do the Nordic top managers and other expatriates seek to implement a Nordic (Swedish, Danish, Norwegian, Finnish) model of co-operation and co-determination in labour-management relations? What is the difference in behaviour between Scandinavian, Japanese, American, German, British, and other transnationals operating abroad, when it comes to cultural adaptation and implementation of management-labour relations; e.g. differences in head-quarters' control over operations, management style, introduction of team-work, work place participation and delegation?

These are some of the questions addressed in a study of 32 companies interviewed in Malaysia between 1992 and 1993. The study is part of a larger research project on 'the Future of the Nordic Model', which focuses on the consequences of company internationalization as it relates to labour-management relations in the Nordic countries; the institutional and legal effects of EEC integration; the scope of action for the trade union movement; and the potential for corporate-wide labour-management co-operation across borders in the Nordic countries and in Europe.

In an effort to further explore the challenges to the 'Nordic model', we initiated a sub-project to learn about the nature of labour relations in Nordic companies located in Malaysia. The objective was to study the experiences of Nordic companies operating in a region outside Europe in a climate of rapid growth, and the extra-European interaction with managerial styles rooted in the traditions of the major economic powers. In Southeast Asia, Malaysia is one of the second-line industrializing countries which, for more than 20 years, has attracted sustained and increasingly technologically advanced foreign investment.

Our approach to the study of labour-management relations is inter-cultural in orientation. There is a significant difference between labour relations in a culture with democratic institutions, which in the Nordic countries developed over a century of struggle and compromise, and the authoritarian tradition in Malaysia. Nordic companies encounter these differences in culture, institutions and labour-management relations in most Third World countries. However, in the course of industrialization and in the presence of transnational companies (TNCs), labour institutions are transformed and influenced by numerous competing actors and models of different cultural origins.

The primary results of our study indicate that Nordic companies have a more open managerial style, practise a stronger delegation of tasks to middle managers, and are more oriented toward trade union co-operation. In contrast,

American and Japanese companies are more hierarchical and managed from the head office of the parent company. However, both of their top-down participatory strategies seem to be more successful.

It is difficult for the Nordic companies to transfer the Nordic, democratic culture and the corresponding institutions in management-labour relations due to the tradition of authoritarian management in Malaysia and to the weak position of the trade union movement. This cultural orientation to labour-management relations makes it difficult to motivate Malaysian middle managers to voluntarily delegate and participate in team work. In contrast, the Nordic model of labour-management relations is based upon strong trade unions, oriented toward co-operation. In Malaysia, this kind of feedback is absent, either because the union is non-existent or passive, or because it is militant and rejects co-operative relationships as they have developed in the Nordic countries. Issues concerning co-determination are, for the most part, missing in trade union policies and labour market institutions. Thus, the vital requirements for the Nordic model of management-labour relations are not met.

We intend to analyse the barriers to and possibilities of the 'Nordic model' of labour-management relations in Malaysia in a context of international 'competition' between managerial strategies, and when new forms of internationalization are emerging. This study may contribute to clarifying the challenges confronting the 'Nordic model', not only on the expanding Asian market, but on the home front as well.

CONCEPTS

In order to highlight the interplay between various cultures and organizational models in labour-management relations, the term *inter-cultural* labour-management relations is used. We will analyse the interplay at the enterprise level – the foreign subsidiary in Malaysia, influenced both by the parent company and by the cultures and labour institutions in Malaysia. Labour institutions are here defined as 'the social institutions which affect or derive from the incorporation of labour in production, the remuneration and working conditions of labour, and associated norms and income guarantees' (Rodgers 1991, p. 8).

The ethnically divided and culturally heterogeneous population in Malaysia makes the management of labour a sensitive inter-cultural process. Foreign companies must observe regulations on ethnic quotas in their recruitment. This is part of the policy of integration and of improving the conditions of the disadvantaged Malay population.

The Malaysian population includes the larger and politically dominant Malay community (approximately 55 per cent), a Chinese population with a strong position in the economy (approximately 35 per cent), and a minority of

28

Indians. These divisions bring an additional dimension to the term 'inter-cultural', as ethnic identity is often employed as a power resource in conflicts.

The concept of *culture*, as defined here, does not refer to a kind of constant phenomenon that is reproduced in ethnic terms; rather culture is understood as the everyday constructed, deconstructed and reconstructed image or under-standing of life, including working life, experience which is influenced by ideologies and value systems. Management and labour are actors forming these changing cultural patterns of work relations.

The global inter-cultural influence can work in the direction of cultural institutional integration or convergence, but it can also raise conflict and resistance, leading to cultural and institutional divergence, as in several Islamic countries or the former USSR. Internationalization and modernization is shaping the 'global village' and the 'global workplace', but its cultural identity can develop in different directions.

The 'company culture' concept represents a rather superficial effort on the part of management to promote certain guiding principles and symbols to enhance the moral spirit of their employees. We prefer to talk about an effort to build an 'organizational identity'.

The term *labour-management relations* as used here includes formal industrial relations, social relations in the labour process, the development of human resources (education and skills), the structure of decision-making in the organization of work, personnel policies and informal labour management practices. The labour market institutions restrict the scope of company policies. Our study focuses on the relations between top and middle manage-ment as well as management and other employees; and the relations between management and trade unions or other employee committees, if any.

In Malaysia, the low level of unionization – an average of 10 per cent of the workforce – means that trade unions are not always involved in labour-management relations. Workers may be represented by a national union, an in-house union (enterprise unions on the plant level), or by a joint consultative council set up by the company itself.

The *Nordic model* of management-labour relations refers to a system based on strong trade union organization and co-operation with management in the company, in the industrial sector, and at the national level. The system of collective bargaining regulates the relationship between the two parties. Unions are organized locally in committees (clubs) that negotiate with management at the enterprise level. On the national level, negotiations are conducted to obtain nation-wide collective agreements. The state intervenes only in case of systemic breakdown in negotiations or open conflict. This collective agreement system is more fundamental to Nordic countries, in con-trast to the dominance of regulation by law in Continental Europe.

The Nordic model of labour-management regulation is founded upon the voluntary co-operation and social responsibility of the major parties in the labour market. This pattern has emerged as a result of specific cultural and historical conditions in the different Nordic countries.

Unions are not split along religious, political or ethnic lines. The extensive unionization of white collar workers in the public and private sectors contributes to the legitimacy of the movement. The strengthening of corporatist structures implies that the role of trade unions is widely accepted and institutionalized at all levels of society.

Thus, the Nordic model of conflict resolution and reform constitutes a tripartite institution of co-operation between trade unions, employers and government. At the company level, a tradition of voluntary, informal co-operation has emerged to promote the interests of the organizing parties, and based upon the system of collective bargaining. Through the development of tripartite labour law and binding regulation, the Nordic countries have transcended the antagonistic labour conflicts so prevalent in many other countries.

The notion of specific *models* of labour-management relations in foreign subsidiaries is based on two rather difficult generalizations. The first one relates to the problem of generalizing from the different individual parent company cultures and labour-management relations to coherent national models (American, Japanese, etc.) or groups of models (European or Nordic). The second problem is to identify and generalize about these models in a foreign culture where the models are either adapted to local practice or only partially exported. At the same time, there is an increasing tendency to move away from national models in favour of more international and company-specific management models (e.g. IBM, Toyota, etc.). How will this trend affect labour-management relations? Will there be a tendency toward global convergence influencing both the foreign models and labour relations in Malaysia?

THE LABOUR MOVEMENT AND STATE POLICIES IN MALAYSIA

From a superficial point of view, there seem to be some institutional similarities between the Nordic countries and Malaysia in terms of the role of the trade union movement. These similarities take the form of the tripartite system, the collective bargaining system, and union organization at enterprise level – the area committees (collective bargaining is mostly carried out at the individual company level only, led by officers from the union head office, which leaves the area committee in a secondary role). Most of the trade unions are affiliated with one national centre, in defiance of internal differences, as well as ethnic and political tensions. Part of the public sector and some services like banking, telecommunications, and electrical power supply have a high percentage of union members. In an earlier period, the trade union movement held a much stronger position in society.

However, a closer historical examination discloses critical differences, which explain the current weak position of the movement in Malaysia. One particularly important difference concerns the fact that the Malaysian government vehemently opposes the trade union movement in the tripartite system, through media propaganda and via the political system. The union movement has no political organization and the government coalition of three ethnic-based parties insists that unions refrain from supporting the opposition. On the other hand, although anti-union policies are a common feature of the authoritarian regimes in Southeast Asia, they tend to be less arbitrary and violently repressive in the parliamentary democracy of Malaysia, where there is some room for public criticism.

The origin of organized labour in Malaysia dates back to the early 1930s. Immigrant Chinese and Indian workers formed general labour unions, based upon geographical criteria. The movement gained in strength and was involved in a number of strikes during the pre-war period. It later became the backbone of the resistance against the Japanese occupation forces, and this was subsequently carried over to the struggle against the British, led by the Malaysian Communist Party.

In 1947, the Pan-Malaysian General Labour Union, established the year before, boasted a membership of 263,598, and represented more than half of the total workforce in Malaysia and 85 per cent of all unions. Faced with militant industrial action and a movement strongly influenced by the Malaysian Communist Party, the British attempted to reconstruct organized labour.

The plantation workers constituted the largest and dominant group. In 1945, a British trade unionist, John Alfred Brazier, was appointed as a trade union advisor. Through a series of legal amendments, federations of unions were prohibited. The colonisers began grooming English-educated, middle-class Indians for leadership positions in the Indian-based plantation unions to break the Chinese dominance. The work force was illiterate, tied to a feudal heritage with no alternative to plantation work, with children who were also destined to become plantation workers because of poor education.

The post-independence period is characterized by successive amendments to tighten the labour laws. In 1969 the first law barred unions and unionists from supporting and participating in political parties. This happened in the same year that racial riots led to a new constellation of power, through which a younger generation of the Malay elite launched a radical policy of economic redistribution in favour of the Malay population. The position of organized labour in national politics declined from a dominant role in the anti-colonial struggle against the Japanese and the British to its present weak standing, with virtually no influence on policies affecting workers' rights and living standards.

The dismantling of the political function of the labour movement was accompanied by an increasing erosion of the unions' economic function, through legal amendments and administrative practices. The Trade Union Act, 1959 and the discretionary powers given to the Director General of Trade Unions (DGTU) define the restrictions on the organization of labour, collective bargaining, and industrial action.

In 1980 a new set of amendments was introduced following major industrial action among the staff of the national airline. When Dr. Mohammed Mahathir became prime minister in 1981, his 'Look East' rhetoric pledged to emulate 'the Japanese model', which included an emphasis on work discipline, industrial harmony, and – more substantially – a preference for limiting union representation to individual plants. In 1989, labour amendments extended the option to form an in-house union to workers in industries that were already covered by a national union. New regulations also seriously affected the economic position of workers through the reduction of overtime rates and the redefinition of the basis for calculating benefits.

Recently, the government has taken additional steps to splinter the labour movement. On the national level, the government intervened following a conference of the Malaysian Trade Union Congress (MTUC) in 1989, where unionists discussed a proposal to field labour candidates in the coming general elections. The government responded through its support for the formation of a rival national centre, the Malaysian Labour Organization (MLO). The Prime Minister declared that 'if MTUC wants to be used as a 'tool for politicians', then trade unions must set up an alternative apex organization to represent them' (New Straits Times, May 5, 1989).

The National Union of Bank Employees (NUBE), which had broken away from MTUC in 1986, appropriated the leadership of this initiative and made its substantial resources available. This third trade union centre (the others being MTUC, covering both the private and public sector unions, and CUEPACS, catering for public sector employees only) was registered in 1990 by the Registrar of Trade Unions.

The end-result of government intervention in the labour market since independence may be summarized in this way:

- The base for building collective strength is limited, as the legal system ensures that unionized labour is barred from effectively increasing its power resources *vis-à-vis* the state and employers.
- Given that the scope for industrial action is narrow, no real escalation of industrial action can take place.

- The employer has the option to stop negotiating at any time by referring a dispute to legal conciliation procedures with discretionary powers given to the authorities.
- The authorities' main strategy for handling labour conflict is to prolong the conflict process (through administrative procedures of the Ministry of Human Resources and via the Industrial Court) – while containing it – so as to erode the support of the union membership involved (Wangel 1991).

While a few individual trade unionists do envisage a socialist programme in their activities, this does not reflect the agenda of the membership. Low basic salaries and rather limited experience with the industrial environment directs members' attention to monetary compensation only. Furthermore, no union has the resources to develop and sustain systematic training programmes. Courses focus on basic trade union skills like collective bargaining, leadership, and labour law. Occupational health and safety courses were introduced in the 1980s, but topics like the implications of new technology, skill upgrading and new managerial strategies for workers' participation, not to mention political education, are absent from the course schedules and union focus.

In the immediate future, the union movement will be preoccupied with trying to head off continuous attacks on the part of the government. The proposal to establish a National Wage Council, similar to the one which has regulated the Singapore labour market for many years, is the most recent attempt to undermine the primary objectives of union activities. The proposal for a flexi-wage, linking remuneration to productivity and company performance, will probably re-emerge. The importation of substantial numbers of foreign workers to the manufacturing sector also bears witness to government efforts to maintain a low-wage investment climate. After 20 years of dispute over the unionization of electronics workers, the government bluntly stated that investors' demand for a union-free environment had absolute priority. This evidence illustrates that the government's tolerance of existing national unions does not imply an endorsement of their further expansion.

The employers are organized in the Malaysian Employers' Federation (MEF) and the Federation of Malaysian Manufacturers (FMM). The former holds the largest membership and focuses on industrial relations issues, e.g. by communicating cases of disputes through a regular newsletter. FMM is the forum of major manufacturing companies addressing issues of industrial policies and conducting its own surveys on, for example, manpower problems. FMM does include proposals for labour law amendments in its recommendations to the government.

Faced with employers' measures to increase numerical and wage flexibility, the state remains passive. The growth strategy of the government insists on a low labour cost climate for foreign investors, as argued by Prime Minister Dr.

Mahathir: 'without the advantage of low-cost labour, there is no way for a developing country to be more productive, that is, to have a lower unit cost in manufacturing than a developed country ... the only real advantage that they have is their low-cost labour ... we enjoy an edge with lower wages' (New Straits Times 9/7/92).

Another significant development is the growth of enterprise-based unions, encouraged by the government. According to Malaysia Economic Report, the percentage of members of in-house unions in total union membership in the private sector rose from 6.5% in 1985 to 19.3% in 1988 (in absolute figures from 28,500 to 61,000 members). Recent figures from the Ministry of Human Resources indicate that the proportion of in-house union members out of total union membership has risen to 41.4 per cent (291,920 members in 344 in-house unions) as of June 30, 1993 (Star 6/10/93). But it should be noted that this trend includes private sector unions that owe their existence to the privatization of statutory bodies, in which only representation covering that particular body is allowed.

In November 1993, Dr. Mahathir commented on the mode of solving industrial disputes, as part of his general criticism of Western society: 'In a civilized society ... the legal system is also devised to help resolve whatever disputes in an organized manner so that the disputing parties do not suffer losses. This approach is not adopted in the settlement of disputes between employers and workers. Instead, a more primitive method is – a 'test of strength' through strikes or other forms of industrial action. Whoever is stronger wins ... the results are obtained not on the basis of work done but rather on the ability to destruct ... That is why their economies remain weak even though other factors such as capital, technology and international market give a certain comparative advantage to them ... This is a manifestation of shallow Western civilization.' (Dato Seri Dr Mahathir Mohammed's speech at the UMNO general assembly 4/11/93, New Straits Times 5/11/93, p. 10)

However, one month later, the procedures for union recognition in companies were simplified. Automatic recognition will be granted, once a union can prove that it has more than 50 per cent of the employees as its members. An employer can no longer delay the process by referring a recognition granted by the Registrar of Trade Unions to the Minister. Recognition cannot be given to a union, if a claim for recognition already filed by another union has yet to be settled.

MTUC has been appointed to the National Advisory Labour Council (NALC), the Social Security Board (SOCSO), which manages compensation for industrial accidents, and the Employment Provident Fund (EPF), which is a pension scheme. All of these are tripartite bodies modelled on the ILO concept. However, they offer little support for trade unions due to infrequent meetings and the fact that they function primarily as a 'testing ground' for new government policies, before they are enacted in Parliament by the government's more than two-thirds majority.

The MLO has joined NALC, and in 1993 it replaced MTUC in SOCSO and EPF due to the alleged 'irresponsible behaviour' of MTUC. MLO has been appointed to the Malaysian Business Council, while the MTUC was left out.

Despite these limitations, it still seems that the labour movement has the potential to play a significant role in the multi-racial Malaysian scene since it is the only major popular organization with the capacity to combine workers' interests across ethnic divisions.

If the trade union movement is to participate as an active partner, i.e. equivalent to the system in the Nordic countries, *vis-à-vis* management, the unions must have a much stronger position in society and a greater interest in co-determination. If there is no breakthrough in unionists' efforts to organize workers, e.g. within the large unorganized semiconductor industry, a stronger position seems rather far-fetched. On the contrary, one must expect an expansion and strengthening of the Japanese, micro-corporatist strategy, and also the American strategy of direct participation without any mediating union organization in the relationship between employees and management.

NORDIC MANAGERS AND MALAYSIAN LABOUR-MANAGEMENT RELATIONS

Originally, the research project from which this paper derives suggested that Nordic managers might transfer a Nordic style of management when operating in subsidiaries established in Malaysia. This hypothesis was almost unanimously criticized and contradicted by Swedish top managers based in Malaysia at a seminar in Kuala Lumpur in February 1991. The Swedish managers' conclusion was that the business idea and technology are decisive factors in transnational operations. These two things are rooted in Sweden, but their transfer to Malaysia does not include a conscious effort to implement Swedish values or management-labour relations.

This practice is distinctly different from Japanese management, which consciously seeks to implement the Japanese model of labour-management relations.

The participants in the seminar characterized the Nordic style of management in Malaysia with the image of the manager 'standing back', leaving much of the decision-making to Malaysian middle managers, particularly with reference to personnel policies and work organization. Nordic managers primarily perform functions related to the overall control and management of finance, technique, and quality in the production process.

This 'standing back' may be related, on the one hand, to a lack of historical and cultural knowledge about the region – other Europeans benefit from experience and tradition since colonial times. On the other hand, Nordic companies cannot expect political and diplomatic intervention by their home governments to apply leverage to their demands in the way that American and Japanese firms can.

Nordic companies in Malaysia face labour institutions that are quite different from Nordic societies. We summarize the institutions in five areas: wage and employment conditions, ethnic balance, the role of middle management, government control, and the work-related value system.

Wages and salaries are rarely determined by piece-rate or productivity-related systems. Normally both blue- and white-collar workers are paid according to a seniority scale: fixed rates for hourly or monthly pay, overtime, and year-end bonuses. The basic pay is increased upon confirmation, most often after three months. As for more indirect incentives, management uses annual extra bonuses (the amount depending on the profit), overtime compensation, allowances for transportation, housing, meals, attendance (to reduce sick leave and absence) and medical service from the company's panel of doctors. Overtime is usually the most important incentive to increase production in temporary peak situations. Rates for work on overtime and public holidays follow the provisions of the Employment Act. The indirect incentives can also be seen as hidden salary increases to keep workers, and to reduce turnover in a market rife with labour shortages.

To the major employers, the labour market is made quite transparent through the surveys conducted by private consultancies. Official wage statistics are published with much delay, and trade unions rely on comparing collective agreements.

An informal frame of wage-fixing is defined by the Consumer Price Index (CPI), the composition of which is much disputed. The awards of the Industrial Court relate closely to the CPI. Organized companies may deliberately choose to stall negotiations for a new collective agreement, in order to achieve the minimal Industrial Court award. The government intends to reduce wage increases to a minimum, i.e. to a lower level than the inflation rate.

Trade unions often have significant insight into the performance of their companies, although there is no provision for sharing of information. Their membership covers middle managers and office staff, through which such financial information can be obtained. Unions observe 'grace periods' to newly organized companies as well as restraint towards companies in financial trouble.

In principle, a rather large number of blue- and white-collar workers and middle managers consider *employment* to be a rather permanent arrangement. This is not just a cultural attitude. Seniority wages promote long-term employment. Also, when workers are laid off, individual compensation at termination is calculated according to length of employment. The amount can be considerable, holding management back from terminating long-time employees. However, these attitudes are shifting as the overheated labour market makes individual 'job-hopping' and career-climbing more popular.

There is also a trend of increasing numerical flexibility. A company can subcontract particular tasks to an agent, who is paying his staff on a piece-rate basis. One example is the short-term, unskilled work of packing finished products before a major shipment. Casual labourers without any contract are not covered by the legal regulation on employers' contribution to the industrial accident compensation and the pension schemes in Malaysia.

Casual labour may also appear on a longer term, when the probation periods of new recruits are extended beyond the normal three months, or when their status as 'trainees' is prolonged indefinitely.

A major part of the recruitment of labour is conducted through the staff already employed. In recent years, the labour shortage has prompted companies to offer monetary rewards to their staff for introducing relatives or friends as job applicants. Personnel officers visit villages and arrange walk-in interviews in rural towns. Some new companies choose to source labour by locating the plant in a rural district, profiting from the significantly lower wage level. However, the female part of this labour force tends to be more unstable, as they are easily attracted by alternative income opportunities in their village or by family commitments.

The supply of technicians and engineers trained in public institutions is far from meeting the demand. Major manufacturing companies have pooled resources to set up private skill development centres. However, the pinching of skilled workers from other companies is still prevalent in industrial estates.

While an increasing part of the labour force will be covered by an employment contract negotiated through a union, the labour market remains non-transparent and highly segmented, including wide regional disparities in wage levels. Mobility and technological change is further impeded by the absence of adequate social protection for workers; i.e. a legally fixed minimum wage would probably ease the shortage of unskilled labour. The long working hours in some companies – up to 60 hours a week – hinders the development of technical skills, and the extensive job-hopping for better pay has similar effects.

Ethnic balancing problems. Originally, the industrial workforce was dominated by the Chinese. Companies and shops were predominantly in foreign or Chinese hands. Most white collar workers and middle managers were also Chinese. Later, when Malays were recruited from rural areas for industry in larger numbers, ethnic tensions increased, exploding into violent riots in 1969.

Chinese people had better and higher positions. Malays had lower status industrial jobs, but as they represented the political majority they demanded better positions and more influence in general.

This situation provides the background for the government's employment quotas and positive discrimination toward Malays, known as the Bumiputra policy, designed to achieve gradual ethnic balance and social equality. Foreign companies are compelled to follow the government's employment policies. Malays have priority in admission to higher education, scholarships, and jobs in public administration. In the private sector, business, and career jobs Malays also have many privileges. It may then come as no surprise that Chinese and Indians feel that these policies discriminate against them. Less qualified Malays get jobs and higher education because of political discrimination. However, to a large extent the practice, even if sometimes used to the extreme, is accepted as a political reality. Since the nation's traumatic experience in 1969, ethnic tension is a very sensitive, almost taboo subject. Social balance has improved, but the Bumiputra economic policy is, in many cases, abused. Chinese businessmen often use Bumiputra partners as fronts.

Due to economic expansion and low salaries Chinese people have almost completely left blue-collar factory jobs, now dominated by Malays. The labour shortage and low wages have also left some hard or low status jobs, like cleaning, construction, domestic service, etc., to the growing number of immigrants from Indonesia, Bangladesh, and other countries. These economic sectors are almost the exclusive domain of immigrants. The government motive for a rather free import of labour is to keep pressure for higher wages and inflation at bay.

Middle managers have, in many ways, a special inter-cultural and intermediate position in foreign companies. Firstly, they have to interpret, translate, and implement decisions made by higher ranking expatriate managers, and explain ethnic, social, or cultural differences back to them. Secondly, they must communicate and mediate in external company relations with the ministries and other administrative authorities involved in public and social events. Their role as cultural intermediaries makes them more than subordinate managers. They become a partner that the expatriates are forced to rely and depend on in relation to the host-country and their own employees. The dependence can be far-reaching. Middle managers represent the continuity in the company, expatriates leaders come and go. A new managing director must rely on information from local-middle managers. After staying two to three years there can still be a substantial information gap. However, this situation is less relevant when there are several expatriates, as in most Japanese subsidiaries.

When problems of co-operation or mistrust arise, middle managers cannot be replaced so easily. Due to seniority, scheduled local management takeover, sensitive political contacts in the system, and other reasons it can be almost impossible to terminate the employment of top middle managers, especially Malays with long seniority.

Government control is very extensive and quite effective through formal channels, i.e. law or guidelines, and informal channels, i.e. personal and political contacts. To counteract these institutional controls many foreign companies use lobbying to achieve their objectives. Here Nordic companies are relatively weak compared to their Japanese or American counterparts.

In part, government control is based upon the priorities of ethnic balance, as in the case of employment quotas. Bumiputra economic privileges are also part of the reason for increased local ownership and profit-sharing. But increased domestic ownership is also consistent with Malaysia's nation-building programme, as it is in other developing nations.

Foreign companies which have no free zone or pioneer status are expected to establish a local partnership in one form or another. Specifically this means that companies are asked to split up activities, localize subcontracting or sales activities, or share ownership and control with a Malay partner. Price control can also be used to regulate the distribution of profits between a foreign owner and a local sales or subcontracting partner. If a transnational corporation is unwilling to follow government guidelines, there can be problems with the importation of components, or the extension of visa permits to expatriate managers or family members. Government guidelines also require the gradual reduction and transfer of permanent expatriate jobs in a company to local managers.

Work related value-system. Because of the patriarchal tradition, employee loyalty toward the company and its top managers is normally quite strong. The loyalty can be supported in personnel policies through various benefits, such as free transportation, medical care, a housing allowance, and individual help with small problems in the family, with the authorities, etc. Compared to other TNCs in this field, Japanese companies seem to be more keen to take responsibility for employees and strengthen paternalist relations. Nordic managers prefer to avoid these extra arrangements. Nordic resistance to this notion is best illustrated in a comment offered by a Swedish manager who didn't want to use an attendance allowance: 'why pay people just for coming to work?'

In Nordic labour-management relations co-operation is often based upon an open dialogue or critical discussion. As part of the normal conflict resolution with the union or decision-making among managers and other work-teams, a kind of 'democratic dialogue' has gradually developed. In most Western countries direct, open, and face to face criticism has become a positive part of problem solving. In Malaysia this open type of criticism is unacceptable (as it was in Western societies in the past). One cannot talk back to one's superior, and one must avoid open criticism so as not to 'lose face'.

The Nordic tradition, combining an anti-authoritarian and openly critical form of co-operation, has significant problems adapting to the Malaysian combination of a patriarchal tradition and face-saving norm. In this society one cannot challenge the decision of one's superior. A person says 'yes', when he actually means no. One cannot admit faults or incompetence. Criticism or questions are taken personally and are not allowed by a subordinate. For delegation, information sharing, team-work and group management decisions this can be a substantial handicap.

Again, Japanese management seems to have an advantage in this cultural context with its more authoritarian and collective form of leadership. Japanese top managers request collective, often time-consuming discussions in the management group and other work teams until full agreement is reached. Discussions are an obligation, not a voluntary, informal process as in the Nordic countries.

In daily work, private life is not as excluded as in the Nordic or Western work place. Employees do not have the same instrumental attitude. Relations to colleagues are often more familiar and close. All information about the company and its employees spreads quickly through informal channels.

Employees are all very aware of the possibilities of ethnic tension, and make consistent efforts to dampen or neutralize them. Identity is double, in that it is characterized by one's department or work-team, and one's own ethnic group. Contrary to the Nordic or European societies, multi-cultural relations are taken as the rule rather than the exception. Although some foreign companies demand English as the working language, in most industries Bahasa Malaysia is normally spoken among the blue-collar workers. Switching between languages is quite common, but among those employees with higher education, English is the dominant language, partly to neutralize ethnic differences in communication.

The collective identity and orientation in Asian countries cannot be taken for granted in a characterization of Malaysian work relations (as it was in Hamzah-Sendut, Madsen and Thong 1989). The collective 'togetherness' and solidarity that characterize Japanese work teams are not typical in Malaysia, regardless of the efforts that are made to transfer and implement the Japanese model. In part, prevalent individualism is due to ethnic divisions, which hinder a collective identification, and to Western influence. Among middle managers rivalry is common. In Malaysia, internal company promotion is not as developed as in Japan. In the present market environment of labour shortage the tendency toward individual job changing and careerism is increasing.

Trade union identification and solidarity has deteriorated considerably, especially in the case of the younger generation. In the eyes of the young, economic boom and high demand for labour make unions superfluous, while negative media attention, government attacks, and unfavourable public opinion further discourage positive associations with unions.

Since colonial days there has been a predominance of Indians in union leadership. One reason for this is that the Indians are more skilled and fluent in English, which is used as the language of negotiation with management. However, ethnic tensions are generally not a problem in the unions. Worksite committees are mixed, although Indians can sometimes be overrepresented. Presently, trade unions are trying to recruit more Malay leaders.

EXAMPLES OF NORDIC TRANSNATIONALS IN MALAYSIA

Our research includes two case-studies of Nordic companies. The first is the assembly plant of Volvo, Swedish Motor Assemblies (SMA), and the second is a subsidiary of Ericsson, Ericsson Telecommunications. The Volvo case represents labour-management relations in a plant on a lower technological level, while Ericsson's production involves a much higher level of technology. Assembly production in SMA is characterized by rather labour-intensive production with very few automated operations. Most of the workers are semi-skilled operators, but some have the advantage of single or multiple skills. Production in Ericsson contrasts with Volvo in most of these areas. Production in the latter plant is capital- and knowledge-intensive. Employees consist of a pool of engineers, technicians, and office staff, with a few semi-skilled factory workers. SMA production is in one of the more competitive sectors, with an extreme degree of variation in the market, while Ericsson has built its business on government contracts of five to ten years in length, and has, until recently, only had one major competitor.

Volvo and Ericsson have been in Malaysia for more than 25 years, and both of these companies were unionized almost from the beginning by rather militant trade unions. The local work site committees of the unions are both relatively strong and autonomous.

Swedish Motor Assemblies (SMA)

Volvo and Ford were the first two foreign automobile assemblers in Malaysia, and both built plants rather close to one another in the industrial district of Shah Alam outside Kuala Lumpur.

The basic labour-management relations in SMA formed very early. In the beginning, Chinese labour dominated the pool of skilled workers, including foremen and staff. In the beginning of the 1970s, newly recruited Malay auto workers pressured the company for more influence. After the riots in May

1969, and the implementation of the Bumiputra policy, the Malays demanded equal treatment and a fair representation in leading positions, but the dominance of the Chinese in SMA caused tensions.

During a period of conflict and deep crisis, Volvo replaced a few Chinese middle managers and the Swedish managing director in order to find a resolution to the conflict. Malaysian middle managers continued the daily leadership of the company during this period. The ethnic and management crisis opened rather deep wounds in the co-operation and labour relations of the company, although the union was not directly involved. Employees of both Malay and Chinese origin who still work at SMA prefer to forget all about the incident, and give the impression that discussion of the subject is almost taboo.

A consequence of the events during this time was that personnel policies and production management at SMA came under the direction of Malay managers. The management's relationship to the militant trade union, Transport Equipment and Allied Industries Workers' Union, and the local area committee consisted of rather constant conflicts and mutual mistrust. Active area committee members could not be promoted. The relationship to the Swedish top managers was characterized more by respect than real co-operation. The combination of union militancy and ethnic tensions proved difficult for Swedish managers, thus they tended to rely on Malay managers in personnel and production to resolve them. But in the past few years the top management has initiated a plan to restructure the leadership and the company's relationship to the union.

The ethnic composition of labour has gradually shifted. Very few Chinese workers are still in the factory. However in the office the majority of the staff is Chinese. In the factory an overwhelming majority is Malay, a minority Indian. Recently a small number of women were employed as operators, partly as an effort to get better, more harmonious labour relations, and to reduce labour turnover.

Car assembly production in Malaysia has long been characterized by tremendous market shifts. During recession many companies chose to shutdown assembly plants to avoid incurring serious losses. It should come as no surprise that this market volatility establishes anything but trusting labour-management co-operation.

The number of employed in SMA has varied according to the market situation, from over 700 employees in 1975 to about 100 in 1985. Production volume reached a maximum of 10,000 cars (which includes contract production for other automobile corporations) in 1974, and a minimum of 400 cars in 1987. Volvo auto production reached its peak with 3,900 cars in 1984.

The market share for Volvo cars is small, especially since the success of a joint Malaysian-Japanese development of a national car project, Proton Saga, which gradually transfers production to Malaysian hands. As a result of this development the market share of all foreign cars has decreased substantially.

However, limiting production to Volvo models concomitantly limits volume, thus SMA has been in continuous negotiation with other automobile firms to contract assembly production. To increase volume and profitability SMA has been involved in production for Datsun, Alfa Romeo, Daihatsu, Subaru, Suzuki, and Renault. The volume on a contract basis varies, from a maximum of 93 percent in 1976 to less than one third in other years.

The competitive environment of automobile production and the government regulations serve to make work processes and labour-management relations in the assembly industry a rather formidable challenge. Flexibility is the first priority. Lines must be rebuilt or altered quickly as new cars or models are contracted, often with very short notice. With so many shifts and short model series, hi-tech investments in automation do not pay. Instead, these conditions force workers to be more flexible. A number of more experienced core workers, skilled or multi-skilled operators, foremen, and technicians, who know about retooling needs, bear the primary responsibility of the ongoing efforts to restructure production.

The demand for flexible workers significantly influences working time and intensity. During boom periods, the company recruits new workers and increases overtime. Recession brings the opposite consequences as the company reduces working hours or temporarily closes down and lays off employees. Overtime compensation is the most important incentive the company has to offer to increase production. There is really no system of piece-rate wages. The SMA experimented with the piece-rate system for a year, linking a rather small proportion of salaries to monthly productivity for all blue and white collar workers, but this attempt proved unsuccessful.

The SMA organizes no programmes for worker training or education, but SMA's partner, Federal Auto, runs an educational programme for auto mechanics from Volvo service and repair shops, led by a Swedish instructor. All training and teaching in SMA takes place at work, and is informally organized by the more experienced workers and foremen. Training could be a more central component of this form of flexible specialization, because when turnover rates are high and many new workers are added, poor training can adversely affect production.

Problems with labour-management relations in the industry are resolved in different ways, according to the level of trade union involvement. In the militant years of the 1970s, employers established a united front, which featured central collective negotiations with the union. In the 1980s, negotiations moved to the local, or company level, and strategies became more decentralized and differentiated. In Proton and two other Japanese auto assembly plants, the companies established in-house unions, and Japanese style, management-led co-operation was the dominant paradigm. In SMA, Malay managers followed a more traditional patriarchal model. The managers kept the works committee of the union at a distance, and co-operation only involved negotiations on collective agreements, and issues such as over-time, vacations, free days, etc. Questions related to production and work environment are excluded from co-operative efforts. Middle managers have not encouraged the committee to take an active part in labour-manage-ment relations, but over the last year, some small changes have taken place. On his own initiative, the works committee chairman has been involved in some experiments and reconstructive work to improve the lines, but in general the committee still remains excluded from labour-management relations.

The trade union that organizes workers in automobile, motorcycle, and com-ponent parts production, the Transport Equipment and Allied Industries Workers' Union, has lost more than half of its membership due to competition from in-house unions. The local committees of the union have a rather strong, and, for Malaysia, unusually autonomous position in relation to the union headquarters. In this way, different local union strategies and patterns of co-operation with management may emerge. For example, management and unionists have sought a more reform-oriented strategy of co-operation which has been successful at a formerly American-owned assembly plant. The plant was taken over by its Malaysian partner during the recession of the mid 1980s, and is now led by a Malay managing director. In close co-operation with the local works committee, the demand for flexible production was resolved in a very satisfactory way. Over 50 different car models are assembled on the lines at this plant, and on the same line there is often a mix of several models. This kind of variation in production demands special skills and flexibility from the workers. Also work tools must be both more specialized and flexible to adapt to local-line demand. The work process and production system has been con-structed in-house through a rather extensive series of experiments. This type of assembly line production contains, in itself, the creative elements that would otherwise be introduced by job rotation. Work and working time flexibility is negotiated by the local union committee and management. New recruitment and retrenchment is kept to an absolute minimum. Overtime can consist of as much working time as normal working hours during peak production time. In recessionary periods, temporary shut downs are planned far in advance. Some employees work in their own shops, while others take on short-term mechanical jobs.

It is very interesting to see a former American subsidiary under Malay management introduce a system of co-operation with the trade union that comes quite close to the Nordic model of labour-management relations. It underlines the necessity for caution when it comes to the application of national labour-management models and generalizations that include cultural and ethnic stereotypes.

Ericsson Telecommunication (ECM) / Perwira Ericsson (PEM)

Ericsson is situated in the same industrial area, Shah Alam, as SMA, but the company culture and working life may as well be from another world. SMA is a normal industrial workplace, which is very noisy and extremely hot, but Ericsson is more of an office-type work place, with air-conditioning and clean, comfortable work space.

The female blue-collar jobs in Ericsson have been reduced in number. The development of the electronic telecommunications industry is moving in the direction of software production and information systems with fewer traditional mechanical jobs. Furthermore, it seems that labour-management problems and cooperation with the union have a diminished priority. The work process and labour productivity are not major problems, as they are in the labour-intensive, competitive automobile industry.

Ericsson's primary problem in the international environment concerns the extent to which it transfers its valuable technological knowledge to partners and host countries abroad. So far, the company's strategy has emphasized strong parent company control, both in terms of ownership and technical knowledge. For Ericsson this means, in principle, to maximize exports and minimize foreign production. This is especially important where ownership and R&D control are concerned. Host countries, like Malaysia, have the opposite strategy. They seek to maximize the transfer of production and technology to domestic partners. In Malaysia, Ericsson faces a dilemma, which pits the parent company against the local-partner strategies. Headquarters limits the Malaysia subsidiary's ability to organize itself in a network type and restricts closer, and more open cooperation with the Malaysian government and the local telecommunication service company. At the same time, Malaysia, like any other state, has a very powerful position as a contract negotiator and monopsonistic buyer of Ericsson products. Buyers have an advantage in that they can sometimes put demands in terms of an ultimatum, asking the oligopolistic competitors (ITT, Siemens, NEC, Ericsson, GEC, etc.) for very good financial packages, local production, and ownership. Coming from a small country, Ericsson can only compete with its advanced technology, and its capacity to compete with financial packages from other major sellers is quite limited. In many industrialized countries these high-tech markets are reserved for national producers. What Ericsson and concerned trade union leaders in Sweden fear the most is a future market full of competing telephone equipment exporters from independent local partners to third countries. South Korea is one such case which may have this capacity very soon.

The dilemma for Ericsson Telecommunication in Malaysia can be illustrated by the situation in 1979 when a new tender competition was announced. The Malaysian Telecommunication Authority (Telecom) sought a new generation of telephone exchange systems that would share the 3 million line order between two major international companies. Telecom also required a high level of local production and local integration. In 1981 Nippon Electric Corporation (NEC) won the bidding for a less sophisticated system for use in rural areas. For the more complex metropolitan exchanges Telecom had to open a new tender, although Ericsson was supposed to have the most advanced system.

The reason for reopening the tender was partly due to the fact that technical specifications were too high, but Ericsson also failed to meet the intended requirements of local production and ownership. The state added a new, political requirement that the company establish a rather remote production facility in Kota Bahru. To comply, Ericsson quickly set up a local partner-controlled company, Perwira Ericsson (PEM), and established the production facility according to the state's guidelines. Ericsson Telecommunication (ECM) remained under unchanged, 70 per cent parent company control, with a 30 per cent share ownership belonging to the local partner, the Army Pension Fund (LTAT). LTAT also obtained a 60 percent majority control in PEM (Laxén-Payrö and Odhnoff 1985).

The reason that NEC won the first bid was probably due to the fact that the Japanese company was in a better position to negotiate and comply with the demand for local partnership.

The consequence for Ericsson was a double ownership and company structure, even though ECM and PEM were located in the very same building. PEM took the responsibility for the installation, testing of exchanges, technical training, and development. Production at the Kota Bahru facility in the north-eastern part of the peninsula became a subsidiary of PEM with about 60 workers.

From the perspective of labour-management relations, especially for the trade unions, the new production contract proved to be a rather negative development. The government defined PEM as an electronic industry firm without the right for trade unions to organize. At this time, the Electrical Industry Workers' Union (EIWU) had organized 85 percent of the total 450 employees at Ericsson. PEM employees were forced to leave the union in exchange for an in-house company union in accordance with the state's request. Furthermore, Ericsson was forced to reduce its staff by 40 workers when jobs were moved to Kota Bahru. Ironically, the collective agreement in PEM was, for the most part, a simple copy of the agreement achieved at ECM.

Co-operation between the management and works committee in ECM began on a positive note, after some initial picketing to receive recognition and reach the first collective agreement in 1975. Management was rather positive toward the works committee. Other informal co-operative efforts centred on sports activities and the social and cultural club.

In 1976, the Swedish Metal Workers' Federation initiated a kind of Swedish-Malaysian 'work council' meeting in the Ericsson company group, which was financially supported by Ericsson. The rationale for this co-operative effort was the fact that Ericsson in Sweden was badly hit by the recession and a subsequent reduction of blue-collar jobs due to technological developments. These factors reduced the number of manual jobs at Ericsson to less than half their original total in 8 years (however technicians and other white collar jobs increased somewhat). The Swedish Metal Workers, and the local union club at the Ericsson parent company wanted some of the jobs in ECM in Shah Alam relocated to Sweden. After a series of negotiations, the EIWU and the local works committee accepted the removal of part of the production in ECM, which corresponded to a reduction of 30 female operators. The Malaysian union people sought to express their solidarity with the crisis situation in Sweden, but in return they expected Swedish solidarity in similar situations should the need arise in the future.

In 1982, when management sought a second reduction in jobs at ECM, due to the transfer to Kota Bahru, the union protested. The Swedish unions couldn't see anything that they could do about the transfer. As a result, an agreement was reached to accept voluntary resignations in exchange for reasonable economic compensation.

After this first period of rather good labour-management relations, co-operation has come to a standstill. Conflicts related to overtime compensation caused very bad feelings in the works committee as a considerable amount of compensation was lacking for a number of workers. After many years of consideration and delay in the Industrial Court, due to company appeals, the parties resolved the dispute in a compromise between EIWU officials and the ECM management that still reduced the amount of compensation.

Production workers' attitudes toward ECM may be characterized by some resignation. Due to technological developments, the amount of work has been gradually reduced, but nothing has been done to upgrade or re-educate the predominately female operators.

In contrast, white collar staff and technicians receive continuous training and education. An important part of the training has also included the Telecom technicians using Ericsson equipment. A regional Ericsson training centre is established in PEM, which features advanced, telephone exchange education for testers and installers. To some extent, the centre is also used for Ericsson seminars outside the scope of the region. Recently, the centre has taken over the human resource department of ECM, and now offers a wide variety of management seminars and educational activities. The Malay female manager has a very open and critical 'Swedish' style of management, closely corresponding to a 'reform-oriented' type of Nordic management. She, like other managers and technicians, has had some specialized training and education during brief periods in Sweden, and has adopted some of the cultural attitudes. The centre views the training and education of installers and testers as an important key to further expansion of Ericsson in China and other countries in the region.

THREE EXAMPLES OF FOREIGN SUBSIDIARIES IN MALAYSIA

The European radio company

This wholly European-owned export-oriented plant is a pioneer operation that was launched in the early 1970s. To take advantage of lower labour costs this firm relocated the production of medium-range products to Malaysia. The original, and rather limited, operation was significantly expanded during the 1980s without any major changes in organization and procedures, but by the end of 1992 the total workforce amounted to almost 4,000 employees. Higher production quotas and the introduction of new radio models required more space as well as a re-arrangement of the production layout, including the introduction of a computerized-material-handling system. At this point, the Malaysian subsidiary began to support the establishment of a new plant in China for the production of low-end radios to enable the Malaysian plant to shift production to more sophisticated models that required greater flexibility and better employee training.

The operators, 80 per cent of which are female, the male foremen, technicians, and engineers work in two shifts during a five-day-work week. The ethnic composition is 60 percent Malay, 25 per cent Indian and 15 per cent Chinese.

The workers are paid a fixed monthly salary according to their grade, plus allowances for shift work and overtime, but no piece-rate. Annual increments are made individually according to a worker's performance review by the foreman.

Due to labour shortages workers received an average pay increase of 20 per cent over a period of nine months in 1990–91. The company has been forced to accept new employees up to the age of 40 with lower basic education since younger workers with better education are recruited by semiconductor companies offering a higher basic wage and more benefits. Management feels that the absence of a night shift, the simple assembly work performed under less work pressure, and most important, job security justify a lower wage. No major lay-offs have taken place; recruits are reminded of the previous downturns and lay-offs in semiconductor companies. There is an internal labour market, but foremen and supervisors are most often recruited from outside. Medical benefits include hospitalization in a second class ward and specialist fees if recommended by the company doctor. A recent advertisement highlighted these features: 'The company always places special emphasis in looking after the welfare of its employees particularly in the area of career development ... We've achieved a harmonious balance between decentralization and unity and derived the best from both – the visibility of working for a smaller firm with the avenues of moving upward in a large organization'.

One area that reflects the somewhat haphazard development of the factory concerns the issue of occupational safety. The original construction of the plant probably sought to provide a reasonable work environment, and the parent company provides some bulky ring binders with guidelines that are seldom used. Safety was given secondary consideration as the main concern was with production. Safety activities have been initiated as part of machine maintenance, but the company has not scheduled periodic machine checks. When a machine malfunctions the head of the tool shop – partly in charge of safety – attends to the breakdown. The machinists had the freedom and the personal interest to form a safety committee, but were not able to sustain a systematic effort. The committee became dormant when the process of plant expansion demanded considerable time. Eventually, the company recruited a full time safety officer who launched a campaign oriented toward good housekeeping along the lines of the Japanese '5 S' system ('Seiri' – to clear; 'Seiton' – to arrange; 'Seiso' – to clean; 'Seiketsu' – hygiene; 'Shitsuke' – discipline).

A passive concern is also reflected by the many complaints about rude foremen. When the foremen shout at the operators, they feel hurt and are afraid to engage in a discussion. The pressure to achieve production quotas is often passed through the chief foreman, who scolds the foreman, who, in turn, becomes angry with the people below him. Foremen promote operators and allocate overtime to them. New recruits experience the most pressure; they often work through break time during their first month to cope with the demands.

One particular conflict between the production line and the sales test department prompted a group of Malaysian middle managers to try to upgrade the organization. Radio parts are tested along the line, and the final product checked at the end. Lot by lot, the units are transferred to a final test before packing. If this 'sales test' identifies one defective unit, the whole lot is returned to the line, and thus reduces the number of completed units. The operators found it difficult to reach the quota as it is, and suspected that the sales test staff deliberately inflict defects to reach their target. The sales test staff on their part, accused the operators of taking short cuts and accepting obvious rejects. This conflict resulted in frustration and conflict that hindered production.

Middle managers launched The Quality Improvement Programme (QIP) to remedy this conflict. Following a seminar on Quality Improvement for Manufacturing, organized by Singapore's Juran Institute in August 1988, a group of middle managers felt that they had sufficient documentation on the success of QIP in big American and Japanese companies to convince their European boss to initiate changes. Middle managers had made a similar attempt in the 1970s, but the senior staff failed to show much interest in the proposal.

Middle managers describe their European superiors as slow-moving, careful planners who tend to focus on long-term objectives. They adjust, compromise, display a certain level of formality and respect, never lose their temper, make others feel at ease, but are also perceived as stingy. They can be approached directly, 'but why not go through your supervisor?' Malaysian managers feel as though they have considerable latitude for decision-making, and are only constrained by the production targets determined by the parent company.

The company is not unionised in spite of several attempts by The Electrical Industry Workers' Union (EIWU). The Malay personnel manager actively employs a very explicit policy aimed at barring national and in-house union organizing. Newcomers are thoroughly screened by a question on the application form that asks the applicant if he/she has 'ever been a member of any registered Trade Union'.

The Japanese Air-conditioner factory

This wholly-owned Japanese company is part of the largest foreign investment group in Malaysia, comprised of 16 manufacturers of electrical appliances and parts. The air-conditioner company was established in 1972 and is now a world leader employing 2000 workers within this product division of the Japanese transnational corporation. The company upgraded the air-conditioner plant since the mid-1980s, which represented the second phase of counter-cyclical overseas Japanese expansion where higher-end products are shifted to Malaysia in an automated production.

The strong Japanese presence is part of the Malaysian government's industrialization project designed to emulate Japanese work ethics, in-house union structures, and the close relationship between state and private sector.

A feasibility study, conducted in the national electricity service, claims Japanization is opposed to Malaysia's work-related values, and highlights the following contradictions:

'Japan: the employee has a commitment beyond wages and fringe benefits

	to the national objective of economic growth as well as to the organization that employs him.
Malaysia:	commitment appears to hinge on a pay packet. Any semblance of commitment is individualistic. Organizational or national objectives are seldom upheld.
Japan:	a shared feeling for the employees and the organization is a positive factor for continuous upgrading of the organization.
Malaysia:	segmented feelings towards professionalism, race and departments retard the progress of the organization.
Japan:	technological improvements that increase productivity benefit everybody. Initiative for this and the changes come from the workers themselves.
Malaysia:	initiative for change generally comes from the top and seldom from the workers.
Japan:	incentive payments have been long used to induce workers to maintain or increase productivity.
Malaysia:	incentive payment as such also long used but paid for overtime and not results.
Japan:	feedback is the natural result of the group orientation of the workers.
Malaysia:	feedback is restricted due to long line levels which become obstacles to effective communications. Very little follow up.'

(Personal communication, November 1992).

Furthermore, structural barriers, particularly the high turnover due to the shortage of skilled labour, imply that the concepts of lifetime employment and seniority wages have, to some extent, become irrelevant. The incidence of job changing, or job 'hopping' continue to increase. Technicians and engineers that have recently graduated are in high demand, but wholly unprepared to bind themselves to one particular company or accept a low starting salary when the prospect of changing jobs could continuously increase salaries.

While Japanese technicians are deeply involved in developing teamwork on the shop floor and expect an extra effort to solve production problems, Malaysian workers tend to abandon overtime work in crisis situations due to family priorities. Every morning the workers assemble in lines for 5–10 minutes to hear a brief talk and do morning exercise in the Japanese style, but the exercise is not popular. Workers claim that they 'have enough exercise just working'. However, another Japanese importation, the karaoke lounge, has been adopted whole-heartedly.

Oral and informal communication is a major part of this company's management style. Small circle meetings are held daily after the morning assembly when the basic business philosophy is read in all subsidiaries world-wide. Once a month, the managing director convenes a general assembly to speak to all employees.

Although job descriptions and job manuals do exist, however only in Japanese, they are considered to be of little use in the actual process of decision-making. Contrary to the Malaysian managers' British-inspired tradition of individual, status-related cubicles, Japanese offices are designed as one large room. To eliminate discord, managers exchange information and engage in broad consultations before making decisions.

The factory operation is taught by Japanese advisors who, unlike expatriates in other foreign companies, stay in Malaysia for a much longer period of time, and become attached to a Malaysian middle-manager. According to the managing director, headquarters in Japan is reluctant to have local management assume higher positions. A few years ago, a group of Malaysian middle-managers protested about this policy in writing because they felt that the Japanese management was not sincerely interested in the qualifications of this group, and failed to offer an appropriate remuneration.

The focus is on achieving high levels of productivity and quality. The slogan 'Catch up with Japan' was launched in the company recently in recognition of the fact that, 'high quality can only be achieved through continuous daily effort and that quality can go down as fast as discipline'. The current managing director recalled the subservient, very reactive and passive Malaysian managers and Japanese expatriates that he met upon his arrival:

'They were looking at Japan for dos and don'ts. The initiative was greatly in the hands of the parent company. I asked, Do you really enjoy this? I tried to cultivate a different attitude. Now we take more of the lead. We have made it happen. The campaign contributes to create initiative and a drive to achieve self-conclusive management'. Through persistent troubleshooting in production, the company has reached its foremost operational capability.

All of the subsidiaries in this company (except for the newest one that enjoys pioneer status) are organized by a national union. This group and one other Japanese group of companies account for 75 per cent of the membership of the Electrical Industry Workers' Union, which is one of the largest trade unions in Malaysia. In contrast, other Japanese investors vehemently reject unionization.

The Japanese company understands the union's role in terms of a metaphor about the two wheels of a cart that must be the same size for the cart to maintain a steady course. The policy states: that workers should be reasonably compensated for their hard work; that interaction with the union should be reserved to the tri-annual renegotiation of the collective agreement; and that the minor, day-to-day problems are best solved when left to a joint consultative council. Bypassing the union means that 'trivial' conflicts can be resolved in an egalitarian atmosphere, as larger issues are easily forgotten by the workers. The personnel manager explains that, 'We were very scared about a possible influence of Western unions; now these are asking for rights concerning management prerogatives like promotion, dismissal, transfer and job rotation. Now the union wants to run the other wheel of the cart too. We foresee problems.' However, the recent example of automation of a television plant showed that longer daily working hours, more shifts, and more intensive work to suit the new machinery were accepted by the union in exchange for substantial monetary compensation (Hing Ai Yun 1990, 81ff).

The American semi-conductor company

This factory was established in 1973 by a transnational corporation based in the United States, with production facilities in several countries. The company belongs to the strategic sector of Malaysia's export-oriented industrialization programme. Due to the presence of large investments by all major manufacturers of semiconductors, Malaysia has established itself as the world's largest exporter, and third largest producer of these electronic components.

The factory has a workforce of 2,400 employees. In spite of the increase in production volume, which was achieved through automation, the total numbers of workers in the plant remained stable for some time. Ninety-five per cent of the production operators are female. The personnel manager claims that in the early days, the high percentage of women working in this sector reflected a preference for female nimbleness, but today, as automation makes this qualification obsolete, the dominance of women in the industry is more a matter of tradition. The ethnic composition is 55 per cent Malay, 30 per cent Chinese, and 15 per cent Indian. The average age is 28, with most of the workers ranging between 20 and 39 years.

During the last two years, the company has been able to choose those applicants with a higher basic education. The personnel manager explained that the earlier 'cheap-labour strategy' has been replaced by a preference for skills and a certain type of person. The factory runs in three shifts, that rotate on a weekly basis. A substantial amount of overtime work is arranged every weekend. Last year, 30 per cent of the employees were at work on every day that factory was open. The turnover is 0.5 per cent a month and 25 per cent of the workforce has been employed since the first day the factory opened.

The basic salary is above average. The company offers individual supplements and increases on the basis of the supervisor's performance evaluation. The level of standard benefits is higher, and the medical coverage, which includes all family members, is the best in the industry. Furthermore, the company grants subsidies for the purchase of a car, a house, and educational assistance. The company maintains an internal labour market. We found that all of the secretaries, with one exception, were former operators who had been promoted after taking classes. The management offers incentive schemes to promote innovative ideas to solve problems, and quality control teams can win holidays for themselves and their families.

Safety activities are clearly defined in the managerial structure, and primarily originate from a concern for smooth production runs as part of the 'Total Quality Control' concept. Safety, environmental issues, and industrial hygiene is monitored by one policy-making body with the plant engineer as chairman. The company claims to follow their own, more strict standards, which are audited world-wide every year by an external insurance company. The production operators are not involved in safety activities, other than being subjected to rules and guidelines for the enforcement of those rules. Since workers can only express their views through attitude surveys and suggestion boxes, problems such as the stress due to the reorganization of work arrangements and increased work pressure in the course of automation are unlikely to be considered.

In principle, the company's 'open door' policy should facilitate direct feedback to top managers, but workers who feel shy may instead choose to put an anonymous note on the bulletin board.

The wages in this company, and all others in the sector, are surveyed every year by an external consulting firm, and their report is used as a yardstick when the overall annual pay increase is determined.

All aspects of the operation are covered by guidelines in thick manuals. For example, concerning plant security, sabotage is defined as, 'mechanical; fire or bomb; germs and poison; labour – deliberate attempts to create unrest', the latter subdivided into: 'stink bombs to damage morale and disrupt routines; rumours to tear down morale and loyalty; labour sabotage: strikes, unrest, personal antagonism, spoilage of work, slow down, provocation of fear on account of false alarms, saboteurs, working to the rule'. The manual advises security guards to enhance their familiarity with the movements in and around the plant and to remain 'Alert, aware, awake, alive'.

The company is indeed alert with regard to trade unions. Like all American companies in this sector, the management claims that a third party is not necessary 'because [the company] can take better care of the people'.

Workers in the semiconductor industry, which accounts for the majority of manufacturing exports of Malaysia, have been denied the right to organize for 20 years. After several unsuccessful US labour organization attempts to convince the Congress to deny Malaysia its current Generalized Special Preferences (GSP) status, the Minister of Human Resources decided to modify the *de facto* ban on unions. The new policy states that in-house unions can be formed in the semiconductor industry.

American companies adamantly reject any third party interference in their paternalistic managerial strategy. However, the threat of relocation outside of

Malaysia seems doubtful considering the huge investments that US companies have already made, and those that continue to pour in. MLO claims that the few in-house unions that formed in the electronic companies in Johore Baru have affiliated with this national centre, but the only example of a worker-initiated in-house union in an American electronic company (RCA, which was later renamed Harris Semiconductor) was subjected to harsh, persistent, and successful union-busting efforts by the employer. The fact that an in-house union in Malaysia covers only a particular plant, not a group of enterprises with the same ownership, enabled this particular company to rename the plant, transfer all employees except the members of the union committee, and then a few months later, terminate the employment of this group due to 'the lack of work.'

MODELS OF LABOUR-MANAGEMENT RELATIONS

In brief, the Japanese approach to inter-cultural management can be characterized as the most comprehensive, and yet the least sensitive to the host culture. The impact of Japanese management in Malaysian factories stems not from 'kinship' between two Asian nationalities, but from a combination of factors: the determination to secure productivity and quality levels comparable to Japanese specifications; limited overseas exposure, including the Japanese managers' lack of foreign language skills; the financial resources available to train Malaysian employees to the extent that employees are reconditioned during long-term stays in Japan; and the support of the Malaysian government through its 'Look East' policy that aspires to emulate Japanese work ethics.

Not only do Japanese expatriates occupy key management positions at the top, but they also dominate the second layer of management, either as 'advisors' to Malaysian managers or as overt superiors. To break the relatively closed circle, within which the Japanese expatriates are making decisions, Malaysian managers will have to make use of their training and exposure to Japanese managerial style. The problem is that the Japanese tend to operate collectively, while the Malaysian managers often compete openly.

Japanese investors are responsible for the lion's share of foreign-owned manufacturing in Malaysia, and their investments span the period from the early days (first half of the 1970s) of labour-intensive, simple assembly to today's higher-end products that are supported by R&D departments within the subsidiary itself. The trend toward the strong Japanese presence in high absolute terms is also apparent when it comes to their observance of the national objective to increase the local content in manufactured products. The problem for potential Malaysian partners is that the Japanese prefer to use their own subcontractors.

American companies maintain even closer links to the state's export-oriented industrialization policy. Their presence in Malaysia covers a shorter span of time, but occupies almost a production sector of its own: the manufacturing of semi-conductors. In helping Malaysia become a world leader in exports, American companies have not only gained strategic importance in the national economy, but are also responsible for subjecting the Malaysian economy to the fluctuations of the global computer industry.

On the enterprise level, the volatility in this sector calls for maximum flexibility in terms of the arrangement of working hours and sudden, massive lay-offs. The high profit ratio in this industry is partly due to the intensity of work imposed upon the employees and to technologically advanced investments. These profits are envied by other foreign companies, claiming that '[the Americans] have all the money in the world'. This makes competitive remuneration possible in a labour market with an acute shortage of female unskilled or semi-skilled production operators, and more importantly gives the company the resources to offer an expansion of welfare benefits and increase training.

The open office landscape style of management that emphasizes fast, direct communication from the top, and scope for equally immediate feedback from the floor, represents a carefully planned managerial strategy of 'compassionate' human relations. There is an effort to soften work pressure and strict discipline with positive encouragement of the individual and periodic 'pats on the back.'

American companies are probably the most thoroughly organized. These firms are fully equipped with thick manuals produced by the parent company offering detailed guidelines to help employees handle any eventuality. American companies are equally consistent in their rejection of any kind of union involvement. It might be the case that the 'intimate' relationships in the companies ranging from top managers to the floor (all addressing each other by first name only and writing memos in a personalized, hand- written style) would collapse as a mere illusion, if a third party was to be involved. But is also true that the stereotyped trade union bogey, and lack of experience in dealing with them in the US have led these companies to fear union organizations in Malaysia.

The patriarchal managerial style that characterizes the American manager lacks an ability to adapt to inter-cultural situations. The blunt, four-letter-word-shouting, American expatriate will obviously offend Malaysian cultural values. He may either choose to hide behind Malaysian middle managers claiming, 'I'm an old bastard, I cannot change' or emphasize the informal 'buddy-buddy' approach which is well received in the Malaysian context. However, there is no evidence of genuine sensitivity to the cultural environment, as the arrogance of modernity *vis-à-vis* indigenous expressions of culture remains unchanged. In the self-perception of many American managers, the direct, open communication between individuals is probably equivalent to democratic labour-management relations, that are only limited by the presence of a collective or trade union organization.

European companies can be divided into two distinct categories: those that were established during colonial times, that produce consumer goods for the domestic market, and whose owners might now well be 'Malaysianized'; and the newcomers who have joined the Japanese and American companies in the quest for cheap labour during the first decade of the 'New Economic Policy' after 1969.

For both types, it seems that the pressure to achieve high productivity, flexibility, and a transformation of labour-management relations arrived somewhat later. It is possible that the colonial experiences with command-oriented labour management of low-salaried labour gives the European a realistic perception of the characteristics of a first-generation industrial workforce, and a more reliable understanding of which kinds of production are the most viable in the initial stages.

The history of colonial administration might also explain the European tendency to post expatriates in subsidiaries for primarily technical reasons. Once qualified Malaysian staff is available, Europeans do not hesitate to replace expatriates to reduce costs.

Likewise, the European attitude toward the cultural environment seems to demonstrate an understanding of the limits of inter-cultural communication with people of a different social and philosophical tradition, and motivate the delegation of tasks and confer a degree of confidence in Malaysian managers.

On the whole, European managers seem to be more pragmatic in their approach. The relationship to headquarters is one of independence, which encourages adaptation to the Malaysian context and autonomy in day-to-day decision-making, with fewer pre-designed procedures. However, the managerial style remains formal, bureaucratic, and top-down, until such a time when the need arises – in some cases through the initiative of Malaysian managers – for European managers to make an effort to appropriate some of the innovative Japanese and American methods of organizing quality activities on the shop floor and promote company culture via social activities and symbolism. In this sense, European companies are 'slow learners', somewhat conservative in outlook, and reliant upon their cross-cultural skills that are moulded by the colonial traditions and the diversity of Europe.

This pragmatism of cultural adaptation also influences European attitudes toward trade unions and co-determination, which, like the Nordic companies, is by and large left to Malaysian middle managers.

CONCLUDING REMARKS

The primary objectives of union activities in Malaysia involve increasing membership through organizing and addressing bread-and-butter issues in collective bargaining. These traditional tasks continue to take the majority of the unions' modest resources. An adversary and potentially aggressive approach to management prevails. Given this background, Nordic-managed companies experience trade unions in Malaysia as a 'missing partner' in any effort to develop long-term, stable relationships that emphasize co-operation and co-determination over a range of issues related to the performance and development of the company. An active, well-organized union partner is missing at the enterprise level and the national level, where welfare policies and industry-wide collective agreements are absent.

The Nordic model fails in Malaysia because its strong point, the *institutionalized* regulation of labour-management relations at the national level, is largely absent. In the Nordic countries, the nature of co-operation between the two parties at enterprise level largely depends upon these labour institutions and mutual public recognition. In Malaysia, trade unions are not considered equal partners. They are met with distrust by the government, most foreign companies and the emerging business class.

The American and Japanese models of labour relations differ substantially from the Nordic model in that they are management-dominated, formed by the company headquarters with little or no labour influence. In an authoritarian culture, companies from the former countries find more success in the implementation of their labour-management relations than their Nordic counterparts.

Western business models all understand labour as a cost of operation, which is recruited for its skills from the external labour market. In contrast, Japanese management conceives of labour as an integral part of the company's permanent resources, continuously under development by the company (Gospel 1992). Thus, personnel policies and human resource development in Japanese companies often emphasizes more advanced and far-sighted planning in Malaysia.

Management's lack of a relevant 'partner' in Malaysia is the result of several phenomena. The scepticism and mistrust that remain a part of the relationship between management and unions in Malaysia, even after negotiating several successive collective agreements, is the likely result of employers' numerous and continuous violations of the minimum requirements stipulated in the Employment Act, which include sudden lay-offs of a large number of workers, factory shut-downs, and the victimization of individual workers. One important feature of the employment relationship is that a high level of productivity is achieved by direct 'despotic' pressure, not by piece-rated wages. In spite of these problems, the seniority-based rate of compensation outlined in the Employment Act, which makes it costly to dismiss employees with seniority, tends to have some stabilizing effect.

The regulation of the labour market and the resolution of conflicts are tightly bound by institutionalized, legal procedures. But unions perceive that this legalism is strongly biased in favour of management; and as such, it does not form an appropriate basis for the development of mutually beneficial, contractual, binding relations to defuse the potential conflict situations when a collective agreement expires.

The persistent struggle for higher wages, bonus, overtime compensation, shift allowances and other benefits also stems from the absence of redistributive welfare policies in Malaysia. Workers that are forced to leave the labour market because of lay-offs, prolonged sickness or retirement are not eligible for social security benefits that, by any standard, match their loss of income. In order to fill the void at the higher end of the workforce, Malaysia's insurance industry is now engaged in a rapid expansion to meet these needs through schemes which are also offered to trade unions on a group basis.

On the national level, the position of the union movement in Malaysia is very different in comparison to the widely accepted and institutionalized role of Nordic unions in all aspects of social, economic, and political affairs. The media engages in a continuous effort to discredit the unions for undermining national development objectives and leaders' alleged tendency to use the unions to advance personal interests and abuse membership fees. One particular cause of the government's crack down on union leaders has to do with their increasing interest in international relations and the alleged smear of the country during frequent overseas trips. The government and the media interpret the struggle to unionize the semiconductor industry as treason and the leadership of MTUC as traitors. The interest of an export industry has become an issue of national security.

Does the Nordic model of close management-labour co-operation and an open, informal management style have any advantages in the global transition of companies and production? In the long run, at the company level, the Nordic model might prove to be more compatible with new imperatives of flexible specialization and the necessity of employee participation in knowledge-based industries.

The old, hierarchical style decision making and organization in transnationals, i.e. from national parent companies to subsidiaries, which focuses its efforts on cost reduction and optimal efficiency in operation and processing, is on the verge of change. Akihiro Okumara shows that even Japanese companies, as the most centralized corporations, are in the midst of profound transformation that follows the paradigmatic change in management and organization of Western companies:

59

(1) from operation—centred to innovation centred,
(2) from pyramidal hierarchy to a network—type organization,
(3) from group to individual—based human resource management, and
(4) from an incremental approach to innovation to an entrepreneurial approach.

(Shibagaki et al. 1991, p.34).

Recent discussions concerning the problems of international management continue to challenge the hierarchical structure of global corporations. The organizational critique offered by management experts is often more radical than trade union suggestions. The implications of the proposed paradigm, especially in knowledge-intensive companies, involve an increase in local autonomy, the delegation of responsibility and individual or group participation in self-reliant teams, which constitutes a radical break-up and reduction of corporate bureaucracies and heavy organizational structure (Peters 1992). In short, this heralds the dawning of increased subsidiary autonomy, open information channels, and opportunities for more creative, innovative work.

In this perspective, transnational companies have the potential to act as *multi-cultural agents of modernization and development*. Local autonomy in global networks has the potential to grant more equal cultural partnership in the construction of multi-cultural teams. However, in this more voluntary, co-operative structure the forces of integration and convergence persist in spite of the corporate principle of cultural pluralism. Thus, while labour-management relations may recognize the local *divergence* of national regulation and cultural traditions, the growth of knowledge-intensive production, increased global information and communication, will lead transnationals to move in the direction of *inter-cultural convergence* to borrow the 'best', i.e. the most productive and profitable practices of human resource management, for global implementation. But the importance of this new human-resource-oriented fragment of the global economy remains to be seen, especially in the Third World context. Malaysia may be somewhat of an exception to the rule of unemployment, misuse, and underdevelopment of human resources in most parts of the world.

In our opinion, in the labour-management field of TNC competition, Nordic companies lack a stronger profile and a more conscious strategy. On the home market, the institutions of the Nordic model have long helped companies to reach an advanced level of democratic participation and human resource development in co-operation with an actively involved union partner. Can the 'democratic dialogue' work in future companies that are organized as networks? Can this model be adopted in other societies and cultures? In Malaysia we have found that the missing trade union partner and authoritarian traditions are substantial barriers to co-operation at the present stage of development.

Rather than discard the authoritarian rule as outdated in Malaysia, it is important to consider the merits of 'soft authoritarianism'. The Malaysian model has managed to suspend class contradictions in an environment of persistent social inequalities.

Irrespective of the prognosis of the Nordic model as such, future industrial relations will depend not only on changing labour market regulations in individual countries, but increasingly on the way that managers are influenced by their experience of foreign cultures and different kinds of labour-management relations. Inter-cultural communication and competence will become a more important factor as managers try to integrate new experiences that enable them to develop their labour resources in global company structures.

NOTE

1. Respectively International Development Studies, Roskilde University, Denmark, and School of Social Science, Universiti Sains Malaysia, Penang.

REFERENCES

Asma Abdullah, 1992. *Understanding the Malaysian workforce. Guidelines for managers*. Kuala Lumpur, Malaysian Institute of Management.

Gospel, Howard, 1992. *Markets, firms and management of labour in modern Britain*. Cambridge, Cambridge University Press.

Hamzah-Sendut; Madsen, John and Thong, Gregory, 1989. *Managing in a plural society*. Singapore, Longman and Malaysian Institute of Management.

Hing Ai Yun, 1990. 'Industrial automation and the transformation of work organization: Three case studies in West Malaysia', in *Economic and Industrial Democracy*, vol. 11, pp. 65–92.

Hofstede, Geert, 1980. *Culture's consequences: International differences in work-related values*. Beverly Hills, Sage.

Kawanishi, Hirosuke, 1992. *Enterprise unionism in Japan*. London and New York, Kegan Paul International.

Laxén-Payrö, Mariana and Odhnoff, Jan, 1985. *The Internationalization of enterprises. Three cases of foreign direct investment decisions*. Stockholm, Arbetslivscentrum.

Peters, Tom, 1992. *Liberation Management*. New York, Random House.

Rodgers, Gerry, 1991. *Labour institutions and economic development*. Discussion paper No. 41. Geneva, International Institute for Labour Studies.

Shibagaki, K.; Trevor, M. and Abo T. (eds.), 1991. *Japanese and European management. Their international adaptability*. Tokyo, University of Tokyo Press.

Wangel, Arne, 1991. *Areas of conflict and patterns of conflict resolution in industrial relations in Malaysia*. Working Paper No.10. Göteborg, Centre for East and Southeast Asian Studies, University of Göteborg.

Williamson, Hugh, 1991. 'Japanese enterprise unions in transnational companies: Prospects for international co-operation', in *Capital and Class*, vol. 45, Autumn, pp. 17–34.

3

Labour Institutions and Flexible Capitalism in Taiwan

LAURIDS S. LAURIDSEN[1]

Labour institutions and state labour policies are frequently referred to in the literature on the industrial success of Asia's economic giants, Japan and South Korea. Normally, three aspects of the Japanese model have been given particular attention in the debate: a) strategically oriented industrial policy and state-business interaction; b) co-operative competition through private business interaction in horizontal networks; c) co-operation between labour and management through particular employment systems. The latter include such elements as life-time employment, the nenko wage system, the particular combination of permanent core workers and flexible contract workers, institutions for joint consultations and enterprise-based unionism. Similarly, the writings on South Korea's rapid economic transformation refer to institutional factors conducive to shop floor productivity and product quality.[2]

Taiwan is probably *the* success story of East Asia, combining economic growth and structural transformation with substantial improvements in education, health and living standards and with a fairly equal distribution of income. What then is the role of labour and labour institutions in Taiwan's successful capitalist development? Did it occur just as the result of industrious and hard working entrepreneurs, diligent state planning and successful timing in relation to the changing 'windows of opportunity' in the world market, or have labour institutions affected the speed and the structure of capitalist industrialization in Taiwan? The present chapter suggests that the high and sustained growth in labour productivity as well as the high level of production flexibility in exporting industries in Taiwan to a substantial degree reflect the underlying micro-institutions in and around the workplace.

FLEXIBLE CAPITALISM UNDER STATE GUIDANCE

As in most cases of capitalist transformation, the *State* in Taiwan has played a crucial role in the four decades of rapid capitalist industrialization. More precisely, state power is being used to 'raise the economy's investable surplus;

insure that a high portion is invested in productive capacity within the national territory; guide investments into industries that are important for the economy's ability to sustain higher wages in the future; and expose the investment projects to international competitive pressure whether directly or indirectly' (Wade 1990, p. 342). This was possible because the state elite had a high degree of relative autonomy from the economic elites, and because it developed a relative high degree of administrative capability. Finally, the commitment of the state elite to capitalist industrial transformation was to a substantial extent an elite survival strategy in a particular political and geo-political context.

Strategic state intervention is thus one core aspect of Taiwan's mode of industrialization. The remaining two are the particular business strategy and the prevailing labour institutions. Let us consider *the business strategy* first. Although Taiwan has both large firms and business conglomerates, it is reasonable to emphasize that the majority consists of small and medium size enterprises (SMEs). In 1986, 91% of all establishments had less than 50 workers employed and the share of employment in manufacturing establishments having less than 50 workers increased from 49% in November 1982 to 54% in November 1990. In all industries, the shares were 54% and 59%, respectively.[3] Moreover, Taiwan's exports have originated predominantly in these locally owned, small to medium enterprises. Large firms are not very export-oriented, and an enormous number of small scale exporters and export traders organize most exports. The number of export traders has kept pace with the overall expansion of manufactured exports and grew from 2,777 in 1973 to 20,597 in 1984. By 1984, Taiwan had almost four times as many export traders as South Korea (Chou 1988; Levy 1988).

Taiwan's myriad small-scale firms are generally following a business strategy based on labour-intensive products. These firms typically operate in markets where the products are standardized, where access barriers are low, where the production technology is well-known and where there is no economies of scale. The critical factor is low input prices, including low unit labour costs. The SMEs have a short profit horizon; seeking niches in new emerging markets; being hyper-flexible and adjusting quickly to changing global opportunities. The competition is excessive and pricing is cut-throat, with most firms operating as price-takers. Therefore, not surprisingly, both the birth rate and the mortality rate of these firms are extremely high (Greenhalgh 1984; Myers 1984; Lam 1989; Mody 1990).

According to among others Biggs and Levy, the competitive advantage of the SMEs in Taiwan has to do with production flexibility and marketing capability. Unlike the South Korean conglomerates, which follow a vertical upgrading strategy of in-house mass-production and aggressively invest in large-scale facilities with the best technology available on global markets,

Taiwanese producers follow a highly flexible 'bootstrap strategy' aimed at market niches for non-standardized products.

> The competitive strategy adopted by most Taiwanese firms followed the highly flexible, niche-producer pattern. Such a strategy concentrates on short product cycles, quick product delivery schedules, short production runs, and mixes of products aimed at the particular market niches. So while the cost leaders compete by extending the length of production runs, and by increasing product standardization, flexible niche producers compete by increasing production flexibility and focusing on market segments (Levy and Kuo, 1991, p. 380).

This difference between the Korean high volume assembly strategy and the Taiwanese niche strategy is well illustrated by an American buyer from a large department store chain: 'When we need five thousand pairs of shoes, we go to a Korean firm for its long production runs and lower cost; when we need five hundred pairs at the end of the season with pink laces, in two weeks, we go to Taiwan' (Levy and Kuo, p. 382).

Thus, the main strategic orientation of Taiwanese small and medium firms is penetration of untapped niches in the early stages of the product cycle. The majority of these SMEs is not in the position of mastering complex technologies, i.e. producing high technology products or applying high-technology processes. While the South Korean firms increasingly master process technologies that permit higher levels of productivity, Taiwanese firms orient themselves towards product innovation – developing new products, differentiating existing products and replicating effort of other firms.

The predominant flexible-niche strategy is facilitated by several factors. First, it is characterized by an extreme form of product specialization and sub-contracting. Taiwanese firms not only procure most components from outside, they often even subcontract a substantial part of their assembly operations. Therefore, they can adjust rapidly to changing market conditions in the main overseas markets. Second, as both fixed costs and inventory costs can be kept at a minimum, it is possible to initiate production with little up-front invest-ment as well as keeping the cost of failure low. Third, as each piece of capital equipment is owned by one entrepreneur, no one is locked with a fixed invest-ment in specialized capital equipment that might be idle most of the time. According to Danny Lam, 'Taiwanese industrial owners tend to see their capital equipment as commodity producers rather than equipment for specific industries. Therefore, there are few institutional barriers to capital mobility, i.e. metal stamping machines that normally stamp buckles can be readily adapted to stamping automobile parts if needed' (Lam 1989, p. 172). Fourth, as far marketing capabilities is concerned, Taiwanese firms can rely on either specialized market information provided by local traders or on overseas kinship linkages. Therefore, direct export is much more usual than in, for instance, South Korea.

Altogether, these characteristics make it possible for Taiwanese firms to earn profits by cultivating flexibility. It is a type of guerrilla industrialization in which firms enter shifting lines of business for shorter periods. In a 'grasshopper-like' fashion they shift horizontally to new designs of existing products, and it is not unlikely that they even shift into new product lines – from electronic components to assembly of 'one-piece' telephones, from TV sets to computer monitors or from video games to satellite receivers.

As mentioned above, the rise and the reproduction of flexible capitalism in Taiwan has not just been left to the market forces. It has been affected by strategic state intervention, both directly through various programmes aiming at promotion of small- and medium-sized enterprises, and indirectly through ownership of, or guidance of, large upstream producers that in turn are input and capital suppliers to and sometimes marketing channels for SMEs. Moreover, production flexibility and networking is embedded in institutional principles of trust, loyalty and predictability rooted in family ties. These family ties include blood and marriage as well as other long-term personal relationships (Orrú et. al 1991; Hamilton and Kao 1990).

How then are *labour institutions* connected with flexible capitalism? How is labour incorporated into surplus production and what are the mechanisms through which labour flexibility is obtained? Although the two are inter-related, it might be fruitful to distinguish between institutions in the labour market and institutions at the workplace. Labour market flexibility here refers to the absence of labour institutions – of legal and/or negotiated restrictions – that protect workers from arbitrary firing, wage reduction, etc. One dimension is *numerical* flexibility, enhancing employers' ability to adjust their labour input. This is done either through adjustment of the number of employees using such mechanisms as turnover, temporary lay-off and recall, temporary workers, part-time workers, subcontracting and homeworking, or through flexible working time (i.e. work shifts and overtime practices) without modifying the number of employees. A second dimension has to do with *wage* flexibility. Such flexibility may rest upon flexible wage systems (performance-linked wages instead of fixed wages), flexible wage structures (ensuring variable wage differentials between different segments of employees) and/or the lack of social wage components in the wage package, i.e. lack of state support for the reproduction of labour power. Workplace *regimes*, in contrast, refer to the existing formal or informal labour arrangements at the workplace. I will turn back to the idea of workplace regimes after having described the prevailing pattern of labour market flexibility in Taiwan.

A FLEXIBLE LABOUR MARKET IN TAIWAN

The Taiwanese labour market is basically open and flexible. During the 1960s and 1970s, a land reform and an organic-chemical revolution in agriculture created a surplus of labour which could find employment in the manufacturing sector, especially in the expanding labour-intensive industries. Young female workers provided the major new source of labour during this period, and in the late 1970s there was even a labour shortage for that type of workers. During the second half of the 1980s, the labour shortage became even more general and married women re-entered the labour market together with immigrant workers.

Numerical flexibility is prevalent in Taiwan. In 1990, labour turnover (measured as the monthly separation rate) was 3.6% in manufacturing, and during the period 1977–89 it oscillated between 3.1% and 4.1%. The turnover rate was higher in labour-intensive industries and among female workers.[4] In May 1990, the average length of job tenure was 7.6 years in all industries, 5.0 years in manufacturing and 5.6 years among blue collar workers. On average female workers had a job tenure of 6.2 years, but among female workers in manufacturing it was only 3.8 years, compared to 5.8 years for men. Among the total employed persons, 26.6% had stayed in their present jobs for more than 10 years. In manufacturing the share was only 14.7% and among blue collar workers 18.3%, while only 8% of female workers in manufacturing reported that they had been employed for more than 10 years in the present job.[5] The high elasticity of female labour relative to male labour also shows up when we look at changes in women's labour participation rates. The pattern shows great fluctuations that correspond to business cycles (Chou 1989; Cheng and Hiung 1992). Numerical flexibility in the form of flexible working hours is also high in Taiwan. According to official labour statistics, average monthly working hours were 223 in 1977, 19 of which were overtime. In 1989 the figure had declined to 204 hours including 13 hours of overtime. However, these average figures conceal large variations in working time and even workers in large enterprises claim to have had 100 hours per month overtime work.[6]

Due to the steady rise in earnings, *wage flexibility* is less manifest in Taiwan.[7] As the wage system combines a basic wage and allowances, it is potentially quite flexible. Normally, the base wage constitutes only about half of the monthly earnings and it can be found as low as one-third or one-fourth. The remainder, then, is extra-hour pay and allowances, including individual work-evaluation allowances. Finally, the traditional practice of giving extra money to employees just before the Chinese New Year still prevails in the form of a year-end bonus normally equal to 5 to 20 percent of the total annual wage (Chao 1991). The flexible wage system is particular important as a disciplinary mechanism, while the flexible wage structure appears to be the main mechanism of labour flexibility on the island. The flexible wage structure manifests itself in the difference in earnings between small and large manufacturing enterprises, and between labour-intensive and capital-intensive enterprises. Concerning the former, workers in enterprises employing 10–29 workers earned only 69% as much as workers in large enterprises with 500 or more employees in 1989.[8] Wage differentials between labour-intensive and capital-intensive industries to a large extent reflect gender positions. In 1989, female workers in manufacturing earned only 65% as much as male workers, which is significantly more than in 1981 when female workers were paid 71% of male wages.[9] As regards income security, the minimum wage level has now been raised to around 50% of the average manufacturing wage, but firms are still paying below that level, especially to women workers (Chang 1990, p. 7). Taiwan has no unemployment benefits and pension systems, although it is in the process of developing some.[10] The social wage component of the wage, therefore, is still almost absent in Taiwan.

Traditionally, Taiwan's *formal labour market institutions* have been *non-effective*. The density of unionization was substantially higher than in South Korea. In 1980, 20.4% of the non-agricultural employees were unionised, and in contrast to South Korea, this share increased, so that the membership share went up to 33% in 1989 (Lee 1991, p. 41). This development, however, appears less impressive when it is found that up to 1987, most workers were joining company unions because the company (under pressure from the state) forced them to join, or entered craft unions in order to get access to labour insurance benefits (Lee 1991, p. 29).

Taiwan has a single union system with compulsory membership. The basic unit of organization is the plant-level industrial union. The Union Act stipulates that all workers in workplaces with 30 or more employees have the right to unionize, and in fact requires them to do so. Staff and workers employed in public administration, schools, research institutes and armament factories, however, are excepted from the right to organize.

As a general rule, wage determination is the sole prerogative of management, which sets wages in the light of the prevailing rates in other companies. Moreover, the management personnel directly supervise plant unions. Finally, unions are subject to more indirect central control from senior unions at a higher level, from public authorities and from the Kuomintang Party apparatus.

Taiwan has for decades been equipped with a variety of formal labour laws. As they are not enforced and have trivial or zero penalty provisions, they have hardly had any real influence. The only exceptions are the Labour Disputes Law, the Labour Insurance Law and the Labour Standard Law. During the period of Martial Law, strikes, lockouts and work slowdowns were not allowed. Since the lifting of Martial Law in July 1987, the Labour Disputes Law in combination with some provisions in the Union Law makes it almost impossible to establish a legal strike. The Labour Standard Law defines working conditions in such areas as working time (including overtime and overtime payment), retirement pay, severance pay, back pay and maternity leave. Generally, the law must be considered as having a relatively high level of provisions compared to other countries at the same level of development.[11] Still, it appears to be thought of as simple window dressing and most companies, even the large firms and public enterprises, do not abide by the law at all.

Altogether, we can conclude that Taiwan's labour market, although segmented, comes close to the non-rigid and 'institutions-free' labour market found in neo-classical economics. Still, that notion evaporates when we take into consideration workplace institutions, too.

WORKPLACE REGIMES: BURAWOY AND DEYO

In order to obtain a more profound understanding of the flexible nature of the Taiwanese workforce and the productivity-enhancing mechanisms, it is necessary to look beyond labour market institutions and consider micro-institutions in and around the workplace. Before turning to the country-specific evidence, I will briefly present Burawoy's approach to factory regimes and Frederic Deyo's analysis of East Asian Labour Systems.

Answering the overall question of how it is possible for capitalist economies to reproduce and stabilize themselves, Burawoy focuses on the political and ideological dimension of production.[12] The fundamental problem of capitalism is not just that of reproduction of relations of production but also of reproduction of relations *in* production. The latter cannot be taken for granted. The general managerial problem is how to translate the capacity of labour (labour power) into actual labour. Moreover, the dilemma of capitalist control is to secure surplus value (and thus reproducing relations of production) while at the same time to obscure it – to keep it hidden. According to Burawoy, these core processes of reproduction are regulated by a 'political apparatus of production' which shapes the ongoing struggles in production and organizes consent at the shop floor. These ongoing struggles in the arena of production, Burawoy refers to as 'production politics', and the overall political-ideological form of production (including both the political and ideological effects of the labour process and the political apparatus of production) he refers to as the *factory regime*. Further he distinguishes between two generic forms of factory regimes: despotic regimes, that are based on the unity of reproduction of labour and the process of production and in which coercion prevails over consent, and hegemonic regimes in which social security legislation guarantees a certain minimum level reproduction of labour, independent of participation in production, and in which labour legislation limits the arbitrary power of managers, the result being that workers must be persuaded to co-operate with management. As demonstrated above, labour legislation and social security legislation are virtually absent in Taiwan and therefore we are here dealing with a despotic type of labour regime.

It is a crucial point in Burawoy's analysis that the specific character of despotic regimes varies with pattern of proletarianisation, character of the labour process, type of state intervention and form of inter-firm competition. Having studied factory regimes, in, among other cases, early cotton industries in England and Russia, Burawoy found that market despotism (Marx's proto-typical form of factory regime) was a rare form of factory regime. By market despotism he refers to the pure capitalist form in which the employer-worker relationship is entirely mediated through the wage – that is through the anarchy and whip of the market which leads to despotism in the factory. In his historical analysis, Burawoy found that patriarchal, paternalist and company state forms of despotic factory regimes were prevalent and that patterns of working-class struggle could be explained by reference to these different factory regimes.

By making a distinction between relations of production and relations in production, and by separating the organization of the work process and the political apparatus of production, Burawoy is able to find similar relations of production combined with different relations in production, and to find the same labour process combined with very different types of politics of production and factory regimes. That opens up possibilities for historically concrete analyses of the various forms of factory regimes according to how they secure and obscure surplus value from workers.

In an East Asian context, Burawoy's work on factory regimes has been extended by Frederic Deyo, who develops a labour property theory of proletarianisation.[13]

> Labour systems define the means through which labor is transformed into products (including services) and more liquid economic assets (e.g. wages, benefits, profits). These systems can best be understood and differentiated by reference to changing and politically contested distributions of economic property rights. First, labor systems differ in the extent to which workers, individually or collectively, have property rights in – that is, social claims on use and disposition of – their own labor (enskilling, job allocation and ownership, control at the point of production, and products and profits). Second, labor systems differ in the distribution of associated property rights in the means of production and in the societal means of economic subsistence. Third, and of particular importance, these systems vary in the nature and distribution

of sanctions and resources employed in expropriating (or contesting) such property rights (Deyo 1989a, pp. 154–155).

Deyo then argues that *labour systems* differ widely in East Asia, and parallel to Burawoy, considers proletarian labour systems to be 'rare, contingent and ephemeral'. In East Asia, full proletarianisation with exclusive reliance on wage sanctions in the expropriation of labour property are found in two labour systems. First, the *hyper-proletarian labour systems* among semi-skilled, mainly female, workers, in the large export industries. This system is based on a short-term market calculus among employers and workers. As the basis of expropriation of property rights is extreme wage dependency, Deyo term these workers a 'hyper-proletariat'. A second proletarian system – *the stable proletarian* – can be found among 'low level white-collar and civil service workers, transportation workers and predominantly male workers in heavy industries, such as auto, steel, oil and shipbuilding, who often have more skill, higher wages, and greater job security than their counterparts in hyper-proletarian light export manufacturing' (Deyo 1989a, pp. 157–8). In both these proletarian labour systems a total expropriation of property rights in means of production and means of subsistence can be found, but they differ in relation to the level of expropriation of other rights.

Apart from these two proletarian labour systems, Deyo suggests that there exists four non-proletarian labour systems, two of which are of particular importance in relation to workers in Taiwan. In the large and medium-sized locally-owned factories in Taiwan and Hong Kong, Deyo detects a *communal paternalist labour system*. Here, control based on wage-labour is combined with an implicit labour contract containing mutual obligations. Workers have significant non-wage claims in such matters as training, job placement advancement, and economic security. Moreover, communal paternalism 'imposes community and associational restraints on employment relations, regulating and legitimating authority while providing a basis for conflict medi-ation and the normative compliance of subordinates' (Deyo 1989a, p. 164). Conflicts are indirect and hidden for outsiders, collective form of action are rare, and Deyo terms the politics of production associated with communal paternalism the 'politics of face'.

Labour systems in the small, often subcontracting family firms in Taiwan and Hong Kong are referred to as *patriarchal* by Deyo. 'Here, personal and kinship rights and obligations govern production relations, secure worker rights to domestic subsistence resources and even establish property claims on capital through family-based management and assistance in setting up one's own firm. Patriarchal authority is tightly regulated by norms of non economic reciprocity and mutual obligations. Controls, based on sanctions of family moral obligation and rights of inheritance, are informal and extensive, applying to non economic as well as economic spheres' (Deyo 1989a, p. 160). Production politics here gets mixed up with family issues, and Deyo has chosen to term it 'kitchen politics'.

Michael Burawoy studies factory regimes in order to explain variations and patterns in working-class struggles. Similarly, Deyo is concerned with the relative weakness of the labour movement in East Asia and cross-country variations in labour struggle in the area. According to Deyo, the predominance of non-proletarian labour sectors at least in part account for the relative weakness of the labour movement in East Asia. Effective labour protest is largely confined to proletarian labour systems, and even here the presence of a fairly large hyper-proletariat in light industries impedes the emergence of a strong and organized class action. The potential for effective and collective labour action and labour movements, therefore, seems to be confined to the stable proletariat in heavy industry and service sectors.

In the following section, I concentrate less on that perspective and more on understanding the institutional relations in and around the workplace (workplace regimes) that constitute the sub-structure of Taiwan's particular model of industrial development.

WORKPLACE REGIMES IN TAIWAN: FAMILISM AND ENTREPRENEURIALISM

Chinese people strongly value, idealize and identify with their *family*. The family performs the economic functions of investment, production and employment as well as the functions of security, welfare and retirement. The family as a property-holding unit is more than the household – it is an extended family related by blood, marriage or adoption, whose defining feature is joint ownership by males in the group. The extended family pools resources, spread risks and maximizes returns across male-related branches and male-related generations. The family makes all important decisions such as investment, education, migration and marriage. Authority relations in the family are arranged hierarchically along gender and seniority lines.

As mentioned above, Taiwan's industrial structure is flexible and marked by the existence of a large majority of small family-owned enterprises. In the lower segment of these enterprises one finds *family workshops* or household enterprises financed, built and staffed by members of individual households, producing on a subcontract basis for larger factories or exporters. The work force is unpaid family labour, which in 1961 constituted 27% of the total labour force. According to official statistics, the share had fallen to 9% in 1989.[14] Following Deyo, it seems reasonable to term the workplace regime in small family-owned enterprises *patriarchal*. The main mechanism of control is patriarchal authority, also providing the ideological preconditions for

71

obscuring surplus and concealing the relations of production. These family households normally do not recognize themselves as being exploited in the sphere of circulation by outside production and export brokers, and inside the household, politics in production takes the form of 'kitchen politics'.

A pattern of family-like authority is also present in *capitalized workshops* above the household level[15]. These workshops are family-owned, too. Moreover, capital and marketing opportunities are found through networks of relatives, friends and neighbours, and apart from family labour, wage labour is recruited from similar network structures. Management-labour relationships in these factories are generally more personalized, work routines being more informal. Workers normally work tirelessly for long hours and under dirty, dark and dangerous working conditions. Deployment of workers is flexible and quick. Although they lack the bonuses, the subsidized meals, the fringe benefits and the insurance and retirement benefits found in large factories, workers are often getting a higher amount of take-home cash in these small enterprises. Overtime opportunities and piece rate payment open possibilities for higher earnings through hard work, and constitute mechanisms which further numerical flexibility, labour productivity and labour docility (Stites 1982; Harrell 1981; Shieh 1990, pp. 205ff).

Familism and personalized relationships are one side of management-labour relations in the capitalized workshops. Another is that industrial work for male workers is an entrepreneurial strategy. In a society lacking effective social security and unemployment insurance, factory work is a risky business in the long term. Male workers normally engage in wage work in order to work hard for the long-term benefit of their families (material well-being and security). At a certain stage of the family cycle, male workers go into manufacturing. They prefer small-scale enterprises in which they, by means of hard work, can get take-home pay no less than that available in large modern industries, and where they can learn how to run a business and establish wider contacts. Seeing their work as a temporary part of an hopefully successful petty-entrepreneurial career, they do not see matters exclusively from a worker's perspective, and accept working conditions which they would not have accepted if they had thought of themselves as lifelong industrial workers.[16] As the bosses often participate in the production line, and as one of the main aspects of production politics relates to the potential spin-off in terms of new bosses, we might refer to this workplace regime as *micro-entrepreneurial*. Contrary to Deyo, who extends the patriarchal labour system to cover these capitalized workshops, I am more inclined to follow Burawoy, who focuses on the mechanisms – the 'work games' – that co-ordinate the interests of workers and management and produces an element of consent.[17]

In sum, these two phenomena – familism and industrial work as an entre-preneurial strategy – produce a substantial amount of consent on the shop floor and form a crucial part of the labour institutions that underpin Taiwan's flexible production structure.

Familism also constitutes an important element in *medium-and large-sized (locally- or foreign-owned) enterprises* which employ *young female workers* on a temporary basis. Recruitment of young women into light, labour-intensive manufacturing has followed early industrialization in most industrialized countries. Taiwan differs only in the extent and in the rapid development of this type of recruitment. In Taiwan, the female labour force participation rate in 1990 was 45%, but among women in the 20–24 age group it reached 64%.[18] Out of 2.2 million female paid employees registered in May 1990, 46% were employed in manufacturing, 32% in services and 14% in trade. In manufacturing, the share of women in total paid employment in private enterprises was 45%.[19] Of all female workers employed in manu-facturing, 52% worked in light industries such as electrical machinery and equipment, clothes and apparel, and textiles.[20]

Within the patrilineal and patrilocal kinship system in Taiwan, the position of daughters is significantly different from that of sons. A kind of implicit intergenerational contract is present in the relationship between children and parents, the latter expecting the children to pay back the 'debts' incurred in their upbringing. In relation to sons, parents invest in their schooling, apprentice training and education as part of a long term strategy. They allow their sons substantial autonomy in decisions on job selection, residence etc., and expect them to take care of them in their old age. Since daughters leave their family of birth permanently upon marriage, they have to repay over a shorter time and are expected to begin repayment early.[21]

In the labour market, these female workers are placed in inferior occupations in the factory or the office. In large factories, they are placed in a hierarchical structure that gives them very limited possibilities for upward mobility. The majority remains 'just factory girls' – a few may be selected to the position of group leaders just above the level of operators. While young male workers are motivated to work hard as an entrepreneurial strategy, such an entrepreneurial ethic makes little sense for young female workers. They just sell 'the spring of their youth' to the companies (Kung 1981). They are not personally committed to the firm and feel no compunction about leaving when their friends leave. Therefore, in order to tie these workers to the company, employers use a rather strict form of labour control, including seniority pay-ments and a variety of performance-based allowances, particularly in periods of labour shortage (see Kung 1981; Arrigo 1980; Gates 1987, pp. 71–73; Diamond 1979).

In short, and as demonstrated earlier, these female workers constitute a highly mobile and flexible section of the workforce. The workplace regime in which these young female workers are placed is *hyper-proletarian* in Deyo's sense, but in a broader perspective it has been revealed above that it is made up of *a particular mixture of patriarchy and factory despotism.*

Medium- and large-sized enterprises not only attract young female workers. They also employ many male workers, particularly in the capital-intensive industries.[22] The latter are normally more skilled, getting higher pay and having more job security.[23] Furthermore, labour turnover in these industries is significantly below the average in manufacturing industries.[24] Accordingly, they constitute the more stable part of Taiwan's industrial working class. As they have been guaranteed de facto life long employment, workers in public enterprises form a particularly stable group.

Unfortunately, few if any researchers have studied relations in production and the politics of production in the larger private, Chinese-owned firms. As mentioned above, Deyo states that one can find a labour system of a communal paternalist type here – a system that imposes community and associational restraints on employment relations. Moreover he stresses the importance of the informal community in channelling, regulating and controlling conflicts. He contrasts that with what he calls the patrimonial labour systems in large South Korean firms, consisting of loose networks of dyadic exchange, the breakdown of which often leads to collective protests.

However, Deyo's communal paternalism was not found by Kang Chao. In analysing a major strike at Far Eastern Chemical Fiber (FECF) in Hsinpu (with strong Hakka communities) he writes: 'According to my field experience, the FECF workers related only to their work mates in a ban consisting of 10–15. They usually went home after work; otherwise they went to eat and drink once a week with their banmates. They do have associations; but these associations (fishing society, pigeon-racing society) were centred around things (and hobbies) and did not facilitate discourse among members; accordingly neither critical consciousness nor solidarity was developed. In the May strike, these associations were not converted into vehicles for union mobilization' (Chao 1991, p. 197). From the scanty knowledge that is available, I would be more inclined to call this workplace regime *authoritarian paternalism.* The particular Chinese form of authoritarian paternalism is well reflected in the way Siu-lun Wong characterizes family firms in Hong Kong:

> My research on the cotton spinners has shown them to be industrial patriarchs who exercised tight control, shunned the delegation of power, conferred welfare benefits on their employees as favors, acted as moral custodians of their subordinates, opposed protective labor legislation, and disapproved of trade union activities...Patron-client relationships are further cultivated to cope with the problems of loyalty and to contain the centrifugal tendency of subordinates to set up on their own and become rival competitors (Wong 1988, p. 137).

The patronizing attitude of managers is also prevalent in relation to year-end bonuses, which they present as a welfare benefit rather than just a part of employees' wages. A more detailed analysis of the workplace regime in the large-scale heavy industries would require a further investigation into 'the explicit and implicit agreements' between workers and management in the enterprises. Capitalist production contains a fundamental tension between the need for labour control and the need for creative participation, giving workers some leverage in the continual process of negotiation with employers. In many more labour-intensive industries in Taiwan, employers have been able to treat workers as 'sheer muscles', but in most heavy industries, active and creative involvement of workers in the operational aspects of the complex labour process is needed. However, how it has worked out under authoritarian paternalism has not yet been researched. What we do know is that, in spite of the authoritarian paternalist workplace regime, the stable male workforce in heavy industries has been able to improve its position in relation to management. One indicator is their disproportionate success in getting wage increases. Another is the higher level of labour activism and independent unionism among these workers, particularly in the 1987–89 period.

In sum, the process of industrialization in Taiwan has been accompanied by the creation of a large working class population, the large majority of which is made up of workers with strong family ties working under patriarchal, micro-entrepreneurial or hyper-proletarian workplace regimes. Altogether these workplace regimes undoubtedly have provided Taiwan's industry, and in particular its export industry, with both hard working and flexible labour. The co-existence of these workplace regimes with an 'unregulated' and thus flexible labour market has made it possible for management to shrink and expand their labour force according to variations in domestic and especially foreign demand. While both strategic state intervention and the particular mode of business organization are important for Taiwan's impressive industrial performance, these labour institutions form a complementary and vital aspect of the impressive flexibility and productivity found in the majority of Taiwan's enterprises.

CONCLUDING REMARKS

Although Taiwan has only 21 million inhabitants it has now the 25th largest GDP in the world and is the 12th largest exporter of manufactured goods. During the last forty years the country has transformed itself from a primarily agrarian society to an industrial society with a growing service sector. Capitalist industrialization never proceeds independently of the concrete institutional context. In an East Asian context, it is crucial to look at the institutional aspects of the state that allowed it to discipline and motivate private capitalists to become efficient and competitive producers, but one should also 'bring labour back in' and study the institutional setting that allowed capital to discipline and motivate labour, and to adjust it to the shifting demand. As demonstrated above, flexible capitalism in Taiwan was embedded in a specific set of flexible labour institutions. Taiwan has up till now virtually avoided 'rigidities', such as trade unions and effective labour legislation, in the labour markets. Therefore, we find a high level of numerical flexibility and considerable wage flexibility, particularly in exporting industries. Moreover, labour arrangements in the workplace – workplace regimes – have to a substantial degree been embedded in familial and micro-entrepreneurial logic. Patriarchal and micro-entrepreneurial workplace regimes in small and medium sized enterprises have contributed substantially to Taiwan's successful flexible niche strategy. Moreover, in part of the large scale industries a particular female hyper-proletarian workplace regime contributed to social control of labour, to substantial extraction of labour and to high yields of labour. Finally, the disproportionate success of male workers in other large public and private enterprises in getting wage increases and fringe benefits, and the paternalist practices of management, were part of a more frail but fungible workplace regime. Across these labour institutions, the rising wages and living standards on the island and the provision of education and health facilities have constituted a powerful instrument of social integration.

Finally, it should be stressed, that the main focus in this chapter has been on the broad institutional patterns. Therefore, processes of social and institutional change in the last decade have not been given sufficient treatment. One such change comes from cost pressure. It derives from higher land costs, increasing wage costs and the rising NT$ which forces producers to search either for 'external solutions' – such as foreign investment in low cost countries (China and Southeast Asia) and import of labour – or for an 'internal solution', that is to switch to high-tech products and substitute brain power for labour power. Another important change is the declining importance of the extended family and growing importance of the nuclear family. Further research on these issues as well as on changing workplace regimes in the large enterprises should have high priority.

NOTES

1. International Development Studies, Roskilde University.
2. See for instance Amsden (1989).
3. Shieh (1990), p. 47. Calculated from *Monthly Bulletin of Labor Statistics, Republic of China,* No. 110, DGBAS, Executive Yuan, table 2–11, p. 23 and *Monthly Bulletin of Manpower Statistics, Taiwan Area, Republic of China,* DGBAS, Executive Yuan, No. 201, June 1990, Table 19, p. 31.
4. *Yearbook of Labor Statistics, Taiwan Area, Republic of China, 1989.* Council of Labour

Affairs, Executive Yuan, Dec. 1990, p. 54 and *Abstracts of Employment and Earnings Statistics in Taiwan Area, Republic of China, 1990.* DGBAS, May 1991, p. 21.

5. Calculated from *Report of the Manpower Utilization Survey, Taiwan Area, Republic of China, 1990.* DGBAS, Executive Yuan, ROC, 1991, table 15–17, pp. 38–45.

6. Yearbook of Labour Statistics 1989, *op.cit.*, p. 198 and p. 204.

7. Manufacturing real wages (average earnings) have increased 55% during the 1973–80 period which was below the rise in labour productivity. Due to labour shortage this pattern changed during the 1980s. In manufacturing, real wages went up by 104% while labour productivity only increased 74% from 1980 to 1990, so that the share of labour in value-added increased. Calculated from *Monthly Statistics of the Republic of China,* 1983, No. 207, March, DGBAS, Executive Yuan and from Abstracts of Employment and Earnings Statistics, 1991, *op. cit.,* p. 18 and p. 22.

8. Calculated from Yearbook of Labor Statistics 1989, *op.cit.*, p. 162.

9. Calculated from *Yearbook of Labor Statistics 1982,* DGBAS, Executive Yuan, table 70 and Yearbook of Labor Statistics 1989, *op.cit.,* p. 153.

10. *The Free China Journal,* June 7 and July 12, 1991.

11. *Labor Laws and Regulations of the Republic of China.* 1988. Council of Labour Affairs of the Executive Yuan, R.O.C., pp. 3–100.

12. The following presentation is based on Burawoy (1985).

13. This presentation is based on Deyo (1989a) and Deyo (1989b).

14. Calculated from *Yearbook of Labour Statistics, Republic of China 1987,* DGBAS, Executive Yuan, 1988, p. 33 and Report on the Manpower Utilization 1989, *op. cit.,* p. 15.

15. The term "capitalized workshops" is borrowed from Fiona Wilson, who introduces the term capitalized workshop production to describe a continuum of production forms which do not fit into either petty commodity production or full capitalist production. For details see Wilson (1991).

16. See Stites (1982); Harrell (1985); and Shieh (1990), chapter 5 and chapter 7. The focus here is on male workers but one should not forget that middle-aged female workers constitute a second and growing category working in the small workshops to supplement family income.

17. Burawoy (1985, pp. 38–39). Gwo-Shyong Shieh has explicitly criticized Deyo for taking into account only labour subordination and for not exploring "the production arrangements and the day-to-day conflicts, compromises, co-operation and competition at points of production that make 'passivity' possible. Among the many processes of manufacturing consent among workers, Shieh's analysis shows that spin-off of bosses is a central process of manufacturing consent in capitalized workshops in Taiwan and that the particular form of subcontracting network production system generates opportunities for such spin-off to appear (Shieh 1990, p. 24).

18. *Yearbook of Manpower Survey Statistics, Taiwan Area, Republic of China,* Executive Yuan, May 1991, p. 17. The increasing role of married female workers in the labour market is shown in the change in their labour force participation rate, which increased from 32% in 1978 to 42% in 1990. Similarly, the increasing number of middle-aged women workers is illustrated by the rise in the labour force participation rate of female workers aged 45–49 years from 37% in 1978 to 48% in 1990.

19. Calculated from Monthly Bulletin of Manpower, no. 201, *op. cit.,* table 11, p. 19.

20. Calculated from *ibid.,* table 9, p. 16. The gender ratios (females as percentage of total) in these industries were: Electrical machinery 56%, textiles 55% and clothing 55%. Probably due to recruitment of more male workers as technology is upgraded, all ratios were lower than in the early 1980s.

21. For detailed arguments along these lines see Greenhalgh (1985) and Gates (1987), pp. 103ff. Diane L. Wolf contrasts Javanese and Taiwanese experiences in Wolf (1990), pp. 43–74.

22. Out of a total of 2.6 million employees in manufacturing industries in 1990, we found 66,000 male workers in large public enterprises and 393,000 in large private enterprises, of which one-third was employed in establishments having more than 500 employees and the remainder in establishments having between 100 and 499 workers. *Monthly Bulletin of Manpower Statistics,* Taiwan Area, R.O.C., No. 201, 1990, DGBAS, Executive Yuan, table 6, p. 28.

23. In 1989, employees in petroleum and coal products, industrial chemicals, primary metals and

transport equipment earned 128%, 54%, 42% and 25% respectively more than the average industrial employee. Calculated from *ibid*, table 23, pp. 46–47.
24. In 1989, the separation ratio was 3.8% in all manufacturing, while the shares in the four industries mentioned above were 0.5%, 1.8%, 2.1% and 2.9% respectively. *Ibid.*, pp. 74–75.

REFERENCES

Amsden, Alice, 1989. *Asia's next giant. South Korea and late industrialization.* New York and Oxford, Oxford University Press.

Arrigo, Linda Gail, 1980. 'The industrial work force of young women in Taiwan', in *Journal of Concerned Asian Scholars*, Vol. 2, No. 2.

Burawoy, Michael, 1985. *The politics of production.* London and New York, Verso.

Chang, Ching-hsi, 1990. *Labor unionism and labor laws in Taiwan*, Department of Economics, National Taiwan University (mimeographed).

Chao, Kang, 1991. *Labor, community, and movement: A case study of labor activism in the Far Eastern Chemical Fiber (FECF) plant at Hsinpu, Taiwan, 1977–89*, unpublished Ph.D. dissertation. University of Kansas.

Cheng, Lucie and Ping-Chun Hiung, 1992. 'Women, export-oriented growth and the State. The case of Taiwan', in Richard P. Appelbaum and Jeffrey Henderson (eds). *States and development in the Asian Pacific Rim.* London and New Delhi, Sage.

Chou, Bi-ar, 1989. 'Industrialization and change in women's status: A reevaluation of some data from Taiwan', in Hsin-huang Michael Hsiao, Wei-yuan Cheng and Hou-sheng Chan (eds). *Taiwan: A newly industrialized state.* Taipei, National Taiwan University, Department of Sociology.

Chou, Tein-Chen, 1988. 'The evolution of market structure in Taiwan', in *Revista Internazionale di Scienze Economiche e Commerciali*, Vol. 35, No. 2.

Deyo, Frederic, 1989a. *Beneath the miracle. Labor subordination in the New Asian Industrialism.* Berkeley, University of California Press.

Deyo, Frederic, 1989b. 'Labour systems, production structures and export-manufacturing: The East Asian NICs', in *Southeast Asian Journal of Social Science*, Vol. 17, No. 2.

Diamond, Norma, 1979. 'Women and industry in Taiwan', in *Modern China*, Vol. 5, No. 3, July.

Gates, Hill, 1987. *Chinese working-class lives. Getting by in Taiwan.* Ithaca and London, Cornell University Press.

Greenhalgh, Susan, 1984. 'Networks and their nodes: Urban society in Taiwan', in *The China Quarterly*, 99, September.

Greenhalgh, Susan, 1985. 'Sexual stratification: The other side of 'Growth with Equity' in East Asia', in *Population and Development Review*, Vol. 11, No. 2, June.

Hamilton, Gary G. and Cheng-Chu Kao, 1990. 'The institutional foundations of Chinese business: The family firm in Taiwan', in *Comparative Social Research*, Vol. 12.

Harrell, Steve, 1981. 'Effects of economic change on two Taiwanese villages', in *Modern China*, Vol. 7, No. 1.

Harrell, Steve, 1985. 'Why do the Chinese work so hard? Reflections on an entrepreneurial ethic', in *Modern China*, Vol. 11, No. 2, April.

Kung, Lydia, 1981. 'Perceptions of work among factory women', in Ahern and Gates (eds), *The anthropology of Taiwanese society.* Stanford.

Lam, Danny Kin-Kong, 1989. 'Guerrilla capitalism: Export-oriented firms and the economic miracle in Taiwan (1973–1987)', in *Journal of Sinology* (Kaoshiung, Taiwan), Vol. 4, No. 1, March.

Lee, Joseph, 1991. *Is there a bona fide labor movement in Taiwan: An economic analysis of trade unions in Taiwan* (mimeographed).

Levy, Brian, 1988. 'Korean and Taiwanese firms as international competitors: The challenges ahead', in *Columbia Journal of World Business*, Spring.

Levy, Brian and Wen-Jeng Kuo, 1991. 'The strategic orientation of firms and the performance of Korea and Taiwan in frontier industries: Lessons from comparative case studies of keyboard and personal computer assembly', in *World Development*, Vol. 19, No. 4.

Mody, Ashoka, 1990. 'Institutions and dynamic comparative advantage: The electronics industry in South Korea and Taiwan', in *Cambridge Journal of Economics*, no. 14.

Myers, Ramon H., 1984. 'The economic transformation of the Republic of China', in *The China Quarterly*, 99, September.

Orrú, Marco; Nicole Woolsey Biggart and Gary C. Hamilton, 1991. 'Organizational isomorphism in East Asia', in Walter W. Powell and Paul DiMaggio, *The new institutionalism in organizational analysis*. Chicago, The University of Chicago Press.

Shieh, Gwo-Shyong, 1990. *Manufacturing 'bosses'. Subcontracting networks under dependent capitalism in Taiwan*. Dissertation. University of California at Berkeley, (unpublished).

Stites, Richard, 1982. 'Small-scale industry in Yingge, Taiwan', in *Modern China*, Vol. 8, No. 2, April.

Wade, Robert, 1990. *Governing the market. Economic theory and the role of government in East Asian industrialization*. Princeton, New Jersey, Princeton University Press.

Wilson, Fiona, 1991. *Sweaters, gender, class and workshop-based industry in Mexico*. Houndmills, Basingstoke, Macmillan.

Wolf, Diane L., 1990. 'Daughters, decisions and domination. An empirical and conceptual critique of household strategies', in *Development and Change*, Vol. 21, pp.43–74.

Wong, Siu-lun, 1988. 'The applicability of Asian family values to other socio-cultural settings', in Peter L. Berger and Hsin-Huang Michael Hsiao, *In search of an East Asian development model*. New Brunswick.

4

Labour Recruitment in an Indian Industry – Historical Roots of a Labour Surplus

ARJAN DE HAAN[1]

Labour in India has evolved, during this century, from being a scarce commodity towards one which is surplus to industrial requirements. At the same time, the institutions through which labour is employed have changed, and these changes have contributed to the emergence of a surplus. This paper describes the historical development of institutions of labour recruitment in the jute industry, and in this way aims to contribute to the understanding of the development of the unemployment problem. It argues that the labour surplus is not a natural phenomenon and is not just related to population growth, but that it is, to some extent, of human making, the result of the pattern of development chosen.

Till the 1930s, labour recruitment was completely along personal lines, and employers had to rely on a number of intermediaries to obtain sufficient labour. Starting before independence, a number of reforms were introduced, with the objective of formalizing labour recruitment. But the reforms have had limited success, and a number of unintended consequences. At present, in theory, labour recruitment in large enterprises is completely formalized, but personalistic forms of intermediation have not disappeared. Labour has become surplus, jobs a valuable commodity, and a number of agents profit from this. Labour recruitment has been taken over by Labour Officers, but they merely add a link to the chain of intermediation. The same applies to some extent to trade union and political leaders.

The first part of this paper contains a brief account of the development of the jute industry in India. Second, the evolution of labour relations and recruitment is described, and it is argued that this has generally happened from 'above'. This is followed by descriptions of the creation of a divide between a permanent and a temporary labour force, and of the exclusion of labour, especially of women. The conclusion describes how formalization of labour relations and exclusion of labour are related.

1. THE JUTE INDUSTRY IN EASTERN INDIA

The early history of the jute industry, of the mills near Calcutta on both sides of the river Hooghly, is one of almost uninterrupted growth and high profits. In Dundee it is said that a part of the city had the largest concentration of millionaires in the world, who became rich by making sandbags in Bengal during the First World War. The industry was situated ideally, near the port of Calcutta, on the most important transit point of cheap labour, it could avail of cheap raw material from what is now Bangladesh, and the market for its goods expanded almost continuously. With the advent of the 1930s, this story changed.

According to Chakrabarty (1989, pp. 36ff), the industry's incapacity or unwillingness to respond to increasing competition was the cause of its crisis. The industry refused to develop its industry on scientific grounds and it continued to focus on low-quality and cheap products. It was able to do so since the mills formed an oligopoly, formalized in the Indian Jute Mills Association (IJMA). In response to the crisis, the industry resorted to limiting its production – a policy which has been followed till long after independence.

Goswami (1991, pp. 237–39) has attacked some dominant ideas about the jute industry in colonial times. He denies that it was an exclusive monopoly of the British, that there were effective barriers to enter the industry. He argues that the industry did not posses oligopolistic power in the market for jute goods because the U.S. bought 40 per cent of the gunny export. The IJMA was not an efficient cartel, since there was a huge amount of free-riding, cheating and quarrelling. In Goswami's opinion, it was 'a primitive, inherently unstable, export oriented, capitalist industry ...'

After the crisis of 1929, a significant restructuring of the industry did not occur. From the industry's point of view, there must have been little immediate alternative but to restrict production. A few years after the crisis, a committee was appointed to investigate the competition faced by the jute mills. A research bureau was set up which tried to improve upon the quality of jute. But by the time the industry had recovered from the crisis – trading conditions reached pre-depression levels in 1937 – the Second World War started, which for years affected the organization of the industry.

With independence, the industry's ideal conditions almost disappeared. Because of partition, the industry was cut off from the supply of cheap and high-quality jute. New mills built in East Pakistan implied increasing competition for India's jute industry. Till the late 1960s, this competition was one of the main factors in its loss of the world market – later to be outdone by the competition from synthetics. East Pakistan's industry had the advantage of better and cheaper material, and of an export subsidy given by Pakistan's government. The industry in India had to pay an export duty for a few years during the 1950s and late 1960s. Labour costs, accounting for around 25 per cent of production costs, increased.

The industry did adjust to the circumstances, but in general the industry has continued its strategy to produce at the lowest possible cost, rather than trying to improve its product and to enter new markets. There were attempts by the Government to increase the quantity and quality of jute produced and India obtained a great amount of self-sufficiency in jute, but the quality remained low. The industry modernized a part of its production process and reduced labour costs. Chatterjee (1962) shows that there was a considerable rise in labour productivity during the 1950s. Nevertheless, the amount of investment spent on modernization remained small. According to Sarkar (1989, p. 79), the industry spent not more than Rs. 50 million in any year for modernization of the mills.[2] The main exception was carpet backing, in which the industry made considerable progress during the 1960s, but this market was lost to synthetics.

Between 1950 and 1965, production showed an upward trend, although a somewhat erratic one. Exports remained at a high level: in 1964 they reached the highest level since independence. In 1961, a spokesman of the industry told the Central Wage Board that they were quite optimistic about future prospects, and the Board concluded that the industry would be able to bear the extra burden of a wage increase.[3]

After 1965, the condition of the industry declined rapidly. One of the main reasons for this was the decline of the export market. In 1965, over 900,000 tons of jute goods were exported; in the 1970s the yearly export varied between 317,000 and 707,000 tons. The export market of sacking was lost first, and the export of hessian declined from 448,000 tons in 1965 to 270,000 tons in 1972; the export of carpet backing, once seen as a saviour of the industry, did not grow nearly as much as was hoped for.

The second reason for the decline is related to government policies. In general, West Bengal did not get priority in India's economic planning, and neither did export-oriented industries. After the devaluation of the rupee in 1966, an export duty was imposed on jute goods. This gave East Pakistan, which subsidized its exports, a large competitive advantage. As a manager told me, the industry's representatives repeatedly tried to convince the government of the harm that was done to the industry, but government seemed to have assumed that the jute industry would always remain what it was.

The third factor which determined the decline of the industry was the withdrawal of British capital. Ownership was slowly taken over by Indian entrepreneurs, but at the moment they actually took over managing power, by the middle of the 1970s, the financial position of the industry had seriously eroded.[4] Only a few companies have been successful over a long period, and they had other reserves from which they could support jute production.

The fourth factor was labour. Since independence, relatively few labour problems had been encountered: negotiations happened in a constitutional manner, there were not too many strikes and wage costs did not rise very much. The situation changed totally around 1970. According to a senior manager, the IJMA made a large mistake in 1969, after the first United Front ministry had come into power and the unions formulated a charter of demands. The IJMA thought it would never come to a general strike, and it did not accept an offer by the government. From then on the IJMA lost control over labour, its strategies to play off the unions against each other failed and within five years they were confronted with four general strikes. In 1970 the IJMA wrote that over a period of 1½ years, the share of wage costs in total manufacturing cost increased from 22 per cent to 27 per cent, which was only the beginning. According to Sarkar (1989, p.41) it increased from 16 per cent to 28 per cent between 1960 and 1980, and labour unrest did not diminish. Further, workers became more secure of work and it became more difficult to dismiss them.

What happened to the industry was, in my opinion, not inevitable. The period since the crisis of 1929 till the mid 1960s shows that adaption was possible, and there were specific reasons why the situation deteriorated after that. Because of its dependence on the world market, the crisis of the 1930s had a very bad effect on the industry. During the 1950s, the industry adjusted to the changed circumstances, but things went wrong in the 1960s. It is, in retrospect, amazing how problems accumulated. As before, because of its dependence on raw jute, the development of the industry remained variable, and 1966 to 1968 were years of bad crops. From 1965 onwards, export markets declined rapidly, and one wonders whether Government could not have done more to stimulate exports; when the export duty was finally removed most of the harm was done. Capital was insufficiently available because of the gradual withdrawal of British money, and from 1970 Indian capital shifted from Bengal towards other places in India. There were additional problems, like the deteriorating condition of Calcutta's port and the worsening supply of electricity. On top of this came the labour problems, the increasing labour costs and increasingly inflexible labour relations.

2. RECRUITMENT OF LABOUR: CHANGE AND CONTINUITY

The study of Indian labour relations presents us with a paradox: on the one hand relations are completely formalized with procedures laid down in industrial acts, etc.; on the other hand personalistic relations are thriving. This section describes the changes in the way labour has been recruited in the jute industry. It shows that the formalization has not done away with the personalistic character of the process and corruption, and it argues that one of the reasons is that the formalization has happened from 'above'.

Jute mills during colonial times and for some time thereafter were managed by British supervisors. Chakrabarty has emphasized the authority of the managers over the workers: it was personalized, excessive, and it bore marks of terror (Chakrabarty, 1989, pp.170–5). Although the power of the manager was supposed to be complete, for its implementation the manager was dependent on labour recruiters as well as Bengali clerks or *babus*.[5]

In the historical studies of industrial labour in Bengal, few subjects have stirred ideas and imagination as much as the process of recruitment, the role of the *sardar*, the labour recruiter and controller.[6] However, the historical material and my field work show a different role of the sardar. In the first place, the sources show that there has been very little active recruitment in the jute industry. Foley, investigating the problems of labour supply in 1906, concluded:

> One naturally asks what recruiting agency is used to supply this constantly increasing enormous demand [for labour – in the year before employment grew by 21,000], and it is somewhat astonishing to find that no recruiting on any systematic method is done at all. A new mill, which will usually employ between two and three thousand hands, is erected and labour comes of itself.[7]

The Royal Commission, in an account of the 1929 strike, noted the ease with which outsiders could persuade workers to go on strike and argued that this arose from the sardar system.[8] But the evidence in the same report does not show such an essential role of the sardar. The Kankinnarah Labour Union wrote:

> Hardly any method is adopted to recruit hands who voluntarily find their way to the mill area in search of employment excepting those who are invited by the sirdars, or Indian supervisors, from their own villages in up country. In some mills, if the Burra sirdar (weaving supervisor) happens to be a native of Chapra district, most of his men (weavers) under him are natives of Chapra (RCLI, Vol. V, pt. 1, p. 262).

The 'oral evidences' of the workers in this report, showing short life histories of twenty jute workers (RCLI, 1931, Vol. 11, pp. 355–65) do not point to an overriding importance of the sardars either. Striking in these stories is the diversity in patterns of recruitment and employment, and only in four of the twenty cases there is explicit reference to recruitment through a sardar.

The most common pattern of migration and recruitment was through personal relations, contacts of families, neighbours or husbands, and it seems that in the past it was not very difficult to get one's wife and other family members employed. Old workers told that much of the recruiting happened at the railway station, where sardars or babus asked incoming migrants where they came from and to come to work in their mills. Many of these migrants, as they had relatives there, did not need to pass through this channel.

My field work indicates that the sardar was a common worker with more experience, who came in charge of a number of workers, ranging from 15 to 50. The sardar often was a relative, a member of the family or a friend who helped a new arrival to obtain employment. This familiarity might have been convenient to managers, but it also constituted a potential source of conflict: sardars have been organisers of strikes as well as strike breakers. To get a job, some money or food often was paid. But, according to old workers, this was not forced: to give a senior person some tea, *pan* (betel leaves) or money was socially accepted. The workers do not perceive to have been controlled by the sardar.

Formalization

Labour relations started to change in the 1920s. Although many of the changes in labour relations have taken place after independence, the change started under colonial rule, and in my opinion these earlier developments are significant to understand the later patterns. As I have argued before (De Haan, 1993a), the main impetus for this did not come from the side of the workers, nor did it come from the employers' side. My hypothesis is that many of the reforms were initiated from outside, and mainly from above.

Studies on jute labour indicate that workers showed a large amount of militancy, and most of their demands were over economic issues.[9] But I would argue that workers' demands were in general not for so-called reform measures like maternity benefit and leave and the regulation of labour recruitment. Nor did employers show much initiative to introduce new forms of labour control. They did not, for example, develop housing schemes to stabilize the working force, and they did not regard bonus schemes and other amenities for labour as potentially productive.[10]

An important factor for the change in labour relations was the changing political climate in late-colonial India, the growing strength of the Nationalist Movement, Congress and Communist parties. In 1937 a local government was elected in Bengal. The labour minister was reformist and pro-employer (Chakrabarty, 1989). It became clear to the managers that something was about to change or was already changing.[11] Although employers created a myth about outside agitation, one cannot deny the relation between general political changes and what happened in the factories. The charter of demands which was the basis for the general strike in 1937, for example, was not formulated by the workers; it was part of the political opposition's strategy against the newly elected local government. The link between political parties and labour has continued after independence: the impetus to changes have often come from 'above' rather than from 'below'.

Finally, international influences have been important for changes in labour relations. In the first place, new ideas have been formulated because of similar problems in the UK. As a reaction to the dislocations of the First World War, various forms of welfare measures were introduced, and reform-minded Britons – and employers, for different reasons – often pleaded for their introduction in the colony. Second, international organizations like the ILO have been influential. At the beginning of this century, India belonged to the ten most industrialized countries in the world, participated in the ILO and became a member of its governing body in 1922. As Sen (1992, p. 179) describes, the policies regarding maternity welfare and child benefit were significantly influenced by this. The demands for these reforms were not formulated by the workers and the policies have had the unintended consequence of excluding women from the factories, as will be described below.

The sardar came under attack in this period. In the late 1930s Labour Bureaux were set up and Labour Officers employed. Apart from establishing better relations between management and employers, the intention was the abolition of the practices of sardars. Since then, employment and retrenchment of workers became subject to regulations. For example, the Bengal Industrial Disputes Rules, 1947, as amended at the end of 1954, prescribed that any case of lay-off should be notified to the Labour Commissioner, the employer should give notice of retrenchment to the Labour Commissioner at least one month before, and vacancies should be notified on the Notice Board with a list of the retrenched workers eligible for the vacancies.[12] Both in the case of retrenchment ('last come, first go') and re-employment, the seniority principle became determining. In principle, recruitment became formalized and the role of sardars diminished.

But it may be questioned whether the personalistic character of recruitment has disappeared. 'The sardar dies hard', Mukherjee wrote in 1945, and according to the LIC (1946) the attempts to eliminate their role were not always successful. The sardars sometimes tried to resist the introduction of the new system of registration. One labour officer became responsible for a few thousand workers, so his control must have remained limited and informal practices of recruitment may have continued. Most of the interviewed people said that they got employment through personal relations, also after 1950, and it seems that the permission of the labour office was merely a formality. The labour office was just one more part in the network through which somebody could get employment, and a table more where a bribe would have to be paid. Management did not show much interest in introducing 'modern' relations of labour. They would try to do away with sardars if they caused them trouble, but generally they did not. They knew about the existence of *baksheesh*, but they did not mind much; moreover they were part of the chain of bribery.

The growth of trade unions has changed the recruitment process. Although one might expect a power struggle between unions on the one hand, and sardars and babus on the other, there are few references to this. It is very likely that unions were formed by or via the people with more power or status in the mill. And even if it were not the same people, I think the unions did not really alter the system of recruitment, but merely formed another intermediary, another link in the process of recruitment.

In the late 1960s, important changes occurred in Bengal. Trade unions had always been formed along political lines, but political power relations changed fundamentally. The countervailing power of the IJMA disappeared. The Communist Government chose the side of the unions, much more than the Congress Government had done. But relations of production did not change and neither did power relations in the mills: the politically powerful became the new intermediaries, the power of the sardar decreased, but the relations remained personalistic and paternalistic.

Despite various attempts to change the process of recruitment, and despite political changes, recruitment and labour relations have remained personalistic. However, in the process, a labour elite was created, as described next.

3. CREATION OF A LABOUR ELITE

Before independence, there was little differentiation among the labourers. Categories of permanent and casual labour did not exist, workers got work easily, became permanent immediately, and could be dismissed easily. With the formalization of labour relations, a labour elite was created. This section describes two aspects of this development – relatively high wages and increasing security of work – and companies' reactions to this.

There is little doubt that wages in the jute industry have been comparatively high. Nowadays an unskilled agricultural labourer in the districts from which the migrant workers have come might earn between Rs.10 and Rs.20; a jute labourers earns more than Rs.60 in the factories which pay the official wage, and around Rs.30 in the factories which do not adhere to central agreements.[13] This wage is sufficient for an individual to live on and a family can be maintained from it. Generally the workers said they could save half of their wage, and often three-quarters. From the present monthly wage of about Rs.1600, a single worker in the town would have to spend around Rs.300 for food and Rs.25 to Rs.50 on house rent. If Rs.800 is sent home, this would still be more than a labourer would earn in Bihar.

From the beginning of this century till the late 1960s, the real wage did not change much.[14] Till the crisis of the 1930s, the nominal wage increased steadily but the real wage remained more or less the same. Because of the reduction of working hours, nominal wages decreased significantly during the depression, and recovered towards the Second World War. During the war, real wages decreased fast because of price rises and employers softened this by supplying rationed food. After the war, wages of industrial labour were linked to the increase in consumer prices. In 1948, the minimum monthly wage in the jute industry was raised from Rs.46 to Rs.58½, although even with that it did not reach the pre-war level.[15] In 1951 and 1955 wages were raised again but the real wage in 1958 was hardly higher than in 1951.[16] In 1958–59, the Occupational Wage Survey concluded that the jute industry was among the low-wage industries.

From 1968, however, wages increased rapidly. In 1970, the real wage was already one-quarter higher than in 1960, as shown in the table below. At the end of the 1980s, the real wage was almost twice as high as in 1960. The wage structure also changed in a remarkable way, and at present production and wages are hardly linked.[17] Unions have strongly resisted linking the wage to production.

REAL WAGES IN THE JUTE INDUSTRY
(Index: 1960=100)

1960	100
1965	107
1970	125
1975	143
1976	149

Source: Central Statistical Organization (1981).

It has been argued that the workers in the organized sector in India do not form a labour elite.[18] However, although there is little information about the development of wages in the so-called informal sector, stories of people who have worked outside the jute industry indicate clearly diverging trends of income. Until the 1960s, many said, it was possible to earn a significantly higher income in, for example, rickshaw pulling. From around 1970, their income has tended to lag behind. Wages in the jute industry were adjusted to price increases – and often more than that – and various benefits were introduced. At the same time, income in the informal sector eroded because of, among other factors, the increasing surplus of labour.

Thus, the jute industry has always paid relatively high wages, and they have increased since the late 1960s, at the same time as the crisis of the industry developed and a labour surplus came into existence. But not only the wage has changed: status and security of employment did also, as is described below.

The creation of a 'citadel'

In the early decades of this century, getting a job was not only easy, it was also an uncomplicated affair. Migrants arriving at the station were approached by sardars and babus who took them by the hand and tried to lure them to their mill. A migrant coming to relatives in the town, or a young boy who wanted to start working, asked a relative or other acquaintance to take him into the mill and this person requested a sardar or a babu. Dismissals were equally easy: sahibs had almost unlimited power.

Nowadays the picture is completely different. The road to employment is a long and costly one. Just to get one's name registered takes a long time and workers have to pay or perform other favours to get work. After the first registration a worker becomes a casual worker, has to report regularly at the factory gate, often has to pay even to get just 14 days work and again has to pay to get permanent employment.[19] The labour market has become, as Holmström called it, a citadel which can be mounted only with a lot of effort and with the help of various intermediaries. In the attempt to regulate recruitment of labour, six categories of workers were created, as shown below.

THE 'CITADEL' OF JUTE LABOUR

- permanent
- special badli (220 days, Provident Fund)
- badli (get Employment Cards/Book)
- casual (no Employment Book, but registered)
- contract labour
- bhagavala

Because of the high rate of absenteeism in the mills, managers would say, the jute mills needed a large number of substitutes: *badlis*.[20] The system of badli labour has been associated with a situation of surplus of labour, in which people trying to get a job have to perform work irregularly before becoming permanent. But the system originated in a period with labour shortages. Especially during the months of May and June many of the workers left and in this period the employers had to rely on substitutes to keep the mills running.

After independence, the position of badlis was regulated and standardized.[21] In the late 1950s, the Labour Directorate (1956–61) concluded that the use of casual labour was increasing and that the Government had to intervene. The Industrial Committee on Jute in 1958 decided that the mills had to prepare a list of badli workers, this list had to be 'frozen', and no fresh recruitment should be made till the badlis were absorbed.[22]

The division between permanent workers, registered substitutes and un-registered workers has been refined gradually and more strict rules have been

89

applied. One of the changes was the creation of a category of *special badlis*, workers who were not permanent but had to get employment for 220 days per year, and got the same rights of holidays and Provident Fund as permanent workers. The percentages of permanent and special badlis to the total working complement were also prescribed. In 1963, the Central Wage Board for the Jute Industry gave the following recommendations. The 'complement' of workers per mill was fixed on the basis of the number of people working in 1963. Eighty per cent of this complement had to become permanent, and this percentage was later increased to 85. The remaining workers of this complement had to become special badlis. Another 10 per cent had to be considered as *leave vacancy badlis*, who had to be employed in 'strict rotation', should get Employment Cards, Employment Books, and badli tokens. The rest of the workers had to be treated as *casual* workers, for whom an Employment register had to be maintained. In later Tripartite Settlements the percentages were changed. In 1972, 90 per cent of the mill's complement had to be made permanent, and 15 per cent special badli, with guaranteed employment for 220 days and Provident Fund membership. In 1979 it was decided that 90 per cent should be permanent and 20 per cent special badlis.

The list of permanent, special badli, badli and casual workers does not yet include all categories of labour in the mill. A fifth category is formed by *contract labour*. In the jute mills, this practice has not been very important and since the 1930s there have been attempts to reduce it.[23] In general, the practice of contract labour is limited to activities peripheral to the main production process, like loading and unloading, and construction. However, there may be a trend towards using more contract labour.

A last category to be found in the jute mills – outside any formal system, hidden and illegal, yet common practice – is formed by bhagavalas (or bhagas, *bhaga* meaning share).[24] They help a registered worker to complete the required production. Old or disabled people employ a bhaga, or an overseer tells them to do so. Sometimes a registered worker employs a bhaga while he goes off to do something else. Bhagas are not employed by the mill, do not get any benefits, and the mill does not have any responsibility for the worker. The bhaga is paid by the registered worker, and when both of them are working all the time, the bhaga gets on average Rs.100 out of a fortnightly wage of over Rs.700.

Rules and practices

Companies try to evade rules and practice deviates from rules and recommendations. For example, in 1979 in one mill it was found that 46 per cent of the workers were casual or badli workers, while 95 per cent should be permanent according to the rules (Mitra, 1985, p. 124). Employers of course tried to limit the number of permanent workers and dismissals were made despite the claim that no retrenchment took place.

The distinction between permanent and temporary or badli labour existed before independence, but it had little significance. Employers could dismiss permanent workers as easily as temporary. It became important when the permanent became legally permanent, when it became more difficult to dismiss workers and workers became entitled to benefits which favoured long-term employees, like unemployment benefits and pension schemes. Jute mills reacted rapidly on the introduction of regulations in the 1950s. Apart from cutting wage costs, they were prone to limit the permanent labour force as much as possible.[25]

Later on, workers have become more secure of work, and the strength of the unions has helped to enforce many of the regulations. It has become difficult to dismiss workers and adjust the daily complement. The available figures show that since the war, the proportion of permanent workers first decreased, and increased later; the number of people who were employed for only a short period increased first, and decreased again later.[26] Figures of the Titaghur No.2 Mill Permanent Workers' Registers show that an increasing part of the labour force has been made permanent and that this was often on demands of labour unions. For example, in 1980, when workers of Titaghur No.2 Mill requested to make more workers permanent, the management wrote: 'The Management had contended that the Mill was already burdened with excess Permanent complement to the tune of 107.3%, in other words excess of 17.3% as compared to the figure of 90% envisaged in the Industrywide tripartite settlement dated 22.2.79.' Still, to maintain 'harmonious industrial relations', management agreed to make a certain number permanent.[27]

Perhaps as a reaction to the increasing difficulties in varying the labour force, owners nowadays resort regularly to total closures of the mills, without any pay to the workers. As said above, labour contractors do not seem to be present on a large scale. It seems that the mills do not need these methods: they close mills when they want to, and actually only a portion of the labour force gets the facilities they are entitled to officially. The status of permanency in this sense has only limited significance, and only a part of the work force gets the prescribed facilities.

As described above, since the 1930s the system of labour recruitment has become increasingly complex, but at the same time labour relations and recruitment have remained personalistic. The same goes for promotion to the higher strata in the citadel. Badlis should get work and become permanent on the basis of seniority, but the same informal means operate: to become permanent one needs a 'source', an acquaintance, union and bribe. It was said that people had become permanent despite seniority rules. The departments in the mill have to report vacancies to the Labour Office, but it was said that departments recruit badlis themselves.[28]

Thus, the increasingly complex regulation, together with the development of a labour shortage and the continuation of personalistic practices of labour recruitment, has made the road to permanent employment a long and costly one. In the first decades after the categories were introduced, people still became permanent relatively quickly and there was still little differentiation among the workers. The differentiation was created with the introduction of labour legislation combined with the increasing surplus of labour. It has become difficult to be registered as badli, and it has become equally difficult to become promoted from badli to casual worker. With the creation of this labour elite, which recently has also lost its security of work, groups of labourers were excluded, particularly women, as described below.

4. EXCLUSION OF LABOUR: THE CASE OF WOMEN

A serious shortage of labour has never existed in the jute industry. The shortages were of a temporary nature, seasonal, and existed in certain segments only. The crisis of 1931, when about a fifth of the labourers were dismissed, marked a final end to the shortages. After 1933, employment slowly recovered. During the War, the pattern was irregular and labour was sometimes scarce because of employment opportunities in American camps, bombing of the industrial area and communal problems. Employment in 1948 was higher than in any year since the crisis of 1931, as the following table shows. The 1950s show a reduction of labour by about 25 per cent, due to rationalization.[29] During the first half of the 1960s, employment and production increased, but declined in the second half of the decade. In the mid 1970s, employment was again on a relatively high level and declined again in the 1980s.

It is difficult to determine exactly when a labour surplus came into existence. On the one hand, historians indicate that the labour market of Calcutta was flooded by labour already at the beginning of the century and they rightly point out that employers' complaint of a shortage does not reflect the reality of an insecure labour market. But on the other hand, studies indicate that a labour surplus came into existence around the 1960s and the jute workers' accounts seem to confirm this. Workers told that up till 1970 it was not difficult to get a job. In the past, it was said, sardars and babus fought at the station to draft arriving migrants. In the early 1960s, loudspeakers on the roof of the mills invited workers to join in the mills. I assume that somewhere in the 1960s, the labour surplus became visible.

EMPLOYMENT IN JUTE MILLS IN BENGAL

	No. of mills	No. of workers
Colonial Bengal		
1912	61	199,725
1915	70	248,725
1920	73	280,321
1925	83	338,297
1930	91	328,177
1935	95	263,399
1940	101	284,720
1944	101	267,193
West Bengal		
1947		303,000
1950		278,000
1955		252,000
1960		208,000
1965		248,000
1970		223,000
1975		246,000
1980		236,000
1985		207,000

Sources: LIC, 1946, p. 6; IJMA, annual reports.

Note: Because of production agreements, the trend in employment in jute mills is irregular, which is concealed even with yearly figures.

The development of this surplus, however, did not affect all people equally. The rationalization in the 1950s implied a reduction of female labour, from over 50,000 in 1930 to less than 9,000 in 1962, as the following table shows.[30] At present, women are almost absent in the jute industry. The reason for this is not the cultural restriction on female labour in the Asian context. Although migration towards the industrial area has been dominated by men, at the turn of the century women constituted a considerable part of the jute-industrial labour force, and Sen (1992, pp. 124–5) concludes that managers did not have strong preferences for or objections against female labour.

The participation of female labour has nevertheless been influenced by cultural considerations. Among local Bengali labourers, only poor and lower-caste women worked (Banerjee 1989). People from North India generally said that women should not work, especially Muslims and upper-caste Hindus. In contrast, women from the South generally have worked and objections against this are much less: 'we came here to earn money, so why should women not work?' These differences were partly caused by economic differences, but not only: people from the South with more land also worked, and the property of

93

Bihari families was often so small that these can hardly be called alternative opportunities. With the decline of female labour these cultural differences have tended to disappear, and objections against women working outside the house have become more general. The idea that women should exclusively take care of household and family has gained ground among the groups from the South also. This has made the declining employment less visible or felt: the decline of female labour is not seen as something entirely negative.

FEMALE LABOUR IN THE JUTE INDUSTRY

Year	Number of women	Percentage of total workforce
1912	31,329	15.7
1920	44,545	15.9
1930	52,144	15.9
1935	37,749	14.3
1940	36,640	13.9
1945	38,789	13.7
1950	35,944	13.6
1955	22,375	8.9
1960	9,419	4.4
1962	8,700	3.0
1971		2.5

Source: Until 1960, IJMA figures; the 1962 and 1971 figures are from Labour Bureau (1975) and are estimates.

But the decline was caused by other factors, and the reasons for it are not far to seek. Legislation introduced in 1891 prohibited night work of women, and made leave during pregnancy compulsory.[31] Women lost their position mainly because and when special legislation for women was introduced, and when the disappearance of a labour shortage made the dismissal of women possible. When employment increased again after the crisis of 1931, men were preferred above women.

It is significant to note that the proportion of women workers to the total factory population dropped at a fast rate immediately after the Bengal Maternity Benefit Act, 1939, was put on the Statute Book and again when the provision for maintenance of a creche by the employer was incorporated ... Women labour were previously employed and are still employed mostly for the reason that they are cheaper than their male counterpart. Progressive labour legislation ... has made women labour costlier these days. Hence the general attitude of factory management regarding employment of women is to 'do away with the women labour

94

with a view to avoid in future expenses on special welfare benefits for women.'[32]

Women were found 'less suitable', because of lower productivity and modernization of the production, particularly the installation of modern spinning machinery.[33] In the mills of Thomas Duff & Co. in the 1960s, there was a drive to reduce the number of female workers. The Chairman of the group told the Labour Officers 'that Victoria and Angus [mills] could do a lot better especially when Victoria had about fifty surplus female workers to their requirement'. A few months later he told the Labour Officer of Victoria Mill that 'he should ensure that the remaining 9 [women] should also resign as early as possible.'[34]

There is little information about the way women were dismissed. The Managers' Reports generally wrote that it was achieved through 'natural wastage' and voluntarily. The Manager of Titaghur No.1 wrote in 1960 that there had been no retrenchment, but that six female workers 'retired voluntarily and were replaced by male workers ...' Also, 6 women (and 125 men) left by way of 'natural wastage and dismissals', and 83 left at the end of the year. In the same year, when Samnuggur South Mill was closed and most of the workers were transferred to Victoria Mill: 'About 650 workers, mostly old people and female workers resigned' (Managers' Report, Samnuggur, 1960). The way they left seem to have been similar to the way people were recruited, through informal networks. As a Labour Officer told, managers asked sardars to tell women to leave. It is noticeable that this did not give rise to organized protest by women, but this is not surprising since they were absent in labour unions.

Thus, initially industrial labour provided new opportunities for women, but these opportunities were lost after the introduction of women-specific labour legislation, combined with a diminishing labour shortage. The fast decline in employment opportunities, which started in the 1930s but gained momentum in the 1950s, hit less hard on the adult male worker than it did on the working population as a whole. Women were forced to retreat from the labour market and this was accompanied by a change in ideas about the desirability of women working outside the household.

5. CONCLUSION: FORMALIZATION OF LABOUR RELATIONS AND EXCLUSION OF LABOUR

The existence of a 'labour surplus' along with workers in the organized sector with good wages and security of work, is not a natural phenomenon, and is not just related to population growth. We might remember Marx' critique of Malthusianism, that unemployment was not caused by population growth, but was related to economic (capitalist) development. In the case described here, unemployment is to some extent of human making, the result of the form of development which was 'chosen' in India. The choice to follow a 'socialist' pattern has resulted in giving a larger part of the product to a smaller part of the population. The increase in wages and job security in the 1950s resulted in saving on labour, especially of women. The Congress government after independence, the communist government in Bengal since the late 1960s, as well as most of the labour unions, while emphasizing the rights of workers, secured the benefits for an increasingly smaller part of the population.

The introduction of rules, although justified from the workers' point of view, have had a number of unintended consequences. Women were forced to retreat from the labour market following the introduction of legislation. Immediately when the employment status was regulated, mills tried to casualize the labour force. And at present, when these strategies are not possible because of the strength of unions, mills simply close down completely and reopen after a long time, on new and employer-friendly terms.

The new rules have not only led to a decreasing number of jobs, but have also initiated a process which strengthens the division between the elite and the 'surplus', because the workers defend the acquired rights. Furthermore, the new rules have given rise to a group of intermediaries, sometimes not directly involved in the industry, who benefit from the new rules. The rules were intended to end the intermediation but only altered the persons involved in it. Since labour recruitment has become more complex, the scope for intermediation has grown; and since jobs have become a scarce commodity, intermediation has become increasingly profitable.

The introduction of labour legislation and rules has not, in general, followed from workers' struggles or initiatives by employers. The creation of a labour elite and a labour surplus did not primarily arise from actions by workers. On the contrary, workers have hardly been involved in the formulation of the rules. Since the start of the organized labour movement in the 1920s, the movement has been influenced by political parties. Often, they formulated the demands, usually based on developments elsewhere. This happened for example in the late 1930s and in the late 1960s: it was general political rather than industry-specific developments which led to unrest. In the 1960s, the consequences for the industry were more serious because the employers lacked countervailing power.

The new rules have not changed the personalistic character of labour relations and recruitment. This, I think, is just because many of the regulations were imposed from above, and adapted from different historical contexts. Implementation of rules need a base, a common ground among the people involved; if not, practices are likely to continue as before. Neither the workers nor the employers perceived an interest in some of the rules. For example, the introduction of a central scheme of sickness insurance (ESI) was delayed because of the resistance on the part of the workers. It was not their demand, they had received the benefits before from the employers, and objected to the payment of the premium. The benefits of the scheme had to be 'explained' to the workers. The same goes for the regulation of labour recruitment. It was not primarily the workers who formulated rules to change labour recruitment, but outsiders, often with plans taken from other parts of the world to be implemented in India. The lack of such a base creates possibilities for corruption. Unlike flowers, institutions cannot easily be grafted onto a different social context.

NOTES

1. Amsterdam School for Social Science Research. This paper was written while the author was at SOAS, Centre of South Asian Studies, University of London. It is based on archival research in the U.K. and India, and field work carried out in an industrial neighbourhood of Calcutta in 1991. The research has been made possible by the Erasmus University Rotterdam and 'NWO', the Dutch foundation for scientific research.
2. Contemporaries often argued that the jute industry did not sufficiently modernize and diversify its production. There is undoubtedly some truth in that. The IJMA admitted that they spent only 0.2 per cent of their sales on Research and Development, while their competitors in the USA spent 4 to 5 per cent (IJMA, Annual Report 1969, p. 13).
3. Report of the Central Wage Board for Jute Industry 1963, reproduced in IJMA (1985). The report shows that the average gross profit of the industry was 9.1 per cent between 1951 and 1955, and 5.6 per cent between 1955 and 1959. The profit rate for all industries were 9.2 and 9.0 per cent in these two periods.
4. The Central Statistical Organization (CSO 1981) shows that the financial capability of the jute industry, while having improved till 1965, eroded quickly after that year.
5. The language barrier was one reason why the manager was dependent on these intermediaries. The complex system of multiple shifts also made an effective control difficult to realize. Registers of employment were not common until the 1940s (Royal Commission of Labour in India [hereafter 'RCLI'], Vol.V, pt.1, p.92; Labour Investigation Committee [hereafter 'LIC'], 1946).
6. Sardar (or *sirdar)* literally means headman. Scholars and many of the reports on industrial labour have created the image of a powerful sardar, a headman from the village who not only recruited labour, but also controlled the workers in mill and town. See for example the 1951 Census (Vol.VI, pt.1A, p. 319): 'A *sirdar*, whose home is in one of these districts brings down to a factory a gang recruited from among the poorer of his co-villagers, maintains some sort of control over them while they are employed and generally looks after them till he takes or sends them home again.' Chakrabarty (1989, pp. 109ff.) emphasizes the sardar's authority, based on fear and the use of naked physical force, although he also notes the sardar's legitimacy. Das Gupta (1981) notes the central importance of the sardari system till 1937, when the first Labour Officers were introduced. '... virtually all the recruitment was made by the sardars at the mill gates. In recruiting labour, kinship, caste and community ties played an important roles. But that was not all. In a situation of limited job availability, the sardars and babus took full advantage of their position.' More recently, in an annual publication of the Government of West Bengal, the Labour Commissioner portrayed a stereotypical picture of the role of the sardar (*Labour in West Bengal*, 1973).
7. Foley (1906, p. 9). Further, he argued (p. 10): 'if the Manager knew his hands intimately, he could surely employ a number of them to bring him in labour from their homes and the neighbourhood, either sending them up as sardars, or inducing them to bring recruits when they

return from leave ... [employers] have no systematic method of recruiting to supply their deficiencies, but after a time labour comes of itself from up-country and they fill up again'. A witness of the Indian Factory Labour Commission of 1908 told that within a month of starting a mill a full complement could be found – without recruiters being involved (IFLC 1908, Vol. II, witness 171).

8. 'The immediate employer of a worker is a sirdar. The sirdar gives him his job, and it is by his will that the worker retains it. The sirdar is the official channel of communication between master and man, and the sirdar's view must be the man's view. Otherwise, the man's job is gone ... dissatisfied or suborned sirdars may initiate and maintain a strike, whatever the workers' view may be ... The sirdars are the real masters of the men. They employ them and dismiss them, and, in many cases, they house them and can unhouse them' (RCLI, Vol.V, pt.I, p.152).

9. The 1920s showed an increase in protests and the *Report of the Committee of Industrial Unrest* (1921) and the Report of the RCLI (1931) were a reaction to this. Both concluded that it was necessary to get in close contact with the workers.

10. Managers almost invariably wrote that the labourers were contented. If there was some labour unrest, which often came as a surprise, this was supposed to be due to outside agitation. Labour unions were regarded unnecessary and unwanted. Advantages of co-operation, in general, were only seen after the introduction of these. For a long time, education was deemed unnecessary, or even counter productive as it was thought that it might give rise to 'babu aspirations'.

11. For example, Murray of Thomas Duff & Co. wrote on 11-1-1938 that he had seen a draft of the Maternity Benefit Rule. The minimum benefit was higher than the average actual earnings of women, 'and is an indication of the Governments's ideas of what a minimum wage ought to be' (Murray to Mason, 11-1-1938, Thomas Duff & Co., 'Correspondence with the Visiting Director', 1937–1938, company archive at the University of Dundee, MS 86/V/7/33).

12. Cited in Thomas Duff & Co., Managers' Reports, Titaghur No.1, 1954, pp. 76–7.

13. In the beginning of this century, in Saran, the major labour-supplying district, a coolie could earn between two annas and three annas three paisa; in the jute mills the wage for an unskilled labourer was over five annas per day (Yang 1989, p. 197).

14. The following is based on the trend described by Mukerji (1960). The earlier figures are quite unreliable (Bagchi 1972, p. 123).

15. Gupta (1953). According to Sanyal (1960), the 1951 real wage level was still below the 1939 level; in 1954 it was 3% higher.

16. These calculations are based on figures from annual Government publications, *Labour in West Bengal* and the West Bengal Labour Year Book.

17. The wage in the industry is composed of various parts. The most important ones are the basic wage and the Dearness Allowance (DA). While the DA is connected to the increase in prices of consumer goods, the basic wage is related to production, and is different per department. In 1963, when the minimum wage was Rs.80 per month, half of this was composed of the basic wage. Since then, the basic wage did not change, only the DA changed. In 1991, while the wage in the mills is over Rs.1600 per month, only Rs.40 is related to production.

18. Tulpule and Datta (1988) deny the existence of an aristocracy: the income of workers in large enterprises has risen only marginally more than the income of workers in other sectors of the economy. In a recent article, Bhattacherjee and Datta Chaudhuri (1994) describe the influence of trade union activities on the movement in real wages, and conclude that unions have got better wage deals in the 'advanced sector', but not in the less organized sector.

19. In 1972, the permanent workers of Titaghur No.2 Mill had been non-permanent workers for 1.4 year on average; in 1991 this was 5.6 years. In the 1972 complement, 53% of the workers had become permanent in the same year as they joined; in 1991 this was 14% (Titaghur No.2 Permanent Workers' Register).

20. Also *budlis*. Substitute seems to be the most appropriate translation. In Bengal, *badli* is also used for a system of labour exchange (Van Schendel and Faraizi 1984, p. 79).

21. The process of recruitment was described as follows by the LIC in 1946 (p. 9): 'A register is

maintained known as the 'Budli' register in which the names of the workers in search of employment are registered. These are mostly former employees of the mill who had left their jobs or over-stayed long leave or had been demoted to a 'budli' from a permanent post ... Those registered have to attend the mill twice a day to ascertain whether a vacancy exists for them ... the Labour Officer selects men from his register in accordance with the attendance put in by the person at the bureau and according to his efficiency ...' The First Tribunal in 1948 defined a badli, as 'a workman who is appointed in the post of a permanent workman or a probationer who is temporarily absent' (Cf. Central Wage Board 1963, p. 230; in: IJMA 1985).

22. In: IJMA (1985). See also Labour Bureau (1965, p. 18) noting that the units maintained registers of badli labour, that they were registered in order of preference on the basis of merit and service experience, and attempts were made to offer equal opportunity to each registered badli worker.

23. E.g. Annual Report Factories Act for 1931; the LIC (1946) noted that only 1.67% of the workers were contract labourers; and the Labour Bureau (1965, p. 15–6) wrote that there was no contract labour in jute mills.

24. It has been estimated that bhagavalas form about 20 per cent of the labour force, but I find this estimate too high (Basu, quoted in *Against the wall. West Bengal labour scenario*, 1991). The number of bhagas is probably quite high at present: the average worker is relatively old, and in the mills that do not pay the retirement benefits, workers above the retirement age continue working.

25. See Duff, Managers' Reports, 1955, Titaghur No.1, p. 62. The report writes that the complement of permanent workers in the sewing department was reduced with 104, and in the batching department, 'as there is no fixed cadre of permanent workers, casual coolies are obtained as and when necessary from the Labour Bureau'.

26. The Managers' Reports of Duff & Co. provide figures of labour turnover and the best indication of the use of *badli* workers is probably provided by the category of newly employed who worked less than one month during the year. Their number increased significantly from the late 1930s onwards: in 1955 there were 11,733 workers (on a complement of 6,432) who worked less than one month in the mill. In the 1960s, this declined significantly and was less than 1,600 in 1969, the last year for which figures are available.

27. Titaghur No.2 Labour Office, Notice file July 1976–August 1980, Notice 7–8–1980.

28. A note on the notice board of the Labour Office of Titaghur No.2 Mill in September 1991 said that badlis go to departments directly instead of to the Labour Office.

29. This seems to represent a more general pattern of the economic development of India after independence and import substitution seems to be related to capital-intensive growth and relatively decreasing employment. The ratio labour-capital is highest for industrial exports, lower for production for the national market, and lowest for import substituting production (cited in Squire 1981, p. 150; see also Roy 1988, for a similar argument regarding industries in Bangladesh; Bhagwati 1988, for a discussion of India's economic strategy; and Lipton and Maxwell 1992, about a new emphasis in poverty reduction, including a shift to a labour-strategy).

30. Child labour also decreased, from ten per cent in 1920 to almost zero in 1935. The unemployment problem is less visible than one might expect because a part of the workers has left the area, and the workers' link with the village 'softens' the effect of unemployment (see De Haan 1992).

31. Sen (1992, pp. 101–7) describes the 'protective' legislation. The legislation introduced in 1891 had little effect because of numerous infractions and the possibility and regular practice of the Government of Bengal to exempt particular mills. The question resurfaced in the 1920s.

32. Annual Report Factories Act for 1953 (p. 10). The report added that the productivity of women workers is much lower than that of male workers. The consequence of the decline, however, was that the family income (of the husband) was not sufficient, and dissatisfaction about this was said to result in wage disputes and strikes.

33. Annual Report Factories Act for 1957 (p. 4). According to the West Bengal Labour Year Book for 1958 (p. 39) employers argued that women could not be suitably employed in factories with two shifts. The Labour Year Book for 1959 (p. 27) added the following reasons

for the decline: restrictions on carrying weights, prohibition of women to work as softener feeder and changes in production.
34. Titaghur No.2 Mill, Labour Office, 'Minutes of the SMLO's', 1952–63, Minutes 30–3–1963 and 17–8–1963. In the minutes of 19–1–1963, it was written that the Chairman of the group asked the Labour Officers of three of the mills to prepare a list of workers of 55 year and older with a view to retire them, and since two of the mills had surplus female workers, the women who attained the age of superannuation should be retired quickly. The Minutes of 4 August 1962 said that there had been no problems in the availability of labour but Titaghur No.2 'had to take on a few female warp winders as males were not available.'

REFERENCES

Primary Sources

Curjel, Dagmar F., 1923. *Enquiry into the conditions of employment of women before and after childbirth, in Bengal industries. Report*, unpublished, West Bengal State Archives.
Foley, B., 1906. *Report on labour in Bengal*, Bengal Secretariat Book Depot, Calcutta.
Government of Bengal. *Annual Report on the working of the Indian Factories Act in Bengal*, various years.
Government of Bengal, 1921. *Report of the Committee of Industrial Unrest*, unpublished, West Bengal State Archives.
Government of West Bengal, Bureau of Applied Economics and Statistics, 1990. *Statistical Abstract. West Bengal 1978 to 1989*.
Government of India, Labour Bureau. *Occupational Wage Survey (1958–59)*, Vol. VI.
Government of West Bengal, Labour Directorate. *West Bengal Labour Year Book*, 1958 and 1959.
Government of West Bengal, Labour Directorate. *Labour In West Bengal*, Annual Reports since 1962.
Indian Factory Labour Commission, 1908. *Report of the Indian Factory Labour Commission*, Government Press, Simla.
Indian Industrial Commission 1916–18 (IIC, Holland Commission). *Report*, Superintendent, Government Printing Press, Calcutta 1918.
Indian Jute Mills Association. *Report of the Committee*, Annual Reports, unpublished, selected years since 1940.
Indian Jute Mills Association, Compilers, 1985. *Industrywise Tripartite Settlements, Report of the Central Wage Board and Summary of Omnibus Tribunal Awards in Jute Industry along with Clarifications*, Calcutta.
Labour Investigation Committee, Government of India (S.R. Deshpande), 1946. *Report on an Enquiry into Conditions of Labour in the Jute Mill Industry in India*, Manager of Publication, Delhi.
Royal Commission on Labour in India, 1931. *Report of the Royal Commission on Labour in India*, Vol. 1, vol. 5, parts 1 and 2, vol. 11, parts 1 and 2. London.
Subdivisional Officer, Barrackpore. 'Notes to successor', a collection of notes, mainly handwritten, from October 1934 to 1950, placed at my disposal by the present S.D.O. of Barrackpore, Mr. K.P. Sinha.
Thomas Duff and Company, University of Dundee, Archive Department, MS 86: MS 86/III, Director Minute Books; MS 86/V/7; MS 86/V/8, Managers' Reports to Directors, 1930–1974.
Titaghur No.2 Mill, Titagarh, Labour Office. Workers' Registers 1972 and 1990 and various notes and memos.

Secondary Sources

Against the Wall. West Bengal Labour Scenario, Nagarik Mancha, Calcutta, 1991.
Bagchi, Amiya Kumar, 1989. *Private investment in India 1900–1939*. New Delhi, Orient Longman.
Banerjee, Nirmala, 1989. 'Working women in Colonial Bengal: Modernization and marginalization', in: Sangari, Kum Kum, and Sudesh Vaid (eds.), *Recasting women: Essays in colonial history*. New Delhi, Kali for Women.

Labour Recruitment in an Indian Industry

Bhagwati, J., 1988. 'Poverty and public policy', in *World Development*, Vol. 16, 1988, No. 5, pp. 539–55.

Bhattacherjee, Debashish and Tamal Datta Chaudhuri, 1994. 'Unions, wages and labour markets in Indian industry, 1960–86', in *Journal of Development Studies*, Vol. 30, No. 2, January, pp. 443–65.

Bhattacharya, N., A.K. Chatterjee, 1973. 'Some characteristics of jute industry Workers in Greater Calcutta', in *Economic and Political Weekly*, February, pp. 297–308.

Central Statistical Organization, Industrial Statistics Division, Ministry of Planning, 1981. *Trends in Indian jute industry 1960 to 1976*, Bulletin No. ISD/7. New Delhi.

Chakrabarty, Dipesh, 1989. *Rethinking working-class history. Bengal 1890–1940.* Delhi, Oxford University Press.

Chatterjee, A.K., 1962.'Trends in labour productivity in jute industry', in *West Bengal Labour Gazette*, January.

Chattopadyay, K.P., 1952. *A socio-economic survey of jute labour.* Calcutta, Department of Social Work, Calcutta University.

Das Gupta, Ranajit, 1987. *Migrant workers, rural connexions and capitalism: The Calcutta jute industrial labour 1890s to 1940s.* Calcutta, Indian Institute of Management.

De Haan, Arjan, 1992. 'Town and village: 100 years of circular migration to Calcutta', Paper for the 12th European Conference on Modern South Asian Studies, Berlin.

De Haan, Arjan, 1993a. 'Migrant labour in Calcutta jute mills: Class, instability and control', in: Peter Robb (ed.), *Dalit movements, and the meanings of labour in India.* Delhi, Oxford University Press.

De Haan, Arjan, 1993b. 'The jute industry and its workers: Changes in stratification in Eastern India', to be published in S. Bandhyopadhyay, A. Dasgupta and W. van Schendel (eds.), *Bengal. Development, Communities and States.*

Goswami, Omkar, 1991. *Industry, trade and peasant society. The jute economy of Eastern India, 1900–47.* Delhi, Oxford University Press.

Gupta, Indrajit, 1953. *Capital and labour in the jute industry.* Bombay, All-India Trade Union Congress.

Holmström, Mark, 1984. *Industry and inequality. The social anthropology of Indian labour.* Cambridge, Cambridge University Press.

Lipton, Michael and Simon Maxwell, with the assistance of Jerker Edstroem and Hiroyuki Hatashima, 1992. *The new poverty agenda: An overview*, Discussion Paper 306. Institute of Development Studies, University of Sussex, August.

Mitri, Sisir, 1985(?). *The jute workers: A micro profile*, Transactions, Vol. 2, nos. 1 and 2. Calcutta, CRESSIDA.

Mukerji, K., 1960. 'Trend in real wages in the jute textile industry from 1900 to 1951', in *Artha Vijnana*, vol. 2, no. 1, March.

Mukherjee, Radhakamal, 1945. *The Indian working Class.* Bombay, Hind Kitabs.

Mukherjee, Indrani, 1985. *Industrial workers in a developing society. A sociological study.* Delhi, Mittal Publications.

Roy, Dilip Kumar, 1988. 'Employment and growth: Empirical results from Bangladesh industries', in *Bangladesh Development Studies*, Vol. 16, No.1, March.

Sanyal, Arun with Shyamal Sen, 1960. 'Labour productivity and shares of wages to production in five selected industries for the First Five-Year Plan period in India', in *Bulletin of the Socio-Economic Research Institute*, no.1, Jan–March, pp. 46–52.

Sen, Samita, 1992. 'Women workers in the Bengal jute industry, 1890–1940: Migration, motherhood and militancy', Ph.D. dissertation. University of Cambridge.

Squire, Lyn, 1981. *Employment policy in developing countries. A survey of issues and evidence.* New York, Oxford University Press, published for the World Bank.

Tulpule, Bagaram and Ramesh C. Datta, 1988. 'Real wages in Indian industry', in *Economic and Political Weekly*, 29 October, pp. 2275–7.

Van Schendel, Willem and Aminul Haque Faraizi, 1984. *Rural labourers in Bengal, 1880 to 1980*, CASP 12. Rotterdam.

Yang, Anand, 1989. *The limited Raj. Agrarian relations in Colonial India, Saran District, 1793–1920.* Delhi, Oxford University Press.

5

Explaining Diverse Labour Arrangements in Rural South Asia

BEN ROGALY[1]

1. INTRODUCTION

Daniel Thorner defined agrarian structure as 'the network of relations among the various groups of persons who draw a livelihood from the soil ... it is the sum total of ways in which each group operates in relation to other groups' (quoted by Harriss 1982, p. 146, n.1). Understanding the relation between agrarian structure and the course of agricultural development has long been a concern of scholars of rural South Asia. In this chapter, I explore the difficulties inherent in explaining a major component of agrarian structure: the relation between buyers and sellers of agricultural labour, in particular its many contractual forms.

This chapter is concerned with diversity in the arrangements for the buying and selling of labour power in rural South Asia. It reviews both theoretical and empirical contributions to the literature in order to assess how mainstream economic theories have coped with diversity in labour arrangements. Drawing further on the literature, the chapter goes on to suggest ways in which research on this topic could be improved.

The persistent diversity in labour arrangements discovered in empirical inquiry indicates the importance of explaining institutions of labour exchange as they exist in practice. The diversity of labour transaction systems between regions and villages and even within villages has been noted by several scholars (including D. and A. Thorner 1962; Ramachandran 1990; Rudra 1992). Such research, characterized by methodological idiosyncrasy and compelled by the need to explain diversity, has found explanation difficult. Gyan Prakash has argued with regard to the historical study of agricultural labourers in India that the very complexity ('multiple fissures') of the subject matter 'demand[s] fractured accounts' (1992a, p. 45).

'Explanation' is defined here as the presentation of a coherent set of causes for a particular event, institution or change (or group of events, institutions or changes). Explanations arrived at through empirical data may be evaluated via an examination of the relationships between the assumptions, the explanations and the data. Typically, this involves analysing how conclusions were reached from the data presented. Should data not contradict the explanation, the latter is tenable. Explanations may also be derived from first principles. In either case, a complete explanation is one which is not only tenable but rules out others.

The particularistic nature of segmented village labour exchange nexi, together with the disciplinary compartmentalization of social science inquiry, may signal the practical impossibility of finding complete explanations at the 'macro' level, say, of a given agroclimatic region of a particular Indian state. However, by critically examining existing approaches, I hope to show how the explanatory power of micro and meso level studies of labour arrangements can be strengthened.

The purpose of this chapter is to review attempts to explain diversity in labour arrangements in rural South Asia. Divergencies in characterizations of change in arrangements also come within this audit. The second and third sections briefly examine two contrasting groups of approaches to explaining arrangements based on the concepts of a labour market and labour relations respectively. In the fourth section, I explore different partial explanations of diversity emerging from recent field studies,[2] through a disaggregation of arrangements into a number of components. The fifth section considers ideological, semantic and substantive divergencies in attempts to characterize the process of change in arrangements. In the sixth section I discuss how the work of Gillian Hart on rural Java could be used to provide a more inclusive framework of analysis. In conclusion, I summarize limitations of the labour market and labour relations approaches and the implications of this chapter for further research.

Labour arrangements are defined here as the totality of formal, informal and implicit terms and conditions which define the relationship between a labourer (or group of labourers) and an employer (or group of employers). Formal (written) and informal (spoken) terms and conditions are those which are explicitly agreed, while implicit ones are those which are understood by both parties, without being stated. They may arise from the nature of other relationships between the same individuals or groups, or from norms associated with a certain arrangement. These definitions do not imply that terms and conditions are necessarily understood in the same way by all who practise them.

Arrangements range from single-stranded daily contracts entered into voluntarily by the worker for a cash return to long term multi-stranded permanent relations under which the worker is obliged to sell labour to a particular employer for an indefinite period (Jagannathan 1987). The multitude of forms in between vary enormously in duration and degrees of obligation. Labour arrangements also include interlocked contracts, whereby a labour contract is partially defined by relations between the same parties in another market or markets.

2. LABOUR MARKET APPROACHES

Neo-classical economic theory has rarely tried to explain the coexistence of diverse labour arrangements. In this section, the perfect competition model of wage determination is briefly outlined, followed by extensions based on the model's core assumptions. One of the extensions explicitly tackles diversity, attempting to include rationales for the coexistence of four types of labour arrangement in a general model of production relations. These examples are then used to illustrate some of the limitations on the explanation of diversity inherent in such models.

2.1 The perfectly competitive model

Neo-classical attempts to explain rural labour arrangements maintain at their core the perfectly competitive model for the determination of wages in the *market* for labour. Although the scale of the studies, the questions asked and the issues raised vary, explanations are sought exclusively on the basis of one or more of the core assumptions of this model.

The core theory explicitly assumes homogeneity of labour, profit maximization by 'producers' and utility maximization by 'consumers'. It also assumes perfect information (where any relevant information is known to all market actors), no uncertainty and thus no transaction costs. As the market always tends to an equilibrium state, the wage on the one hand and the quantities supplied and demanded for labour on the other, are simultaneously determined such that a change in demand or supply functions would lead to a change in equilibrium wages and thus a change in actual wage, while a movement in actual wage, due to any exogenous factors, would entail similar adjustments in the quantities demanded and/or supplied.

At equilibrium, the value of the marginal product of labour – the incremental value added to the product by addition of one unit of labour – is equal to the wage – the incremental increase in returns to labour from addition of the same unit – and also to the labourer's marginal rate of substitution between income and leisure. The latter refers to that quantity of leisure a labourer would be willing to forego to gain an extra unit of income.

2.2 Neo-classical extensions

Neo-classical economists have extended the perfectly competitive model for analysis of rural labour markets in South Asia. Lal conceded that labour had unique qualities, which distinguished its behaviour from that of other 'commodities'.[3] Partly as a consequence of this, a 'multiplicity of contractual arrangements' existed which did not fit the perfectly competitive model, the dynamics of which required sequential spot contracts. Dropping the assumptions of perfect information and no uncertainty, 'second best' solutions could be identified as rationales for particular contract types (1989, p. 111). According to Binswanger and Rosenzweig in their critical review of literature on contractual arrangements in agriculture, non-competitive behaviour could then be explained by such factors as:

(i) the costs to both labourers and employers associated with frequent job search;
(ii) dislike for wage employment and/or social pressure against it; and
(iii) the costs to the employer of supervising hired labour (Binswanger and Rosenzweig 1984, p. 14).

Binswanger and Rosenzweig also implied that market structure, in particular the oligopolistic and oligopsonistic structure they attributed to rural markets in South Asia, had to be accounted for in extensions of the competitive model (pp. 3 and 34–5).

The main concerns of applied neo-classical work have been to test the extent to which supply and demand determine rural wages, to explain downward rigidity and to provide rationales for the existence of particular contractual forms. Here I summarize specific theoretical propositions, drawing on their presentation in Lal (1989).

The uncertainty of demand for labour and the notion of implicit contracts has been used to explain the coexistence of rigid wages and unemployment. The notion of implicit insurance contracts between employer and labourer was shown to be able to explain how, as production and exchange in other markets fluctuated, wages were protected. The labourer paid an implicit insurance premium in good years when the wage was less than the value of the marginal product of labour, and received an implicit insurance benefit in bad years when the opposite was the case. The insurance contract could not have been underwritten by an insurance company because it would have run into moral hazard problems. Rather, employers had to monitor the contract as only they had access to the information required – the value of the marginal product of labour (Dreze 1979, p. 10, quoted by Lal, p. 118).

Turning to explanations of specific contractual forms, Lal's model of interlinked credit and labour markets [following the work of Braverman and Srinivasan (1981) and Braverman and Stiglitz (1982)] posited landlord-moneylenders as tying credit to commitments of labour to reduce the risk of default. Lal showed how this led to monopolistic lending (as labourers could now borrow only from landlords to whom they sold labour), but that as the credit and labour markets were jointly determined (relatively high rates of interest being compensated for by wages at above the marginal product of labour), the solution was both efficient and equitable.

Without defining 'attached' labourers, Lal then drew on Bardhan's formulation (1984, p. 80) which showed that the attachment could be explained by assuming that workers were risk averse (and thus wanted to smooth inter-seasonal consumption) and that employers were risk neutral (with regard to climatically induced changes in labour demand) and wanted to ensure adequate labour in the peak season. The 'greater the *mean* demand relative to supply', the greater was the importance of attached labour (Lal, p. 125, his emphasis).

The phenomenon of caste-homogeneous work groups has been explained as employers' response to 'idiosyncratic' tasks, which require the ability to cooperate and work in a team (Lal, p. 117). Binswanger and Rosenzweig interpreted employers' use of a *mukadam* (middleman) to hire gangs of migrant labourers (Breman 1984) as the solution to an informational problem regarding the quality of the work force.

In a later article, Binswanger and Rosenzweig criticized the 'highly model-specific' attempts made by neo-classical economists to explain particular labour market phenomena. Each model, built on a combination of assumptions, was seen to emphasize the consequences of the assumptions (and the individual phenomenon explained by them) for economic efficiency, rather than 'on the establishment of testable implications' (1986, p. 504). Binswanger and Rosenzweig went on to build a model for the analysis of production relations,[4] which could 'assist in explaining the diverse set of actual production relations observed in a particular rural environment in an internally consistent way' (p. 503). They explicitly invited empirical testing of their general analytical framework (p. 535). Rationales for the coexistence of four distinct contractual types were built into the model (pp. 520–1; see also Rosenzweig et al 1988, pp. 79–86 for a similar attempt and Stiglitz 1989, p. 27, for an example of another call for the explanation of diverse arrangements from within the neo-classical school).

The model involved combining the analysis of the 'behavioral determinants' of production relations (risk, risk aversion and information problems) with that of the 'material determinants' ('the material features of agriculture and the material attributes of its factors of production') (p. 505). Asserting that a knowledge of the history and agro-ecological specificities of a region were necessary for such an analysis, Binswanger and Rosenzweig chose one region: South Asia. Crucially they assumed that all economic decisions made by individuals, whether allocative or distributive, were based on the objective of income maximization and a concern to avoid seasonal dips in consumption (p. 505).

Binswanger and Rosenzweig used just a few of the stated assumptions of their general model of production relations to build their rationales for the coexistence of diverse labour arrangements (pp. 519–521). They assumed risk in production and exchange as well as health risks, costly information, individual self interest, dislike for effort and risk aversion. From these assumptions they derived the general consequence of asymmetric information (a combination of self interest with costly information), and from that the existence of incentive problems (p. 507). On the 'material' side, they assumed seasonality (involving seasonal fluctuation in the demand for inputs, including labour) and, a need to synchronize the timing of agricultural operations (due to spatially dispersed production).

Four types of labour arrangement were compared on the bases of incentives to worker effort, other costs (such as the cost of recruitment) and risks. These were: unpaid family labour; and hired labour on short term piece and time rate and permanent contracts. The coexistence of piece rates and time rates in short term contracts was explained by the general incentive superiority of piece rates (less supervision was required to ensure worker effort) only being feasible when the worker's output was measurable both quantitatively and qualitatively. Thus where output was not measurable, time rates would be expected to obtain (for example in the case of weeding); and where it was measurable, piece rates would be expected.

Binswanger and Rosenzweig went on to argue that, while there were much fewer costs associated with the labour of family members, the larger the family size, the lower the share of each individual in the profits and thus the lower the incentive to work. Moreover, complete reliance on 'family' labour was avoided because of its 'committed' cost of consumption throughout the year and because of the seasonality of farm operations and associated fluctuations in the demand for labour. Thus it was optimal to hire in non family labour on a short term basis in the peak season, such that the quantity of family and hired permanent labour would be less than peak season demand.

However, because of the risks associated with the need to synchronize the timing of agricultural activities 'across farms' and the importance of performing them on time, it would not be optimal to rely on hired [implicit daily] labour alone. Thus it would be optimal also to employ permanent labourers at above the number demanded in the lowest trough of the lean season. This argument, although constructed for a different purpose, provides a neo-classical explanation for the coexistence of four contractual arrangements for the employment of agricultural labour.

In the application of their 1986 model, Binswanger and Rosenzweig first attempted to characterize regional characteristics of South Asian agriculture by adding further assumptions. Thus they assumed land to be scarce and land titles to exist, that the use of draft animals was common, that transport and communication costs were high, that slavery and other forms of 'extra-economic coercion' did not exist and that competition characterized relations among all agents in the economy (pp. 523–4). The rationales for the co-existence of diverse labour arrangements outlined above were then used to predict changes in labour arrangements following the introduction of new agricultural technology. The authors concluded that the demand for short term relative to long term labour would increase because the seasonality of labour demand would be enhanced by the use of higher yielding varieties.[5] There would also be an absolute increase in demand for all labour and higher peak season wage rates. The latter would lead to 'an increase in the use of migrant labour and an inducement to invest in harvesting or harvest processing machinery' (p. 533).

2.3 Testing the rural labour market theories

In their review, Binswanger and Rosenzweig argued that the failure of theories of wage determination to *take into account contractual realities* rendered them empirically untestable. Thus the predictive powers of different models could not be ranked (Binswanger and Rosenzweig 1984, pp. 38–9, n.20, emphasis added). Binswanger and Rosenzweig did not test their predictions for the coexistence of certain types of labour arrangement. However, tests have been carried out to establish the extent to which supply and demand for labour can explain wages.

Lal cited three tests on money wages using National Sample Survey (NSS) data, which explore inter-village, inter-district and inter-state variations and found 51–72 per cent of the variation to be explained by supply or demand factors. He went on to use NSS data himself to explain inter-state variation in real wages between 1956–57 and 1970–71 (op. cit., pp. 127–129 and 135). However, as he admitted, the tests were 'crude' and the results 'suggestive'. The identification of percentage increase in cereal output as sole demand variable is ambiguous as increased output has come about in some areas through labour displacing mechanization. The sole supply variable – percentage increase in the male agricultural labour force – is also questionable, as it leaves no room for estimating different trends for women, which, given their large numbers in the agricultural labour force, may affect the overall trends in labour supply.

In a micro study of Aurepalle, a village in Mahbubnagar District, Maharashtra, a regression was run to try to explain the variation in wages between different 'regular farm servants' (defined as those agricultural labourers with contracts of three months or more duration) (Binswanger et al 1984). The most significant explanatory variable was the one which distinguished between those who worked primarily as cowherds and others. Grazing livestock and ploughing involve contrasting work intensity and have been commonly found (in micro studies from other regions) to be distinguished by different local terms. Defining the contracts in indigenous terms would have avoided this result, which 'finds' an 'explanation' due simply to misspecification.

2.4 Some problems with labour market approaches

Labour market approaches alone have not succeeded in explaining diversity in labour arrangements. With the exception of Binswanger and Rosenzweig's model, attempts to explain the existence of particular contractual systems in terms of market imperfections have proved unable to account for the co-existence of heterogenous systems of exchange (Bharadwaj 1989a, p. 17). Bharadwaj argued that the efficient profit maximizing choices of a free decision maker should not be assumed (1979). To analyse a contract, it was important to study exchange over a whole nexus of markets, to make explicit the social heterogeneity of the peasantry and to know which decisions have been foregone as well as those actually taken. Elsewhere Bharadwaj regretted the attention given to optimality of contracts in the growing literature on inter-linked markets, as it neglected the dynamic consequences (1985, p. 13).

Bardhan also criticized models designed to explain the rationale of particular institutional forms for overlooking 'how in the historical-evolutionary process the underlying rationale changes and the same institutional forms adapt and mutate in response to changed circumstances' (1988). Srivastava's empirical study showed that 'certain aspects of ... (inter-locked transactions) ... change systematically with the penetration of capitalism, even though the outward form of interlocking may appear to be similar' (see section 5.2).

The process of exchange of labour is crucially informed by what Rudra termed 'village society' (1984, p. 256; 1992, ch. 16). This includes manifestations of power relations such as the operation of social sanctions and caste ideology.[6] However, the neo-classical approaches explored here do not attempt to endogenize social institutions, such as caste or gender, nor the 'tastes' or 'preferences' of agents. Binswanger and Rosenzweig and Lal all routinely subordinated cultural/institutional to economic explanations of diversity and change. Binswanger and Rosenzweig conceded that 'culture and institutions' may be important 'since these factors can affect the supply or demand for labor' (1984, p. 30). Lal saw labour market processes as resulting from the mediation of '..'institutions' into the interplay of supply and demand'. This privileged economic over social explanatory factors from the outset, reflecting the economistic bias which has characterized historical work on rural labour in India (Prakash 1992a).

In the analysis of data from the Aurepalle study, Binswanger et al found it 'astonishing' that the lowest caste group should have the majority of 'rural farm servant' (agricultural labour contracts of over three months duration) jobs (op. cit., p. 159). There is no room in their analytical framework for an ideology of domination nor any attempt to *explain* a labour market segmented by caste.

The possible explanations for non-competitive behaviour given by Binswanger and Rosenzweig imply an assumption that 'prejudices' are exogenous. Thus they need not be explained. Moreover, the statement that 'small farmers may 'dislike' [wage] employment' (1984, p. 14) is an absurd proposition. Empirical work has not shown wage employment in agriculture to be 'liked' by anybody. It has an association with low status, both as manual labour and because it is subject to authority. (This is not inconsistent with variations in the social and economic status of different operations and the social status of employment by particular employers in specific contexts.)

Another inadequacy of Binswanger and Rosenzweig's review arises from the assumption that the heterogeneity of labour is based on inherent efficiency differences (p. 8), just as Lal based his consideration on skill differences (1989, p. 107). Even in their later consideration of the heterogeneity of labour as one of the 'neglected themes' in literature on wages and contractual arrangements, they did not consider personal relations with employers developed on the bases of location of residence and settlement history and mediated by class and caste. Although gender segmentation of the labour market was discussed, no explanations were offered (p. 31).

Lal's ideological agenda, though not explicitly stated, was betrayed by his paraphraseology of Bardhan's findings on labour tying, which he used to support his version of Bardhan's theory. In reporting that Bardhan found land productivity to be positively associated with attached labour, he left out the adverb 'weakly'. Further, where Bardhan has inferred attached labour contracts to be 'frequently' associated with employer credit, Lal preferred 'usually' (see Bardhan 1984, p. 80).

Careful choice of qualifiers also added weight to the conclusions Binswanger and Rosenzweig reached regarding the studies they reviewed on employer collusion. The studies they reported did not find 'much' indication of collusive behaviour. They did not define 'important' when they reported that 'there [was] little evidence in the market for daily labour, of important departures from competitive behaviour' (1984, p. 35).

Binswanger and Rosenzweig did not present a theory of collusion between labourers either. They described any agricultural 'agitation' as 'sporadic' in contrast to what they saw as the persistent organized activities of industrial unions. In stating that 'efforts to organize rural labour unions have been confined to Kerala, Tamil Nadu and West Bengal', they were both grossly inaccurate and understated the absolute significance of these states in terms of rural population (ibid, p. 36). Above all, they omitted to analyse the solidarities formed among hirers out of labour resisting wage cuts, observed by a number of studies and termed 'mutuality' by Harriss (1992) and Kapadia (1990). The means of resistance can be hypothesized to be provided by the observed 'occupational multiplicity' (Comitas 1973, cited in White 1976) of rural households. Invoking 'mutuality' and 'occupational multiplicity' could be introduced into a neo-classical analysis to argue that the observed 'unemployment' at equilibrium wages is not necessarily 'involuntary'. A hirer out of labour may prefer to earn nothing and retain her/his association with other labourers in the locality. Wage labour is only one possible source of livelihood – other productive and reproductive activities may be engaged in for survival, both valorized and unvalorized.

The frequently observed geographical immobility of labourers was attributed in part to asymmetrical information (Binswanger and Rosenzweig 1984, pp. 33–34). Employers were reluctant to employ strangers because of the possibility of shirking. Thus the familiar unitary explanation appeared again: 'Immobility here does not imply absence of choice; instead it may reflect a *second-best adjustment* to the informational and land market problems' (pp. 33–34, emphasis added). Several recent studies from different regions of South Asia have shown the importance of seasonal migration both to migrant labourers and to employers (Breman 1985; Datta 1991; my study). Binswanger and Rosenzweig's interpretation of Breman (summarized in section 2.2 above) does not explain the coexistence of a variety of modes of migrant labour recruitment, such as direct employer hiring of anonymous seasonal migrant labour gangs found to be so common in agriculturally dynamic districts of West Bengal in my field study.

In their attempt at a general model of production relations, Binswanger and Rosenzweig did not identify or resolve some of the main problems with 'labour market' approaches discussed above. Their model presented useful and coherent sets of consequences for agriculture of seasonality, the requirements for synchronicity and timeliness, and the associated risks of all three. It further showed how supervision costs to employers were exacerbated by widely dispersed production. However, their assumption of individual self interest limited the usefulness of the behavioral part of the model. One consequence of this assumption, which was not acknowledged, was that it led to household decision-making being treated as if it were synonymous with the decision-making of a single individual. Moreover, the identification of South Asian agriculture with unitary material and behavioral characteristics obscured the diversity of agrarian structures and rural social relations in that region.

The internal consistency of their reasoning is questionable. For example, they question why households should not rely entirely on 'family labour' without providing the first obvious answer of differential farm size. They view the 'committed' consumption of family workers as a cost of using such labour without spelling out the necessary concomitant of their opportunity cost in terms of alternative earnings foregone. In application the model again falls down first by its assumption that 'extra-economic coercion' does not exist (followed by a statement that it might do but the model will ignore it) and secondly by its assumption of 'competition among all agents in the economy'.

This section has raised serious doubts about the capacity of neo-classical economics to explain the coexistence of diverse labour arrangements in South Asian agriculture. Its failure in this regard can be attributed to restrictive assumptions rooted in the model of perfect competition. In the following section, I examine some of the central assumptions of orthodox Marxian approaches and ask whether these too have hindered such explanation.

3. LABOUR RELATIONS APPROACHES

Scholarship in political economy has focused on explaining labour relations in terms of conflicts of interest. Thus Adam Smith viewed wage determination as a bargaining process between unequally endowed agents. 'It is not difficult to foresee which of the two parties must, upon all ordinary occasions, have the advantage in the dispute' (1976, I.viii.II, cited by Rothschild 1992, p. 87). Thornton concluded that 'the labour of uncombined labourers is ... sold at a disadvantage' (Bharadwaj 1989b, p. 142) because unlike 'tangible commodities', where the price is determined by 'the competition of dealers, the price of labour may be determined by the competition of customers' (Thornton, 1886, p. 93, quoted by Bharadwaj, loc. cit.).

In classical Marxist theory, social relations of production are defined by the mode of appropriation of surplus labour with a corresponding structure of ownership of the forces of production (Harriss 1982, p. 110). The empirical complexity of production relations in a given space and time is an outcome of the coexistence and interpenetration of modes of production in a process of transition (Patnaik 1987, p. 2).

Using this conceptual framework, classical Marxist scholarship of rural South Asia has commonly made the following assumptions:

> (i) in analysing and characterizing empirically observable production relations, the most important explanatory parameter is class;[7]
> (ii) that history is an *inevitable* process of transition from slavery through feudalism and capitalism to socialism, with struggle between classes as the motor (a form of historical determinism);
> (iii) that each of these stages is *progressive* in relation to its predecessor (history as progress).

3.1 Class reductionism

As class is usually assumed to be the most important parameter for social differentiation, other sources of conflict (including age, gender, caste, religion, language and region) are interpreted in the light of this single insight.

Brass presented a case study from Haryana to challenge the notion that 'attached' labour relations, which he treated as single category, were entered into by labourers voluntarily and for their own 'particular reason[s]'. Moreover he argued that attached labour could only be understood in terms of the 'class/decomposition/recomposition (or restructuring) that accompanie[d] class struggle'. Thus the persistence or reappearance of these apparently 'feudal' production relations was explained as capitalists' 'deproletarianization' strategy to counter growing labour power (1990, pp. 36–7).[8]

Repeatedly, empirical studies have squeezed complex societal relations into class categories based on land ownership and the extent to which labour power is hired in or out. Ramachandran's richly detailed study of wage labour in the Cumbum Valley, Tamil Nadu, separated out the propertyless as a class, dealing exclusively with *their* material condition, and terms and conditions of employment. For the sake of his study he created a class homogeneity of labour as defined by the ownership of the means of production and net labour hiring practice. Yet there is no *a priori* reason why the first criterion for group loyalty should be class (Elster 1986, see below). In one contemporary study of rivalry in a West Bengal village, status was 'shown' to be the prime cause for competitions (Davis 1983).

Banaji in another context (1990, p. 297) emphasized the distortions implicit in the division of the peasantry into rich, middle, poor and landless, when wage labourers were often subsumed into the poor peasant category.[9] He rightly insisted that the peasantry is both 'amorphous *and* profoundly divided' (his emphasis) and such a rigid stratification terminology was not the most appropriate way of trying to make sense of this 'shifting and ambiguous reality'.

Elster has emphasized the difference between the *relevance* and the *centrality* of class in analysis of labour relations (1986, pp 160–1). In order to do this he posited class as one basis for group solidarity and collective action. While he argued that in any class society, class is likely to be a source of conflict and that class issues would pervade other sources of conflict, he disagreed with the orthodox Marxian view that class was always the most salient issue. Prakash extended this in his critique of the historiography of agricultural labourers to specify the intertwining of 'class, caste, 'tribe', gender and religion' in determining the category 'labourers' (1992, p. 45). Such critiques have enabled political economic analysis to go beyond orthodox Marxist categories to explain the reproduction of relations of domination and, in the process, to start to account for diversity in labour arrangements.

Bose's work on agrarian relations in late colonial Bengal (1986) provided a more than convincing case for a *regionally* differentiated analysis. He demonstrated the dangers of generalizing agrarian change too broadly with examples of the distinct processes of change in north, west/central and east Bengal.[10] Mohapatra has argued explicitly that regional differentiation is required to account for distinct processes of change due to 'local ecological context[s]' and 'the structure of power' (1991).

3.2 Freedom versus unfreedom

Echoing the assumption of history-as-progress, a number of Marxian studies positioned labour arrangements on a continuum between unfreedom and freedom (Ramachandran made this the central concern of his study (1990)). Freedom was used in the sense that, not bound to a particular employer, labourers could *choose* to whom they would sell their labour power. Ramachandran acknowledged that his definition of free labour did not imply that a worker under capitalism was completely free (p. 1 n.2). The unfreedom-freedom opposition and the notion of history-as-progress from one to the other have been criticized by Prakash. 'Neither rooted in history nor complicit in power, the analysis of bondage, servitude and slavery as different degrees of unfreedom presents itself as self-evident distinctions while privileging free labor as outside the reach of power relations ... Although it is true that these statuses represent historically given categories, their arrangement as a spectrum of conditions makes sense only in that it suggests a progressive restoration of a lost essence – freedom' (1990, pp. 6–7; see also 1992b).[11]

It is important to distinguish between the economic compulsion to sell labour power and the social compulsion to sell to a particular employer. The latter (pure unfreedom) is now rare in agriculture according to most contemporary field studies. This however, does not imply the opposite – that freedom of labour is the norm. Despite the low social status involved in hiring out labour power for agricultural fieldwork (which varies by region, gender, caste and religion), hundreds of millions of individuals in South Asia are not free to choose not to be agricultural labourers.

Moreover, seasonal fluctuations in volume of employment and access to earnings, makes many people dependent for advances, loans or employment in the lean seasons on the *group* patronage of local employers who have claims on their labour in return in the peak season. Thus individuals, households, descent lines and hamlets may be dependent for their livelihood on a single employer or group of employers as descent line, hamlet or subcaste. Conversely, an individual employer or group of employers may rely on local labourers for peak season labour power.

The process of production and the requirements of reproduction create a mutual dependency. However, the unequal distribution of economic power, reinforced by cultural and religious domination (Prakash 1992a, p. 36) is manifest in labour arrangements that themselves contribute to the reproduction of existing power relations and to changes in those relations.

In this section I have shown that contrary to orthodox Marxian assumptions, class need not be the central axis of domination or subordination in employer-employee relations. Moreover the assumption that wage labour becomes fully emancipated over time cannot be sustained. In the following sections, I use further examples from the literature to argue that explanations of the diversity in labour arrangements and the changes in their array over time, require disaggregation of the wage 'package' and proper definition of arrangement types.

4. EXPLAINING INTER- AND INTRA-CONTRACTUAL DIVERSITY: THE NEED FOR DISAGGREGATION

An investigation of the coexistence of diverse labour arrangements requires each arrangement to be properly specified. Power relations are indicated not only by the type of contract via which an individual buys or sells labour power but also by the precise terms and conditions of the contract, where these are not predefined by the contract type. Empirical studies of labour arrangements need to investigate whether arrangement types which have been represented as being indicative of a particular asymmetry in employer:employee relations, do not themselves also exhibit intra-contractual variation.

Just as dividing labour contracts into 'casual' and 'attached' (see section 5) disguises the overall power configuration between parties to the arrangement, a focus on wage rates alone neither distinguishes which party has the balance of advantage nor indicates the 'price' of labour.[12] Thus Rudra and Bardhan state at the start of their book that it is 'necessary to take account of all the ... attributes or aspects of employer-employee relations to understand the nature and degree of attachment of labourers to employers' (1983, p. 1; see also Bardhan and Rudra 1981, p. 89). Ramachandran also describes specific forms of intra-contractual variation (p. 189).

However, some attributes or components of labour arrangements such as the degree of obligation between employers and employees, and the actual duration of a loose priority relationship,[13] are not quantifiable. Here evidence is considered from a number of studies (including mine, see p.2, n.2, above) on variation in the following (measurable) attributes of labour arrangements:

- earnings, effective wages, and hours
- form of payment
- time of payment

- type of work
- payment regime
- work organization.

The studies have been selected to show how divergent (but not always conflicting) explanations have been put forward for similar types of variation. They serve as a warning against the careless use of general theory in diverse social, economic and agro-ecological environments in the South Asian region and for proper contextualizations. One pair of studies serves to illustrate how differing methodologies result in divergent explanations for variation in one attribute of diversity (work organization) in a single area. After separate consideration of each component, an outline is given of how these insights might feed into future research.

4.1 Wages and daily earnings

Daily earnings are defined as the material reward due to a worker following the hiring out of his or her labour power in a particular twenty-four hour period. The wage is the amount due per unit of work. In the case of time rate work, the effective wage is measured per hour, which often connotes a standard number of hours. For piece rate, the wage is paid per unit land area or other physical unit.

Inter-contractual variation (wages and earnings). Several studies have found earnings per day to be lower on average for annual than for daily contracts. Others have commented on premium payments to those in long duration contracts.

Annual arrangements may be actually paid annually, seasonally, monthly, daily or in a combination of these. Calculating the equivalent material payment per day has shown *lower earnings* than for daily rate contracts. Lower earnings have been explained variously by the compulsion to work for the same employer who sets the wages, by revealed preference by certain labourers for surety of subsistence (Kapadia 1992, p. 7) and by unvalorizable patronage benefits over a perhaps higher daily rate without such benefits (Davis 1983, pp 202–3).

On the other hand, Bardhan's recruitment cost theory explained the incidence of *higher earnings* per day for long duration contracts by employers paying a premium to ensure supply of workers when time was very short in the peak seasons. As more land was brought into irrigated cultivation in West Bengal and cropping intensity increased, Bardhan argued that the cost of labour hoarding diminished, negatively related to the flattening out of seasonal labour peaks (1984, p. 77).

Hart explained observed higher wages for long duration contracts in Java in terms of labour management and control. The creation of a tier of privilege among the labour force was used as a mechanism of social control. Labourers were then divided, with those in apparently advantaged positions having more to lose from acting against the interests of the employer. She also showed how groups of labourers with 'long-standing social ties with the village elite', based on settlement history, had access to arrangements with higher pay (1986a, pp. 175–7; see also section 5, below).

Intra-contractual variation (wages and earnings). Variation has been observed within the same contractual form between the wages as well as earnings of men and women, young and old. The amount earned has also been shown to be related to type of work done, which may be organized, inter alia, by caste and gender. Furthermore, variation in wages has been found to occur when payment is imperfectly related to hours worked, when some workers have to travel further than others; and in one study according to the supply and timing of seasonal migration.

Most studies concur that when there is gender differentiation in daily time rated arrangements, men do better than women. However, in one of the localities in my study, women earned more for transplanting than most men earned at any time.[14] The narrowing of wage differentials between the sexes in seasonally tight labour markets has been shown to vary by agricultural region in West Bengal (Kynch, undated).

In certain circumstances agricultural daily-rated wages also varied according to the type of work performed (see also section 4.4 below, which briefly considers type of work itself as a yardstick of diversity). In one locality of my study, this often reflected seasonal variation in the demand for labour and labourers' requirement for earnings. Access to particular types of work are commonly proscribed in a number of areas by gender and caste (Beteille 1974, p. 122), though to differing degrees. This has been stated in many studies but rarely explained (see Prakash 1992, p. 31–4 and 45 for an attempt).

Sarap found wage differentials according to age, strength and skill among men and boys in *guti* and *khutia* arrangements in Orissa (1991, p. A170).[15] He identified three types of *guti* arrangement, attributing the differences in terms and conditions of contract to employer household characteristics. Others have sought to identify those contracts where daily earnings vary, dividing arrangements into negotiable and non-negotiable categories (Dreze and Mukherjee 1987; Kapadia 1992). Kapadia identified piece rates for gang labour as negotiable, in contrast to daily time rates, which were fixed. My data showed daily equivalent earnings for *bagal* and *bhatua*[16] arrangements in the Purulia locality to be negotiable; however, in Bardhaman, daily rates for seasonally migrant harvest labourers varied in one segment only, reflecting the party political orientation of the employers concerned.[17]

Ramachandran found that labourers apparently employed on a 'casual' daily basis would perform extra unpaid duties for an employer before returning home. This had the effect of extending the working day beyond eight hours, signifying a reduction in *wages* though not in earnings. Although for other analyses, Ramachandran standardized the eight hour day, he did not explicitly consider earnings per hour. Thus his statement that a 'general practice' of time rated work was that a single wage rate existed for each type of work (p. 191). The 'continuation of labour services' was explained by the presence of a 'despotic dominant landlord' on the one hand and the desperation of labourers arising from 'poverty, unemployment and land hunger' on the other. Ramachandran also noted variation in wages in Gudalur (not his main study village), where in the 1976–7 peak seasons, workers often received premium payments for travelling longer distances to the fields.

Sarap observed harvest piece rates to vary for the same work according to the supply and timing of seasonal migration (p. A172). Farmers' interests in completing the work as early as possible were reflected in the higher piece rates available for those groups which could complete in good time, and generally in times of scarce supply of migrant labour.

4.2 The form of payment

The form of payment refers to the substance in which the work is rewarded: i.e. cash, kind, food, clothes or a combination of these. Other forms include the use of a small plot for cultivation and/or the provision of homestead land.

If one form of payment is seen as advantageous to employers and neutral or disadvantageous to labourers or vice versa then the actual form may reflect the balance of bargaining power. Form of payment is part of the arrangement 'package', whether contested or not.

Ramachandran asserted that workers 'in Gokilapuram, as elsewhere' preferred payment in kind, particularly in the main harvesting, threshing and transplanting seasons. This he argued was due to the workers' perception that kind wages protected them against the decline in real cash wages. However, Ramachandran showed that for piece rate gang work, where the number in the group had increased but the payment per unit land has stayed the same, this was an illusion.

In my study, daily-waged, time-rated labour was materially rewarded in cash, kind, cash and kind or cash and food. Supplements included tobacco and bath oil. Form of payment differed considerably between the two localities and in Purulia between seasons, types of work, arrangement types and employers. There was no consistent preference by labourers for payment in kind. Some employers differentiated in payment form between different categories of labourers (usually by the location of the labourers' residences). The reality was diverse and it would be wrong to extrapolate from this that labourers consistently prefer payment in kind. For example, in the main seasonal migration to Bardhaman from Purulia for the (*aman*) paddy harvest, the cash payment was valued as a means of recovering from debt and celebrating the forthcoming *mela*,[18] while the kind portion was consumed in the camp. On the other hand, seasonal fluctuations in paddy prices caused labourers to prefer payment in kind in the lean season when prices were particularly high.[19] Petty purchases were made using paddy as currency from village shops.

Sarap described variation in the pay form of *guti* labourers in combinations of cash, kind, food and homestead. He distinguished three common combinations and associated the differences with employer characteristics based on place of employer's origin and level of education. Employers who recently immigrated from a neighbouring state retained some of their old contractual arrangements, while of indigenous employers, the more educated feared the new legislation under the Bonded Labour Abolition Law (1976) and converted the form of payment to cash as well as routinizing payment time.

4.3 The time of payment

Payment may be made to the worker in full on the day of work. It can take place partly the same day and partly in advance or in arrears. Sometimes payment is made fully in advance or arrears. Arrangements as institutions lead workers to expect patterns such as receipt of a kind portion immediately and a cash portion later.

In my study both labourers and employers were asked each day when they would receive payment for that day's work. In this way it was learned that the timing of payment for daily time rate contracts varied according to season and locality. In the Bardhaman locality, the kind portion was consistently paid on the day of work and the cash portion adjusted against advances at the end of the month or season. In Purulia later cash payment was expected at harvest when employers tried to wait as long as possible to receive the best price for their crop.

In the peak seasons when seasonal migrant workers were employed in the Bardhaman locality, arrears payment of the cash portion of cash and kind wages was standard practice. Although workers who migrated from the other locality expressed preference for this as it acted as a saving mechanism, some employers refused to pay the arrears until the seasonal duration agreed had terminated. During unseasonal rains some such employers did not pay migrant labour any wage, nor provide subsistence; yet they were not free to leave as they were refused the balance due for work already completed.

In the Purulia locality, most long duration contracts (seasonal or annual) were paid at the end. Deductions were made for any 'advances'.[20] At harvest, daily arrangements were often not rewarded on the day of work. Employers waited as long as possible, as payment was mostly in cash and this depended on crop sales. The later the sale, the higher the price gained for the crop. As Marx has pointed out this amounted to an interest free advance from labourers to employers[21] (Bharadwaj 1989b, p. 16). The practice of *berhun* loans continued, whereby loans were made to particularly vulnerable labourers in wet[22] lean season, which had to be repaid by labour at harvest. The debt was reduced by much less than the minimum received by other workers for the same tasks. Thus intra-contractual diversity in timing of payment may be partly explained as an exercise in employer power and partly as the outcome of labourer livelihood strategies (see section 6).

Sarap found advances common for 'farm servants' (both *guti* and *khutia*). The worker would be expected to work off the advance within the agreed duration of the contract. This was explained by employers' desire to cement the relationship between the parties. The advances were paid in only 75 per cent of cases (p. A170). He found that the practice was more common among indigenous employers in contrast to those who had migrated recently from Andhra Pradesh. One explanation offered was the slightly higher value of overall payments offered to *guti* by the latter group of employers. Other possible explanations were not explored, such as the need to build alliances and increase influence in local affairs by these employers (see section 6).

Ramachandran found that daily time rated work was not always paid on the same day or on completion of the task. Timely payment was related to the wealth of the employer, with richer employers tending to pay wages on time (p. 200).

· 4.4 Type of work

Types of work carried out can be crudely divided into three categories: agricultural, livestock and non-agricultural. Agricultural work here refers to all activities connected with the production of crops from preparation of land to storage and transport. Livestock associated work refers to livestock rearing and milk production activities, including grazing, cleaning out dung, preparing food, feeding and milking. Other tasks are classified by the umbrella term non-agricultural arrangements.

Type of work may be associated with a particular labour arrangement. Thus, for example, separate arrangements were found by Sarap and in my study for grazing livestock (see section 2.3). Moreover, certain crop associated tasks are institutionally tied to a particular payment regime and/or work organization (see 4.5 and 4.6). Sarap explained the predominance of piece rate contracts for the transplanting, weeding, harvesting and threshing of paddy by the employers' need to complete the task quickly. The same argument (that some paddy activities were time-bound) was used by Bardhan to explain the increased popularity of long duration daily or seasonally rated arrangements (1984, p. 77).

4.5 Payment regime

The payment regime refers to the unit by which payment is calculated. In short duration contracts payment may be calculated either by time rate or by piece rate. Workers paid per day, per hour or other unit of time are being paid at a time rate, while those paid according to a physical quantity of work done are being paid at piece rate. In the Purulia locality of my study transplanting involved both a piece rate (for uprooting paddy seedlings) and a time rate (for transplanting them).

Payment regime, like duration and degree of obligation was usually indicated in both the study localities by the indigenous term for an arrangement. Thus inter-contractual diversity existed by definition.

In separate discussions of paddy cultivation in southern Tamil Nadu, Ramachandran and Kapadia reached separate conclusions on whether piece rates were in the interests of the worker. The implication of Ramachandran's argument was that piece rates were forced on reluctant employers by supervision requirements (p. 187). Workers benefitted from the higher earnings available per day (p. 193). Kapadia found that the Pallar caste landless women labourers with whom she lived preferred time rates over piece rates (1992, p. 5). Piece rates represented an 'internalization of discipline' (p. 28) and a 'powerful extension of employers' control of the workforce'. In a situation of excess supply of labourers employers benefitted whenever contracts were negotiable, as in the case of piece rate contracts (loc. cit.). The increased incidence of piece rate contracts signalled increasing employer power.

My study found piece rates to be favoured by workers in the Purulia locality due to the higher potential earnings. Therefore employers had less difficulty recruiting on piece rates than time rates in the peak season. In the Bardhaman locality, workers for employers resident in the CPI(M) stronghold area (see section 4.1, n.14) demanded fixed hours as compensation for being denied the possibility of working on piece rates. Workers resident in the Congress dominated area, where employers did not adhere so strictly to the CPI(M) brokered floor, had access to much higher earnings through lucrative piece rate arrangements.

4.6 Work organization

Work organization is also usually defined in the indigenous term for an arrangement. It refers to whether labourers are to be employed as a group (with a single payment made by the employer to a gang leader, or contractor) or individually. Thus inter-contractual variation again occurs by definition.

Here the contrast between the description and analyses of Kapadia and Ramachandran is highly informative. They both provided aspects of a regional picture, not simply based on spatial differences in work organization, but in the different parts of an explanation that emerged from distinctive field methodologies. Ramachandran described the composition of, and recruitment to, several work groups, only one of which was limited to a single caste. Supervision was observed to be required by the contractor at harvest, when coordination of cutting, binding and loading onto trailers was essential. At transplanting, on the other hand, supervision was not required even by the contractor. Thus technical differences between operations informed the extent of supervision necessary.

Kapadia specifically considered the recruitment of Pallar caste women into workgroups. While Ramachandran explained the one single caste (Pallar) work group in terms of the work ability of this caste as perceived by employers, Kapadia examined the internal composition of Pallar groups and explained them in terms of the power and patronage of the group leaders. Thus the inclusion of elderly women was not fully explained by Ramachandran, though one reads between the lines that he viewed it as an intra-caste social security mechanism (p. 214). One contractor reported that he punished workers from his own community if they complained that the less productive elderly were paid equal shares (op. cit.). Kapadia explained the inclusion of the elderly as patronage favouring of their own kin by contractors (pp. 19–21).

Sarap attributed the increase in gang labour in his area to the decrease in control through personal relations *which accompanied the inflow of migrant labour.* 'Homogeneity' of labour groups due to common 'place of origin' decreased the employer's supervision costs (p. A172). Unlike Lal (see section 2.2), he did not spell out the mechanism whereby commonality of origin decreased the need for supervision.

4.7 Implications for future research

Future empirical research could build on the notion that there are measurable components of labour arrangements which form part of any remuneration package. Wages and earnings may reflect the balance of advantage but can be bolstered by measurement of the form of payment, time of payment, payment regime and work organization. Explanations for the existence of diverse labour arrangements in a confined area is textured by consideration of the components of each arrangement and the intra-contractual variation which they reveal. It will be important to identify the relative incidence of whole packages or combinations of components in order to begin to understand the processes involved in the negotiation of labour arrangements.[23] However, before making further suggestions regarding the future research agenda, I explore problems arising from an over-aggregated typology of labour arrangements for the analysis of contractual change.

5. DISTINGUISHING IDEOLOGICAL, SEMANTIC AND SUBSTANTIVE DIVERGENCIES IN THE CHARACTERIZATION OF CONTRACTUAL CHANGE

Ambiguity over the meaning of the terms 'attached' and 'casual' labour, together with different uses of 'exploitation' and 'coercion' based on unstated ideological divergencies increase the lack of clarity in the literature. This is marked in analyses of *change* in labour arrangements. A contract is experienced along more than one axis, including duration, interlinkage and degree of obligation/freedom (as defined by Ramachandran, see section 3.1), and these are not necessarily correlated. While some authors specify the yardstick by which attached and casual arrangements should be distinguished (e.g. D. and A. Thorner 1962, pp. 21–23, and Ramachandran 1990, pp. 169–70, who use freedom; and Binswanger et al 1984, p. 143, n.1, who use duration), some of the authors discussed in this section allow the blurred distinction of the categories to remain in place.

There is no necessary empirical correspondence between contracts of a particular duration and the existence or extent of interlinkage with other markets, nor between either of these and the degree of unfreedom.[24] Indeed, long duration, interlinkage and coercion do not necessarily correlate negatively with the commercialization of agriculture or the development of capitalism (Hart 1986b, p. 189; Brass 1990, p. 37; Rudra 1987; Bhalla 1976, p. A29). Nevertheless, 'attached' or 'tied' labour arrangements are generally distinguished from 'casual' arrangements by their duration and/or by their degree of unfreedom and/or by the extent of interlinkage with other markets. This presents problems for comparison of the findings of different authors on change in their relative incidence over time. As a consequence, I examine in turn the evidence for the increase of short duration relative to long duration, free relative to unfree and multi-stranded relative to single-stranded attached labour contracts.

5.1 Duration

There is considerable evidence that the incidence of *long duration* arrangements as a proportion of total labour contracts has increased since the onset of the Green Revolution both in northern and eastern India. In the early 1970s a survey of three contrasting regions in Haryana (northwest India) was carried out to investigate changes in relations of production following the recent and continuing rapid changes in technology (Bhalla 1976). The regions were selected according to degree of adoption of the new technology, the most 'advanced' of the three being the region in which the forces of production had changed the most. Bhalla found that in this region more than half of male agricultural labourers were employed under some form of long term (one year or more) contract. In the intermediate region, the proportion was 30 per cent and in the backward region, 9 per cent (p. A25).

A survey conducted in West Bengal by Bardhan and Rudra in 1979 found that the proportion of tied labour households to the total number of labour households was twice as high in agriculturally more advanced villages (Bardhan 1984, p. 78; as predicted by Binswanger and Rosenzweig 1986, p. 533, see section 2.2 above). Moreover, a later smaller survey in the same State compared a group of four villages in a relatively backward District (Bankura) with two large villages in a relatively advanced one (Bardhaman). Longer association was found to be more common in the advanced villages (35 per cent as opposed to 20 per cent) (Rudra 1987, p. 760).

In contrast to these results, an historical study of rural labourers in Bengal between 1880 and 1980 found that short term employment was 'the only type of labour contract which (had) increased decisively' (van Schendel and Faraizi 1984, p. 96). Life long contracts[25] had disappeared by the end of the nineteenth century though annual and seasonal contracts had continued with no clear evidence of a significant increase or decrease.[26] Ramachandran judged the literature to indicate a clear trend away from long term towards 'daily paid' and 'piece rate' work (1990, pp. 14–15). He attributed shifts in incidence of long duration contracts to the 'nature of the crop grown and the way the market for labour has evolved in a region' (p. 237). He thus explained trends in predominantly technological and economic terms, illustrating how green revolution technology could be consistent with the sharpening of seasonal peaks in labour demand, while expansion in the size of the rural labour force could maintain a surplus of labour throughout the agricultural year.

5.2 Freedom

A second yardstick by which the incidence of tied labour is measured concerns the relative *freedom* of labour over time. Section 3.2 above notwithstanding, this reveals further contradictions in the literature. At the heart of the disagreement lie ideological differences over the meaning of 'exploitation' and 'coercion'. 'In the economics of orthodox Marxism, the existence of exploitation under capitalism is assumed. In neo-classical economics it is assumed away' (Hodgson 1982, p. 202).[27] *Exploitation* for a conventional Marxist is the appropriation of the surplus value of labour in the production process. This is equal to the value of the total product minus the labourers' needs for his/her reproduction.[28] For conventional neo-classical analysis exploitation occurs when a labourer is paid less than his/her marginal product.

Similarly, economic as opposed to extra-economic *coercion* does not exist for some neo-classical authors because coercion is taken to imply the use of physical force. A contract may be regarded as 'voluntary' even when the employer has used superior bargaining power to offer a labourer an 'all or nothing' choice. At the limit, where the employer is a perfect monopsonist and there is no labour mobility this may be akin to the 'freedom to starve' (Bardhan 1984, p. 82). For Ramachandran, workers are unfree when they are forced by a social or economic obligation to hire out labour to a specific employer or group of employers (1990, p. 1; see also previous section). This may be termed 'economic coercion'.

In a study of five villages in Haryana in 1987, Brass found that labourers were unfree whenever they took a loan from an employer, whether the repayment of the debt through labour was due intermittently on different days or in a continuous block (Brass 1990). Attachment was 'coercive' by its very nature as 'only through a debt would a free labourer become attached' (p. 53). Brass identified the increase of indebtedness among casual as well as longer term labourers as a strategy used by employers to counter the bargaining power of labour (see section 3.1).

In contrast, Bardhan considered those tied contracts which benefitted employers without involving extra-economic coercion as voluntary on the part of labourers and not necessarily to the latter's disadvantage. Whether a contract is voluntarily entered into and whether it is to one or other party's objective material advantage are of course separate issues. Clearly, part of the contradiction here is due first to the very different production and exchange relations in the two regions and secondly to the authors' different ideological frameworks.

Substantive differences remain, however, regarding the extent to which labour is obliged to work for a particular employer under disadvantageous conditions. While Bardhan argued that increased attachment was a response to higher recruitment costs in the peak season as demand for labour increased and the labour market tightened,[29] Brass viewed the higher incidence of tying as an employers' strategy to exercise more effective control over the labour force.

Earlier evidence from north India was also divergent. Bhalla (1976) identified changes in the form of tied labour contracts as reflecting a 'counterattack' by employers on the increased bargaining power of labour following a sharp rise in labour demand. Taking the form of indebtedness, the involvement of a panel of powerful village individuals in the increasingly formalized written contracts and the individual, personalized basis on which precise terms and conditions were designed, the strategy had been 'entirely successful' (p. A29). Bhalla termed the outcome of these strategies the 'redesigned fabric of conservative rural power' (p. A27). Although labourers were materially better off in the villages where the green revolution had penetrated furthest, at the time of the fieldwork they had not organized any kind of collective action.

In contrast, Singh, in a study of two Districts in Punjab, attributed the predominance of the *siri* (crop-sharing) contractual form directly to the increased bargaining power of labour (Singh 1976, p. 97). In conditions of increasing yields and agricultural commodity prices, it was advantageous to labour to continue to receive payment (a) as a share of the harvest and (b) in kind (p. 96).

Srivastava compared production relations in three villages in Uttar Pradesh (Srivastava 1989). The relatively advanced village was situated in western Uttar Pradesh, which more closely resembles developed agriculture of archetypal north Indian conditions. The others, in eastern Uttar Pradesh, may have had more resemblance to the backward agriculture of eastern India than to the western part of the same state. Srivastava found that new forms of interlinked contract developing out of 'more recent strategies of surplus producers'[30] did not in themselves constitute a decline in freedom for the labour force (p. 518). The relative constraint which they imposed on the mobility of labour was more to do with 'direct economic processes' (labourers could and did opt to leave interlocked contracts) than the effects of labour relations in the agriculturally more backward village, where 'several types of interlocked relationships (were) derived from traditional relationships' (p. 517). Thus tied contracts could have the same form but reflect different accumulation strategies. Interlinking the credit and labour markets did not necessarily indicate 'additional' surplus appropriation. Although Srivastava concluded that the persistence of certain such forms could lead to 'the more adverse forms of interlocked relationships', he provided no evidence from the study to support this assertion, basing it rather on other authors' work. A more reasonable conclusion from his work might have been that labour in the advanced village, despite the extent to which it was tied, was relatively free in relation to labour in the backward villages. However, contrary to the implications of Srivastava's final sentence, the study does not actually contradict Bardhan's findings on the issue of freedom (see above and Srivastava, p. 519).

Other findings for West Bengal, however, have brought Bardhan's optimism into question. Rudra (1987) found that tied labourers in the advanced villages were less free than those in the backward ones. This was evidenced by the terms of the contract, which in the advanced village involved being at the 'beck and call' of the employer for any task when required. However, payment was only received for days when the labourer worked for the employer. The predominant form of tied labour in the backward villages, on the other hand, stipulated a continuous period of employment for a specific task. Moreover the higher incidence of longer duration contracts in the advanced villages (cited above) often implied a 'more servile relation' (1987, pp. 759–760). The problem here is that Rudra's concept of freedom differs from Ramachandran's (1990). In the latter's conceptualization, a continuous tie in the backward village would be considered less free than the advanced village's 'beck and call', because of the absolute constraint on working for another employer.

Although van Schendel and Faraizi reported that 'extra-economic coercion' gave way to 'economic coercion' at the end of the nineteenth century, 'the particularistic basis of rural employment and labour control is ... retained to the extent that the interests of smaller employers are served' (1984, pp. 97–8). Here it is the dependence on employers for credit, though no longer as personalized in that more than one source may be available, which restricts the freedom of labourers. Economic coercion here refers to the practice of tying employment contracts to consumption loans, obliging the worker to supply labour as repayment.

The use of the free/unfree axis, particularly by Srivastava (1989) and Ramachandran (1990) distinguishes a world view which holds that as agricultural labourers come to approximate a rural proletariat, they can be said to be emancipated (following assumption (iii) of classical Marxist approaches (section 3.1)). This 'emancipatory' perspective is contrasted with the 'moral economism' of anthropologists Kapadia (1990) and Davis (1983). These scholars interpreted long term contracts in villages in Tamil Nadu and West Bengal respectively as in the interests of labourers. The world is seen as moving away from mutual obligation (good) towards commoditization of labour (bad). Kapadia attributes the declining incidence of long duration labour arrangements to the exercise of employer power.

5.3 Interlinkage

The changing incidence of tied contracts when defined by interlinkage has already been discussed in the previous section in as much as it relates to the 'freedom' of labour. It is important to reemphasize here, however, that changes or lack of them in the *form* of interlinkage do not necessarily signify the domination of one party's agenda. Although Adnan argued that interlocked markets were 'contractually imposed by one agent upon another' (1984, Section 3.1.2), there is no *a priori* reason why this should be so. The interlocking of product and labour markets documented by Singh as being in some labourers' interests under a particular set of economic conditions, were lobbied for by workers (Singh, 1976; see also Bhalla, 1976, p. A25, for evidence of similar lobbying in Haryana). Moreover, in the advanced village in western Uttar Pradesh, Srivastava argued that certain forms of interlocking could facilitate 'subsistence (of the direct producers) and production' (1989, p. 517). Interlocked transactions were shown by Srivastava to arise both out of new (i.e. more commercialized) and 'traditional' relations (see above). Labourers may perceive interlocking to be to their advantage and seek it out. Thus the use of interlocked contracts as a category may be fairly redundant as they cannot be ranked as a group against single-stranded contracts. The

127

advantage of micro-studies is that they enable the economic and power relations behind different arrangements and different manifestations of the same arrangements to be specified.

6. 'POWER, LABOR AND LIVELIHOOD': GILLIAN HART'S FRAME-WORK FOR THE ANALYSIS OF RURAL LABOUR ARRANGEMENTS

Gillian Hart's study of labour arrangements in the village of Sukodono in rural Java addressed several of the limitations of labour market and labour relations approaches summarized in sections 2 and 3 above (Hart 1986a). Contrary to the choice-theoretic neo-classical models, she did not focus on finding rationales for particular contract types; nor did she externalize the practice of power relationships. Hart's framework diverted from orthodox Marxian methods in its avoidance of class reductionism and explicit opposition to an historically determinist approach. Hart set out in her analysis of Sukodono to account for 'the coexistence of a wide variety of different institutional arrangements' (i.e. *diversity*) viewing *change* as a 'process through which particular institutions, in turn, give rise to opposing tensions and contradictions' (1984, pp. 55–56).

Hart has produced a framework for analysis, which can be used in widely differing contexts. In her Java study, she considered the labour deployment strategies of households which hired out labour and the accumulation strategies of employer households. With respect to the former, Hart looked for relationships between the income of a labour household on the one hand and its asset position and age structure on the other. She found that asset holding (a proxy for class) and the number of adult workers in a household were positively related to the number of income earning possibilities faced by that household. Daily earnings varied according both to the crop produced and to the location of the employment (whether inside or outside the village). Poorer households and those with a smaller number of adult workers required job security; however, the longer duration arrangements available to them tended to be the ones with lower earnings. Households with land, or with a larger number of adult workers, were able to deploy at least one individual into riskier but higher paid work. In one case relatively advantageous long duration arrangements were accessed by lower asset class labour households. This was explained by the long standing personal ties of a particular residence grouping with local employers due to their earlier settlement in the village.

Hart explored the relationship between the exercise of power at the village level and the effect of macro political and economic factors on employer strategies. She discussed how the interaction between the rural power structure on the one hand, and local bureaucrats on the other, could influence labour arrangements in different ways in different national political systems.

Whereas in Bangladesh, for example, the competitiveness of local politics meant that gaining access to state resources was contingent on client support, in Java such access depended more on forces external to the village (1984). The military and bureaucracy maintained law and order and granted concessions to the rural elite in the form of non-agricultural investment opportunities. In Sukodono, major employers used the provision of job security as an indirect means of organizing and disciplining labour, partly to allow themselves more time to cultivate relations with bureaucrats (1986a, p. 178).

Hart explained employers' preference for landed labourers as an exclusionary device to segment the labour force, for reasons of both *labour management* (to ensure worker effort) and of *social control* (to bring about worker docility). Those in the relatively privileged arrangements were motivated by the fear of losing the 'privileges' they had – and landed labourers, who generally came from higher economic and social strata, would have had more to fear from the ensuing loss of esteem than others. They had no class affinity with other workers and could thus be expected to supervise them with the employers' interests at heart. Landless workers were kept docile and hardworking both by their economic vulnerability, which was perpetuated by the segmentation of the labour force, and by their knowledge that they could not get access to the privileged employer-employee relations if they resisted.

In tackling change, Hart acknowledged the importance of technological and demographic explanations, but set herself the task of explaining the residual. This entailed an historical narrative, mainly from secondary sources, tracing the sharp changes in regime type over the last three decades. It showed crucially that changes in the balance of power between employers and labourers and changes in the extent to which elite rural households were expected to maintain law and order in the countryside were not unidirectional. At the same time, they were not arbitrary, but closely related to changes in regime type.

Although Hart's framework provides a coherent and attractive foundation for the study of labour arrangements elsewhere, it contains at least one conceptual and two field methodology problems. There is an unaddressed conceptual problem with the separation of labour management and social control. Social control is defined as 'an attempt to exercise power in *non labor spheres*' (1986c, p. 190, emphasis added). Hart has not considered that labour management can be a form of social control. Moreover, the desire to prevent the rural poor from behaving disruptively (used by Hart as an illustration of motivations for developing social control) may also be seen as a labour management tool.

Hart used 30 day recall to establish the extent to which each individual employer and labourer hired in or out labour power and in which types of arrangements. Thus she was unable to look closely at intra-contractual diversity. The division of work of greater and lesser privilege into crops rather than types of operation further reduced the fine tuning of the analysis.

Nevertheless, our attempts to characterize the relation between agrarian structure and agricultural growth can benefit greatly from the framework of analysis used by Hart. The investigation and proper specification of the agricultural, ecological, social, economic and political contexts at the village and higher levels and the objective of explaining the empirical data she collected, rather than trying to pin them to one or other abstract theory, represent advances on much of the other work in this field. Moreover, she tackled the issue of power at a number of levels, without reducing it either to the imperfect structure of markets or to class relations alone. The framework could and should be used in South Asia as a basis for a series of comparable micro and meso level studies of labour arrangements, and their aggregative use in building up a typology of agrarian structures.

7. SUMMARY AND CONCLUSION

This chapter set out first to evaluate the success of mainstream economic theories in explaining the coexistence of diverse labour arrangements in rural South Asia. Secondly it has tried to outline three avenues by which empirical studies could sharpen their analyses of diversity.

Sections 2 and 3 concentrated on assessing labour market and labour relations approaches to the problem. The limitations of neo-classical approaches were identified as:

(i) restrictive assumptions derived from the perfect competition model, in particular the assumption that individual behaviour is always based on self-interest;

(ii) the focus on constructing rationales for specific contractual arrangements, rather than seeking to explain the concurrent existence of a variety of arrangements (with the exception of Binswanger and Rosenzweig 1986);

(iii) the neglect or externalization of power relations – both economic and social (mediated, for example, through caste and gender);

(iv) the subordination of cultural to economic explanatory factors by implication;

(v) not taking sufficient account of the heterogeneity of labour; and

(vi) discounting of the importance and possibility of labourer solidarity, expressed through resistance to wage cuts.

Classical Marxian approaches were criticized for:

(i) their class reductionism, through which class was assumed to be not just relevant but central as a parameter of social differentiation, sub-ordinating and neglecting other parameters such as age, gender, caste and religion;

(ii) the implicit assumption of history-as-progress, which was flawed in its veiling of the power relations inherent in 'free wage labour', including the economic compulsion to sell labour power in low status work and the social compulsion to sell to particular groups of employers.

In the fourth section, I argued that variation within arrangement types (intra-contractual diversity) required explanation as much as the coexistence of diverse contracts (inter-contractual diversity). Units of measurement applicable to both types were identified and used to illustrate how very different explanations have been found for similar forms of diversity. These are summarized in Table 1, serving to illustrate the requirement for con-textualization of investigations of diversity as well as the need for clear statements of method.

The fifth section discussed how changes in labour arrangements have been represented via divergent explanations in the literature. Semantic, ideological and substantive differences in accounts of change in similar and contrasting regions were drawn on to illustrate the importance of careful prior definition of arrangement type.

In the sixth section, the work of Gillian Hart on contractual diversity and change in rural Java was summarized. It was shown to be able to resolve several of the problems of mainstream economic approaches identified in sections 2 and 3. Her simultaneous consideration of the differentiated agendas of both employers and employees in the context of asymmetrical distribution of power locally, and the effects on this of a changing regime type at the national level lead us towards a more inclusive framework for the study of diversity in rural labour arrangements.

The number of possible explanations illustrated in section 4 and Table 1 is evidence enough that more micro and meso level inductive studies of labour arrangements are required, if the understanding of agrarian structure and its relation with agricultural development in any one region is to be improved. As well as answering the criticisms I have made of neo-classical and orthodox Marxian approaches, the framework of analysis should place the objective of explaining empirically encountered diversity first. This would be incom-patible with an agenda which sought simply to validate one particular general theory.

TABLE 1

A SUMMARY OF THE EXPLANATIONS OF DIVERSITY IN LABOUR
ARRANGEMENTS PRESENTED IN THIS CHAPTER

Type of Diversity	Author	Explanation
Wage		*Higher wage in long duration contracts explained by:*
	Bardhan	Recruitment cost – high in peak season
	Hart	Labour management/ social control
		Lower wage in long duration contracts explained by:
	Kapadia	Security of subsistence preference
	Davis	Unvalorizable patronage benefits
		Intra-contractual inter-seasonal swings (manifest in differences between types of work) explained by:
	this study	Shifts in demand for labour and relation to supply
		Intra-contractual (harvest wages); variation in part of one locality vs rigidity in the other part explained by:
	this study	Party political orientation of employers
		Variation in wage (not earnings) due to labour service explained by:
	Ramachandran	Despotic landlord and poor, unemployed, land hungry labourers
		Intra-seasonal variation in harvest piece rates explained by:
	Sarap	Coordination of number & timing of arrival of seasonal migrants (supply) with demand.
Form of Payment		*Labourers' preference for kind payments explained by*
	Ramachandran	Perceived protection against inflation
		No evidence for constant labourers' preference for any one form explained by:
	this study, Binswanger et al	Lump sum cash from seasonal migration valued for repaying debt, celebrating *mela* versus kind preferred in lean season when cost of paddy high.
		Employer preference for cash payments explained by
	Sarap	Fear of legal action – Bonded Labour Abolition Law
Time of Payment		*Employer preference for late payments explained by:*
	this study	Cash payments required sale of crop. Post harvest prices lowest
		Employer use of arrears payment with migrant labour explained by:
	this study	Tying mechanism. Prevents departure

Type of Diversity	Author	Explanation
Time of Payment		*Loan tied to work at lower than going rate (implicit interest) explained by:*
	this study	Employer power and labourer livelihood strategies
		Variation in whether advances paid (inter-contractual) explained by:
	Sarap	Employers' desire to cement relationship
		Variation in whether advances paid (which employers of farm servants were among 75% who paid advances) explained by:
	Sarap	Compensates for lower value of annual payment
		Variation in timeliness of payment for daily rated work explained by:
	Ramachandran	Variation in wealth of employer
Type of Work		*Specific payment regimes for certain work type*
	Sarap	Piece rate explained by need to complete task quickly – transplanting, weeding, harvesting, threshing.
	Bardhan	Long duration arrangements explained by need to ensure timely labour supply so that work could be done on time and at appropriate time.
Payment Regime		*Piece rates vs time rates explained by:*
	Ramachandran	Piece rates forced on reluctant employer by supervision requirements. Otherwise work too slow (see section 4.4 above).
	Kapadia	Piece rates reflect internalization of discipline within work group – powerful employers' control of work force.
	this study	Piece rates favoured by workers – because of higher earnings – employer again reluctant
	this study	Piece rates available (& otherwise higher earnings) according to orientation of dominant political party.
Work Organization		*Internal composition of Pallar work group – inclusion of elderly explained by:*
	Kapadia	Patronage of own kin by Pallar female contractors
	Ramachandran	Social security: intra-caste mechanism
	Lal	Caste-homogenous group to enable necessary team work/cooperation for 'idiosyncratic' tasks where supervision costs otherwise high.

NOTES

1. International Development Centre, Queen Elizabeth House, Oxford University. This chapter is reprinted with minor changes from *Journal für Entwicklungspolitik* (Vienna), Vol. IX, No. 3, 1993, with permission.
2. Findings from my study of two localities in West Bengal carried out between June 1991 and March 1992 are drawn on heavily in that section. The objectives of the study were to explain diversity and change in labour arrangements within and between the two localities in two contrasting seasons. The two research areas are referred to here by the names of their respective

districts: Purulia and Bardhaman. Agriculture in the Purulia locality (more than one village as it was composed of two whole *mouza* – smallest administrative unit – and parts of two others) was characterized by a single paddy crop and hardly any assured irrigation. Most land in the Bardhaman locality (two *mouza*) was cultivated two to three times per year and had access to either groundwater irrigation or surface water from the Badamjal river, which acted as a drainage channel for the Damodar canal irrigation system. In both localities most employers of labour belonged to the *goala* caste, involved in both dairying and cultivation. In Purulia the landowning structure was characterized by smallholdings; most hirers out of labour also managed their own cultivation. In Bardhaman, the structure was slightly more skewed, the main difference being that most labour days hired in by employers were from seasonally migrant labourers. The two localities were strongly connected by the huge flow of migrant labourers out of the Purulia locality towards Bardhaman and Hooghly districts, though none were directly employed in the sample villages. Daily records of hiring in and out of labour were kept by ninety-three sample households, together with detailed information on other transactions.

3. See Samuelson (1966, p. 1567) and Hodgson (1982, p. 182) for elaborations of this point.
4. Production relations were defined in the paper as 'the relations of people to factors of production in terms of their rights of ownership and use in production, and the corresponding relations of people among each other as factor owners and renters, as landlords, tenants, workers, employers, creditors and debtors' (1986, p. 503). The concept of production relations as used by Binswanger and Rosenzweig should not be confused with the 'labour relations' approach discussed in section 3.
5. This prediction is the opposite of Lal's. Lal argued that green revolution technology would increase the ratio of demand to supply and thus the proportion of 'attached' labourers in the workforce (see above and Lal 1989, p. 125).
6. However, Rudra's (1984, pp. 252–253) conception of ideological forces applying to all sections of village society omitted the important distinctions between the ideologies of different castes, classes and genders (see Kapadia 1990). Aware that in attempting complete explanation, they would have to consider ideological as well as material variables, Binswanger et al referred to the views of one caste about another as an ideology (1984). However, the views of higher castes about the 'weak, lazy, and unthinkable' Madiga group (ibid., p. 159) was the product of a system of ideas, rather than a system in itself. Ideology is defined in the Shorter Oxford English Dictionary as 'a system of ideas concerning phenomena, especially those of social life; the manner of thinking characteristic of a class or an individual'. Explaining how and why a system of ideas came into being would better enable us to understand what Binswanger et al refer to as the caste segmentation of the labour market than reporting on one of its manifestations.
7. Marx himself did not define class. However, the groups that appeared as classes in his writing were unique to each theoretical mode of production (e.g. lord, serf, guild-master and journeyman under feudalism; industrial capitalists, financial capitalists, landlords, peasants, petty bourgeoisie and workers under capitalism). It has been defined variously according to ownership of the means of production, net labour hiring practice, and 'exploitation status' (Elster 1986, pp. 142–3).
8. Although the reverse was implied by the quotations from Smith and Thornton (above), Brass's reasoning in his argument that proletarianization (the creation of a propertyless class dependent on selling labour power and 'free' to do so) could be seen by capitalists as leading to increased power for labourers, relied on the assumed concurrent loosening of personal relations, credit ties and tenancy relations. With the success or failure of a crop at stake, together with the capital invested in it, the new class of labourers (if organized) could hold the capitalist farmer to ransom. Moreover, the capitalist could fear losing the social control he was once able to exercise over former clients.
9. See, for example, Bharadwaj (1974, pp. 62–5; 1985, p. 11).
10. Van Schendel (1991) closely followed Bose's regions in his attempt to identify changes in employer-labourer relations in the same period. Beteille (1974) illustrated the problems of trying to generalize insights on agrarian relations over the whole of West Bengal in his discussion of the contrary meanings of 'jotedar'. These studies cast further doubt on the

134

validity of taking the whole South Asian subcontinent as a region in the characterization of production relations (see 2.2 and 2.4 above for details of the Binswanger and Rosenzweig model, which tackles South Asia as a single region).

11. For an opposite view to that of Prakash, see Brass's attack on post-modernism, for its denial of 'the possibility of a universal process of socio-economic development', and for signalling 'the abolition' of 'emancipation as the object and attainable end of historical transformation, and along with it socialism and communism' (1991, p. 177).

12. Contrary to the implicit equivalence between wage and utility made by Datta et al (1989, p. 93).

13. As Rudra and Bardhan point out (1983, p. 2) there is no strict division between those employees who are obliged to an employer and those who are without such an obligation. 'Loose priority relationship' refers to the grey area in between.

14. Transplanting was usually rewarded at piece rate; however, those employers paying a time rate equivalent paid much more than to any other agricultural worker at any time of year, except ploughmen who brought their own plough and animal power.

15. *Guti* and *khutia* are two categories of 'farm servant' in Sarap's study. A *guti* arrangement involves daily work on the employer's fields, while *khutia* labourers work as herdsmen.

16. *Bagal* is defined for the present purposes as an annual arrangement concerned almost exclusively with grazing livestock. *Bhatua* refers to an annual fieldwork oriented arrangement.

17. The locality was split by a river with dwellings on either bank. On the south side, a CPI(M) stronghold, wages were kept rigidly at the norm brokered by that party. Employers from the north side of the river, where Congress dominated, were observed to negotiate with groups of seasonal migrants, using the CPI(M) brokered wage as a floor.

18. Country fair.

19. Preference for particular forms of payment were found to vary annually for similar reasons in the study of the village in Mahbubnagar District, Maharashtra reported by Binswanger et al (1984, p. 161).

20. I distinguish between loans and wage advances, the latter referring to prior payment against work to be done in the future where there is to be no implicit or other interest charged.

21. James Mill, on the other hand, referring to payment at regular intervals, saw the capitalist as paying the labourer in advance of the final sale of the product (cited by Bharadwaj, 1989b, p. 51).

22. The wet lean season refers to the period during the monsoonal rains (in the months of Bhadra and Aswin – mid August to mid October) in between transplanting and harvesting of the main *aus* and *aman* paddy crops. The dry lean season occurs in the period immediately preceding transplanting (ie in the months of Chaitra and Baisakh – mid March to mid May). In contrast to the loans made in the wet lean season against 'cheap' harvest labour, dry lean season advances against transplanting and land preparation carried no implicit interest.

23. This goes further than Dreze and Mukherjee's (1987, p. 39) call for an identification of which contracts are and are not negotiable. Diversity in components as well as arrangements needs to be explained and the processes involved in negotiation as well as the existence of negotiation per se need to be identified.

24. See van Schendel and Faraizi (1984), p. 96 for an example of short duration interlinked contracts; and Rudra (1987), p. 759; Breman also argues that the distinction between attached and casual labourers is not as clear in practice as it might seem (1985, p. 262).

25. Also termed 'bonded labour' by the authors. I have avoided using this concept in the text where possible because of its association with other yardsticks used to discuss tied contracts (degree of freedom/unfreedom and extent of interlinkage with other markets).

26. Elsewhere, however, van Schendel explicitly considers daily paid contracts of seasonal duration as casual (1991, pp. 190–191).

27. Roemer clarifies the distinction in game theoretical terms (1986a, pp. 104–9).

28. A labourer's needs and those of those dependent on his/her (necessary product) are analogous to the concept of 'natural price of labour' discussed by Ricardo (1971, p. 118). He argued that this price varies according to societal norms and individual expectations – it was not simply biological.

29. Bardhan's (1979) 'recruitment cost' explanation held that employers placed a 'high premium on quick and ready availability of labour'. Bardhan argued that higher recruitment costs were incurred hiring landed labourers who were reluctant to commit labour time during peak agricultural activity. Thus landless workers received higher wages. While Bardhan's prediction did not hold for her village, Hart accepted that the concept of recruitment cost could provide a partial explanation of why *small landowners* were preferred at times of peak labour demand. In her study of a Javanese village, the *landless* presented higher recruitment costs because of their preference for long duration contracts. However, according to Hart, Bardhan's theory still did not explain a) why landed labourers had access to slack season jobs of relatively long duration and high wages, and b) why at the intermediate stage following peak labour demand, small landholders should have been preferred by employers over the landless (Hart, 1986a, pp. 170–3).

30. The segmentation of the labour market which followed was classified into four groups:

   (i) those who work for the employer on priority because of debt considerations;

   (ii) those who work for the employer because of credit considerations and because of kinship ties to a group;

   (iii) those who opt for the employer because such employment facilitates certain transactions; and

   (iv) those who do not work for a particular employer(s); are not indebted or for whom settlement of debt takes place outside employment or tenancy markets (Srivastava 1989, p. 518).

REFERENCES

Adnan, S., 1984. *Peasant production and capitalist development: A model with relation to Bangladesh*, unpublished Ph.D thesis, University of Cambridge.

Banaji, J., 1990. 'Illusions about the peasantry: Karl Kautsky and the Agrarian Question'. Review of *The Agrarian Question* by Karl Kautsky (London: Zwan Publications, 1988), in *Journal of Peasant Studies*, vol. 17, no. 2.

Bardhan, P., 1979. 'Wages and employment in a poor agrarian economy: A theoretical and empirical analysis, in *Journal of Political Economy*, vol. 87, no. 3, pp. 479–500.

Bardhan, P., 1984. *Land, labor and rural poverty: Essays in development economics*. New Delhi, Oxford University Press.

Bardhan, P., 1988. 'Alternative approaches to development economics', in Chenery and Srinivasan (1988).

Bardhan, P. (ed.), 1989a. *The economics of agrarian institutions*. Oxford, Clarendon Press.

Bardhan, P., 1989b. 'Interlinked rural economic transactions', in P. Bardhan (1989a).

Bardhan, P. and A. Rudra, 1981. 'Terms and conditions of labour contracts in agriculture: Results of a survey in West Bengal 1979', in *Oxford Bulletin of Economics and Statistics*, vol. 43, pp. 89–111.

Beteille, A., 1974. *Studies in agrarian social structure*. Delhi, Oxford University Press.

Bhalla, S., 1976. 'New relations of production in Haryana agriculture', in *Economic and Political Weekly*, vol. 11, no. 13, 27th March.

Bharadwaj, K., 1974. *Production conditions in Indian agriculture: A study based on farm management surveys*. Cambridge, Cambridge University Press.

Bharadwaj, K., 1979. 'Towards a macroeconomic framework for a developing economy: The Indian case', in *Manchester School*, September.

Bharadwaj, K., 1985. 'A view on commercialization in Indian agriculture', in *Journal of Peasant Studies*, vol. 12, no. 4, pp. 2–26, July.

Bharadwaj, K., 1989a. *The formation of rural labour markets: An analysis with special reference to Asia*, WEP 10–6/WP98. Geneva, ILO.

Bharadwaj, K., 1989b. *Themes in value and distribution: Classical theory revisited*. London, Unwin Hyman.

Binswanger, H., Doherty, V., Balaramaiah, T., Bhende, M., Kshirsagar, K., Rao, V. and P. Raju,

1984. 'Common features and contrasts in labor relations in the semiarid tropics of India', in H. Binswanger and M. Rosenzweig (1984a).

Binswanger, H. and M. Rosenzweig (eds.), 1984a. *Contractual arrangements, employment, and wages in rural labor markets in Asia.* New Haven, Yale University Press.

Binswanger, H. and M. Rosenzweig, 1984. 'Contractual arrangements, employment and wages in rural labor markets: A critical review', in H. Binswanger and M. Rosenzweig (1984a).

Binswanger, H. and M. Rosenzweig, 1986. 'Behavioral and material determinants of production relations in agriculture', in *Journal of Development Studies*, vol. 22, pp. 503–539.

Bose, S, 1986. *Agrarian Bengal: Economy, social structure and politics, 1919–1947.* Cambridge, Cambridge University Press.

Brass, T., 1990. 'Class struggle and the deproletarianisation of agricultural labour in Haryana (India)', in *Journal of Peasant Studies*, vol. 18, no. 1, October.

Brass, T., 1991. 'Moral economists, subalterns new social movements, and the (re-) emergence of a (post-) modernised (middle) peasant', in *Journal of Peasant Studies*, vol. 18, no. 2, January.

Braverman, A. and T.N. Srinivasan, 1981. 'Credit and share cropping in agrarian societies', in *Journal of Development Economics*, vol. 9.

Braverman, A. and J.E. Stiglitz, 1982. 'Sharecropping and the interlinking of agrarian markets, in *American Economic Review*, vol. 72, no. 4.

Breman, J., 1984. 'Seasonal migration and cooperative capitalism: The crushing of cane and labor by the sugar factories of Bardoli, South Gujerat', in H. Binswanger and M. Rosenzweig (1984a).

Breman, J., 1985. *Of peasants, migrants and paupers: Rural labour circulation and capitalist production in West India.* Delhi, Oxford University Press.

Chenery, H. and T.N. Srinivasan (eds.), 1988. *A handbook of development economics.* Amsterdam, North-Holland.

Comitas, L., 1973. 'Occupational multiplicity in rural Jamaica', in L. Comitas and D. Lowenthal (eds), *Work and family life: West Indian perspectives.* New York, Doubleday-Anchor.

Datta, A. K., 1991. *Control, conflict and alliance: An analysis of land and labour relations in two Bangladesh villages*, unpublished Ph.D thesis. The Hague, Institute of Social Studies.

Datta, B., D. Ray and K. Sengupta, 1989. 'Contracts with eviction in infinitely repeated principal-agent relationships', in Bardhan (1989a).

Davis, M., 1983. *Rank and rivalry: The politics of inequality in rural West Bengal.* Cambridge, Cambridge University Press.

Desai, M., Rudolph, S. and A. Rudra (eds), 1984. *Agrarian power and agricultural productivity in South Asia.* Delhi, Oxford University Press.

Dreze, J., 1979. *Human capital and risk taking,* Stanford Institute for Mathematical Studies in the Social Sciences, Reprint Series, No. 288. Stanford.

Dreze, J., and A. Mukherjee, 1987. *Labour contracts in rural India: Theories and evidence,* Discussion Paper No. 7, Development Research Programme, London School of Economics, February.

Elster, J., 1986. 'Three challenges to class', in J. Roemer (1986).

Harriss, J., 1982. *Capitalism and peasant farming: Agrarian structure and ideology in Northern Tamil Nadu.* Bombay, Oxford University Press.

Harriss, J., 1983. *The mode of production controversy: Themes and problems of the debate,* Discussion Paper No. 60, University of East Anglia, School of Development Studies, March.

Harriss, J., 1992. 'Does the 'depressor' still work? Agrarian structure and development in India: a review of evidence and argument', in *Journal of Peasant Studies*, vol. 19, no 2.

Hart, G., 1984. *Agrarian labour arrangements and structural change: Lessons from Java and Bangladesh*, WEP 10–6/WP65. Geneva, International Labour Organization.

Hart, G. 1986a. *Power, labor and livelihood: Processes of change in rural Java.* Berkeley, University of California Press.

Hart, G, 1986b. 'Interlocking transactions: Obstacles, precursors or instruments of agrarian capitalism', in *Journal of Development Economics*, vol. 23.

Hart, G., 1991. 'Engendering everyday resistance: Gender, patronage and production politics in rural Malaysia', in *Journal of Peasant Studies*, vol. 19, no. 1.

Hart, G., 1992. 'Household production reconsidered: Gender, labor conflict and technological change in Malaysia's Muda Region', in *World Development*, vol. 20, no. 6, pp. 809–23.

Hodgson, G., 1982. *Capitalism, value and exploitation: A radical theory*. Oxford, Martin Robertson.

Jagannathan, N. V., 1987. *Informal markets in developing countries*. New York, Oxford University Press.

Kapadia, K. 1990. *Gender, class and caste in rural South India*, unpublished PhD dissertation, University of London.

Kapadia, K., 1992. 'Discipline and control: Labour contracts and rural female labour', draft paper presented to 'Meanings of Agriculture' Workshop, Centre of South Asian Studies, SOAS, London, July.

Kynch, J., undated. 'Agricultural wage rates in West Bengal and their trends over time'. Helsinki, WIDER (mimeo).

Lal, D., 1989. *The Hindu equilibrium (Vol II): Aspects of Indian labour*. Oxford, Clarendon Press.

Mohapatra, P., 1991. 'Some aspects of arable expansion in Chotanagpur: 1880–1950', in *Economic and Political Weekly*, vol. 26, no. 16.

Patnaik, U., 1990. *Agrarian relations and accumulation: The 'mode of production' debate in India*. Bombay, Oxford University Press for the Sameeksha Trust.

Prakash, G., 1990. *Bonded histories: Genealogies of labour servitude in colonial India*. Cambridge, Cambridge University Press.

Prakash, G. (ed), 1992. *The world of the rural labourer in colonial India*. Delhi, Oxford University Press.

Prakash, G., 1992a. 'The history and historiography of rural labourers in colonial India', in Prakash (1992).

Prakash, G., 1992b. Review of Ramachandran (1990), in *Journal of Asian Studies*, vol. 51, no. 2, May.

Prakash, G., 1992c. 'Reproducing inequality: Spirit cults and labour relations in colonial Eastern India', in Prakash (1992).

Ramachandran, V.K., 1990. *Wage labour and unfreedom in agriculture: An Indian case study*. Oxford, Clarendon Press.

Ricardo, D., 1971. *On the principles of political economy, and taxation* (ed. R. M. Hartwell). Harmondsworth, Pelican.

Roemer, J. (ed), 1986. *Analytical Marxism*. Cambridge, Cambridge University Press.

Roemer, J., 1986a. 'New directions in the Marxian theory of exploitation and class', in Roemer (1986).

Rosenzweig, M., 1984, 'Determinants of wage rates and labor supply behaviour in the rural sector of a developing country', in Binswanger and Rosenzweig (1984a).

Rosenzweig, M., H. Binswanger and J. McIntire, 1988. 'From land abundance to land scarcity: The effects of population growth on production relations in agrarian economies', in R. Lee, W.A. Arthur, A.C. Kelley, G. Rodgers and T.N. Srinivasan (eds.), *Population, food and rural development*. Oxford, Clarendon Press.

Rothschild, E., 1992. 'Adam Smith and conservative economics', in *Economic History Review*, vol. 45, no. 1, pp. 74–96.

Rudra, A., 1984. 'Local power and farm level decision making', in Desai, M. et al (1984).

Rudra, A., 1987. 'Labour relations in agriculture – A study in contrasts', in *Economic and Political Weekly*, vol. 22, no. 17, April 25th, pp. 757–760.

Rudra, A., 1992. *Political economy of Indian agriculture*. Calcutta, K.P. Bagchi.

Rudra, A. and P. Bardhan, 1983. *Agrarian relations in West Bengal: Results of two surveys*. Bombay, Somaiya Publications.

Samuelson, P., 1966. 'Economic theory and wages', in *Collected scientific papers of P.A. Samuelson*, vol ii. Cambridge (Mass.).

Sarap, K., 1991. 'Changing contractual arrangement in agriculture labour market: Evidence from Orissa', in *Economic and Political Weekly*, vol. 26, no. 52, pp. A167–176, December 28.

van Schendel, W. and A. Faraizi, 1984. *Rural labourers in Bengal, 1880 to 1980*, Comparative Asian Studies Programme, Publication 12. Rotterdam.

Singh, P., 1976. *Some aspects of labour use in Punjab agriculture: A study of Ferozepore District*

1967–68, 1968–69 and 1969–70, unpublished M.Phil. thesis, Jawaharlal Nehru University. New Delhi.

Smith, A., 1976. *An inquiry into the nature and causes of the wealth of nations* (edited by R.H. Campbell, A.S. Skinner and W.B. Todd). Oxford.

Srivastava, R., 1989. 'Interlinked modes of exploitation in Indian agriculture during transition: A case study', in *Journal of Peasant Studies*, vol. 16, no. 4, pp. 493–522.

Thorner, D. and A. Thorner, 1962. *Land and labour in India*. London, Asia Publishing House.

Thornton, W.T., 1886. *On labour: Its wrongful claims and rightful duties*. London, MacMillan, 2nd edition.

White, B., 1976. 'Population, involution and employment in rural Java', in *Development and Change*, vol. 7, pp. 267–290.

139

6

Eastward Ho!
Leapfrogging and Seasonal
Migration in Eastern India

ARJAN DE HAAN and BEN ROGALY[1]

1. INTRODUCTION

Contradicting images of an immobile rural population in India, studies of migration movements show an almost continuous flux, not only at present but throughout this century. In eastern India, there has been a massive movement of labour in an eastward direction.

This paper focuses on two contrasting settings within this stream: rice cultivation in a Green Revolution area in West Bengal, and industrial production in Calcutta.[2] The comparison reveals a surprising picture: while agriculture draws much of its labour force from relatively less productive adjacent districts, this movement is leapfrogged by the industrial labour force. Clearly these parallel movements could not have been predicted by conventional models of migration and economic development.

In his model of rural-urban migration, Todaro assumed that migrants acted individually according to a rationality of economic self-interest. Rather than simply moving to cities because of a simple wage difference, however, the decision to migrate took into account the expected probability of employment at the destination. Implicitly a personal cost benefit analysis took place in the prospective migrant's mind, weighing up the difference between the present value of expected earnings from formal sector urban employment (and an initial period of informal sector employment) and the present value of expected earnings in the village (Todaro 1969; Harriss and Todaro 1970). Later modifications have not changed the fundamental individual maximizing assumption of the original model (Todaro 1976; 1980), although Thadani and Todaro explore some of the social determinants of migration (1984).

The Todaro models have consistently assumed global rationality (migrants do not suffer cognitive limits on the amount of information they can retain), perfect information (migrants are fully informed regarding employment prospects and remuneration rates in both source and destination areas), and no transaction costs (e.g., searching for work or travelling between areas).

Other economists in the neo-classical tradition have extended Todaro's models to take account of incomplete and imperfect information (see Chapter 13 in Stark 1991) and transaction costs. Nevertheless, with honourable exceptions, there has been a consistent focus on instrumentally rational decision makers responding to differences in earnings.

Another body of theory emphasizes the structural nature of the migration process, not just in the context of permanent rural-urban migration, but also with respect to the migration of workers between rural areas, including on a temporary basis (for example, Das Gupta 1981; Breman 1985; Standing 1985; Shrestha 1990). Migration of labour is seen as inevitable in the transition to capitalism. Migration was not a choice for poor people, but rather the only option for survival after alienation from the land following technological change in agriculture (Shrestha 1990). The structural literature draws attention to the advantages of migrant labour for capitalist production: in particular, if labour power is produced and reproduced in source areas under conditions of petty commodity production, capitalist employers in destination areas do not bear that cost in wages (Meillassoux 1981, Ch. 5). Further, the opposing class interests of migrant labourers and their employers are emphasized (Standing 1985, pp. 5–6).

According to Breman, migrants did not and could not opt for departure. Recruitment was organized through recruiting agents, jobbers and *sardars*. In colonial India, 'demand and supply [did] not come together in an open market', and 'the inequality of power [was] expressed not only in the price of labour but also in extra-economic coercion as a significant aspect of the relations between parties' (Breman 1990, p. 70). The urban labour market in India at present is strongly segmented, due to scarcity of work. 'Some economic functions are linked so much to particular groups that penetration by outsiders is almost inconceivable. It is too simple to seek the reason for evident cases of self-restraint in cultural inhibition. Apart from the unfamiliarity with the type of work and insufficient knowledge of opportunities, lack of access is one of the most important structurally determined impediments' (Breman 1989).

Although structural theories emphasize the segmentation of the labour market, there is little knowledge about how segmentation operates (see also Banerjee 1992). The analysis of this paper is not situated either in the behavioural or the structural camp. Rather, we assert that in order to explain 'choices' made by potential migrant individuals and their households, it is necessary to understand the economic and social structures of which they are a part. This paper stresses the embeddedness of the two migration streams in the agrarian structure of source areas, in the industrial labour recruitment process, and in the social institutions of gender, caste and locality. The importance of earnings differentials in the decision to migrate is also explored.

The rest of the paper is structured as follows. Section 2 compares recent trends in the growth of agriculture and registered manufacturing in West Bengal, indicating that agriculture has been the more dynamic of the two. As a consequence, labour mobility between rural areas has been more marked of late than migration for manufacturing employment. However, the rural-rural migration within West Bengal continues to be leapfrogged by the migration to Calcutta. Section 3 shows how the pattern of the two migration streams can only be explained by considering the interplay of a number of causal factors and is not reducible to either of the theories outlined above. Section 4 concludes the paper.

2. AGRICULTURAL GROWTH, INDUSTRIAL STAGNATION AND MIGRATION IN CONTEMPORARY WEST BENGAL

Over the last twenty years agriculture in West Bengal has shown significant growth, especially in the last decade, when the share of agriculture in state domestic product increased while that of manufacturing industry declined (see Figure 1). As a consequence, the mobility of labourers *between* rural areas in this period appears more dynamic than current trends in migration from the countryside for employment in urban manufacturing.[3]

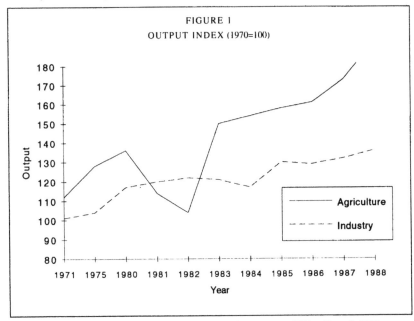

FIGURE 1
OUTPUT INDEX (1970=100)

Source: Bureau of Applied Economics and Statistics, Government of West Bengal, 1990.

Moreover, contrary to the assumptions of modernist theories of economic growth, the industries which developed in Bengal did not draw their labour force from the immediately surrounding countryside but from further away. The immediate hinterland was left virtually 'untouched'. We describe two streams of migrant labour – one to the jute industry in Calcutta and the other to areas of intensive agricultural production in Bardhaman and Hooghly districts of West Bengal. This illustration of leapfrogging over seasonal rural migrants by urban-bound industrial migrants will serve as a basis for the critique of mainstream migration theories in the following section.

2.1 Agricultural Production in West Bengal

Since 1980 agriculture's share in West Bengal's State Domestic Product has steadily increased. The Centre for Monitoring the Indian Economy reported an average annual growth rate of foodgrains production of 6.5 per cent in the decade to 1992. This is supported by Table 1.

TABLE 1
INDEX OF AGRICULTURAL PRODUCTION AND PRODUCTIVITY
GROWTH IN WEST BENGAL

Year	Net cropped area	Production	Productivity
1969–70	100	100	100
1975–76	115	128	106
1980–81	109	136	115
1984–85	109	154	126
1988–89	114	193	146

Source: Bureau of Applied Economics and Statistics, Government of West Bengal, 1990.
Note: Productivity refers to output per unit land area.

This growth is associated with the relatively late but rapid uptake of Green Revolution technology (HYV seeds, chemical fertilisers and mechanized irrigation), particularly in paddy production in the Gangetic areas of the state, such as Bardhaman district. Most importantly the increase in private investment in shallow tubewells has facilitated the expansion of summer (*boro*) paddy (see table 2).

TABLE 2
NUMBER OF SHALLOW TUBEWELLS IN WEST BENGAL

Year	No. of wells	Increase on 1981
1981	155,000	
1985	220,000	42 %
1988	340,000	119 %

Source: Bureau of Applied Economics and Statistics, Government of West Bengal, 1990.

While double and triple cropping have now become commonplace in the plains, mechanization has been restricted to irrigation and ploughing. Transplanting, weeding, cutting, binding and threshing paddy have not been mechanized, so that increases in paddy production are associated with increases in the seasonal demand for labour for these activities.

West Bengal has the highest population density in India (766 per square kilometre according to the 1991 Census). Yet the area of land owned by households whose main source of income was agricultural labour increased between 1977 and 1983. Moreover, the ratio of agricultural labour households to total rural households declined. This suggests a reverse in the trend towards 'proletarianization' inferred from the 1971 Census, which showed the percentage of agricultural labourers in the total rural workforce to have increased. Lieten has termed this 'repeasantization' (1992). The supply of *local* labourers may not therefore be adequate to cope with increasing demand.

2.2 Seasonal rural-rural migration for paddy production in West Bengal

Seasonal migration for agricultural work into and across parts of Bengal was common in the late nineteenth and early twentieth centuries (Yang 1979; van Schendel and Faraizi 1984, pp. 50–57; Sen 1992, p. 26; Bose 1993, p. 86). Today, when travelling into and out of Bardhaman District during the *aman* and *boro* paddy transplanting and harvesting seasons,[4] it is impossible to ignore the groups of mainly *adivasi* (tribal) labourers carrying cooking implements and/or 'savings' of hulled rice and vying for space on buses and trains.

Four times a year hundreds of thousands of agricultural labourers enter the Gangetic plains of central southern West Bengal from the largely unirrigated districts to the west and north to take part in the transplanting and harvesting of *aman* and *boro* paddy (see Map 1). Yet no official data exist to indicate the precise numbers of workers, the timing of migration or changes in the numbers of migrants, and the pattern of migration over time. This stream of migration is also under-researched.[5]

Our data from one locality in Bardhaman District suggest that the migrants come from diverse districts of origin in West Bengal and Bihar. These include, moving in a swathe from south to north in Map 1, Singhbhum, Santhal Parganas and Purnea districts in Bihar and Bankura, Purulia, Birbhum, Murshidabad, Malda and West Dinajpur districts in West Bengal.

At the start of the *aman* paddy transplanting of June–July 1991, one observer counted 70,000 migrants leaving from just one 'market place' – the Govinda Nagar bus stand in Bankura town. On the other hand, the district authorities estimated that the annual migration for the *aman* harvest had declined from approximately 50,000 in the mid 1980s to 15,000 in 1989 and 1990. This decline, they argued, was due to the successful development policies implemented in the district. They acknowledged that there had been a resurgence of the earlier scale of migration in the *aman* harvest at the end of 1991. This was attributed to the temporary restrictions imposed on development expenditure following attempts to reduce the budget deficit by the central government after the general elections earlier in the year.[6]

A further indication of the scale of the seasonal migration in the source districts is found in the Purulia District Plan for 1991–92. The authorities in Purulia regarded it as a 'menacing problem' and dedicated their development efforts to reducing the 'alarming exodus of labourers' (Government of West Bengal, Purulia District Draft Annual Plan, 1991–92, pp. 1 and 6).[7]

The evidence reported here is taken from a pair of simultaneous micro studies conducted in one source and one destination for seasonal migrants during the agricultural year 1991–92 (see Rogaly, chapter 5 in this volume). Most of our data refers to just one season – the *aman* paddy harvest of November–December 1991. In that season 110 individuals migrated out of the 247 households resident in the source locality in Purulia District. Of our sample of 17 employer households in the destination locality in Bardhaman District, 11 hired in a total of 66 migrant labourers from 9 source districts.

Although most of the sample of 38 local labourers in the destination locality found almost full employment in the harvest season (a mean of 22 days per worker), the majority of labour days hired in were worked by migrants (1142 out of 2013). At the same time, more was earned outside the source locality by seasonally migrating labourers than inside by non-migrating labourers, although the *aman* harvests in the Purulia and Bardhaman localities coincided.

The means by which migrant labourers are matched with employers vary, as will become clear in section 3. Our study of one migrant source locality in Purulia District suggests three main avenues of recruitment: via 'market places'; through established connections with particular employers often maintained by migrant labour gang leaders; and through networks based on kin and *jati*.[8]

2.3 Manufacturing industry in West Bengal

In 1947, West Bengal was much more industrialized than the Indian economy as a whole, and much of the industry was export-oriented. Jute manufacturing was the main industry, and tea and coal were important export products. Other industries had also developed, including chemicals and machine manufacture.

Following independence, India pursued an import substitution policy, with growing intervention by the central government. Industrial production in India as a whole did grow significantly. Even in West Bengal, between 1951 and 1965, the value added in manufacture rose at a mean annual rate of 6.9 per cent. Growth of employment, however, lagged behind. Industrial growth in the context of import substitution was predominantly capital-intensive. The number of jobs grew slower than both output and growth of the population. In the same period, employment in registered factories rose at a rate of just 2.1 per cent per annum (Lubell 1974, p. 7).

In 1951, there were 652,000 workers in registered factories, of which the largest part (278,000) worked in jute mills and 158,000 worked in engineering. By 1969, the total number of workers had grown to 791,000 and engineering had become the largest sector (295,000); the number of jute workers had decreased to 204,000 (Lubell, 1974, p. 18).

Since the middle of the 1960s, the growth of industrial production has decelerated – in West Bengal as well as the rest of India – as did industrial employment, even in the new industries like engineering. The index number of industrial production grew from 100 in 1970 to 117 in 1980 and 136 in 1988. Employment in registered factories grew slowly during the 1970s, reaching 859,000 in 1980 and stagnating thereafter (879,000 in 1987; Bureau of Applied Economics and Statistics, Statistical Abstract).

2.4 From North West Bihar to the jute mills of Calcutta

One of the surprises of the research in the industrial area was the continuing predominance of migrant, non-Bengali labour in unskilled occupations. Table 3 presents the number of migrants – defined by place of birth – in the state of West Bengal and in the districts of Calcutta and 24 Parganas, which are the main areas of urban occupations.

TABLE 3
MIGRANTS IN WEST BENGAL, 1981 (000s)

Born in	West Bengal	24 Parganas	Calcutta district
Outside West Bengal	2,204	419	468
– Bihar	1,348	228	249
– UP	364	102	89
Bangladesh	3,292	1,074	221
Total Population	54,581	10,739	3,305

Source: Census 1981

About 10 per cent of the people present during the 1981 Census were born outside the state. The largest group is formed by refugees from what is now Bangladesh, who generally came with whole families and were forced to settle in West Bengal. At least in the case of the jute mills, the influx of refugees did not change the composition of the labour force. Over 2 million people had migrated towards West Bengal from other parts of India. The major stream comes from Bihar, and the second largest from Uttar Pradesh.[9]

The 1971 Census provides figures on economic activities of migrants, and in Table 4 we focus on the people from Bihar. The table shows the predominance of males among the migrants, indicating the importance of migration for work rather than for marriage. The largest single category is industrial occupations, which are mainly concentrated in Calcutta. More migrants than before, however, were working in the tertiary sector.

TABLE 4

ACTIVITIES OF MIGRANTS FROM BIHAR, 1971 (000s)

	West Bengal	*Calcutta Urban Agglomeration*
Total Workers	748	385
Mining	52	0
Household Ind.	14	3
Other Industry	225	164
Construction	14	14
Trade/Commerce	102	72
Transport etc.	98	63
Other Services	108	68
Other	129	7
Total Migrant Workers	1,316	546
of which, male	896	444

Source: Census 1971.
Notes: According to the definition used in the Census, a migrant is somebody whose former residence was outside the state of West Bengal. The category 'other' includes rural activities, which strongly underestimates seasonal migration.

Of the migrants who came to manufacturing industry, a large proportion came to work in the jute mills. With the expansion of the jute industry at the turn of the century, migrants, mainly from Bihar and Uttar Pradesh, replaced local labour: neither people from the surrounding areas, nor from the western districts of Bengal, went for the jute industry in large numbers.[10] The most reliable recent survey (Bhattacharjee and Chatterjee 1973) shows that around 1970, 87 per cent of the jute workers came from outside Bengal. The field study confirms that the labour force is still predominantly non-Bengali, and a computation from a workers' register of a jute mill shows that in 1991 only 12 per cent of the labour force was local.

Within this stream of migration the main source areas were districts of north-west Bihar and eastern UP (Chapra or Saran – at present forming three districts – Arrah, Azamgarh and Ghazipur; see Map 1). Smaller numbers of people came from Orissa, Andhra Pradesh and Madhya Pradesh in the south and south-west. The extent of segmentation is shown in extreme form by the percentage of workers in one jute mill for which the workers' register was available: over 40 per cent of its workers came from Saran.

As described elsewhere (de Haan 1992), the pattern of migration has remained circular, implying that the workers in the industry have maintained strong links with their villages of origin. In the next section we attempt to explain why the leapfrogging of the rural-rural migrants by the urban-rural migrants continues.

3. EXPLAINING THE TWO MIGRATION STREAMS

In this section, we show how the decision to migrate is based *both* on individual and 'household' choice informed by expected earnings differentials (as predicted by behavioural models) and embedded in the agrarian structure and the social institutions of gender, caste and locality.[11]

3.1 Earnings differentials

Expected daily earnings from harvest season agricultural employment in the Purulia locality were much lower than in the Bardhaman locality. In the former area, payments for work hired under daily time rate arrangements were made either in cash or in kind. The modal range of payment in December 1991 was equivalent to 2.1 to 3 kg (approximately Rs.10 to 15) of hulled rice for a six hour working day net of breaks.

In the Bardhaman locality, most migrant labourers were remunerated in a mixture of cash (usually Rs 12) and kind (usually 1.5 kg of hulled rice) as well as cooking fuel, oil, tobacco and vegetables each day (equivalent to 4.1 to 5 kg of hulled rice in total – approximately Rs.20 to 25) and were provided accommodation by the employer. They worked days of eight and nine hours duration net of breaks.

Agricultural labourers in the Purulia locality were aware of the much higher *potential* earnings in Bardhaman District. Indeed they expected continuous employment in the migration destination, which was not available in their own villages even in the peak seasons. Clearly this difference explains part of the decision to migrate.

However, potential migrants were not completely informed and the migration was not risk free. Even if potential migrants in a hinterland area had developed regular seasonal employment relations with a specific employer or destination area, they did not necessarily know whether or where other, better terms and conditions existed. Indeed, in canal-irrigated parts of Bardhaman District, employers themselves did not know the timing of *boro* paddy cultivation in advance. Moreover, in the case of migration via 'market places', the precise decision on which 'market place' to negotiate in, and which employer to hire out to once there, was often a group rather than an individual one, in which the *sardar* (gang leader) played an important role.

Moreover, although an offer of employment at high daily rates was very probable if a group of migrants presented itself at a busy labour 'market place' in the peak season, hours of work, living conditions and timeliness of final settlement varied. Several groups of migrants were unpaid for several days at the end of the season and left with no choice but to wait without pay. During five days of unseasonably heavy rain, when the harvest work had to be postponed, some employers provided a ration of 1 kg of rice per day, while others provided nothing and prevented labourers returning home by withholding arrears payments.

Thus although the large earnings differential explains part of the seasonal migration stream, the movement is not frictionless. Potential migrants possess incomplete information and face uncertainty regarding the timing of payment and climatic conditions.

Wage differentials have been the main reason for people from north west Bihar to migrate to the industrial area in Bengal. In the beginning of this century, daily wages in the jute mills were almost twice as high as the wages for unskilled labour in many parts of Bihar, and this difference has probably increased over the century. At present, the official wage in the jute industry comes to Rs.70 a day, which makes it an attractive option for unskilled workers.

But this does not explain the leapfrogging. In the intermediate areas, the western part of Bengal, wages were and are almost as low as in Bihar. The Dufferin report of 1888 (quoted in Van Schendel and Faraizi 1984) shows that a considerable portion of the population had to rely only on labour for its income, particularly in Medinipur, Malda and Murshidabad. At the end of the nineteenth century, depeasantization accelerated and real wages of labourers in Bengal declined (Kabir 1992). And, as mentioned in Section 2.2, there was substantial migration within Bengal; there is no evidence that people in western Bihar were freer to migrate than in other areas. However, the migrants from the intermediate areas generally did not go to the industrial area (see also de Haan 1994).

Channels of information and contact explain the existence of particular streams of migration. In Saran at the turn of the century, according to one district report, there was a high level of knowledge about possibilities of work and the wage rates in Calcutta. But while channels of information may correspond to different migration streams, they do not explain *why* these streams came into existence, why, for example, Saran became a major recruitment district, and why the districts in the western part of Bengal did not; nor why relatively few *adivasis* came to the jute industry, despite their heavy presence in the coal mines of Bardhaman.

3.2 Agrarian structure and the industrial recruitment process

Agrarian structure, including the distribution of land and the types of hired labour arrangements, varies across rural Bengal and Bihar. In the Purulia locality, the distribution of landholdings was skewed, although very few households were completely landless. The results of logistic regression analysis of factors affecting the likelihood of migration suggested that migration was more likely for those from households with less land and assets, and with few dependants.[12]

Data collected on the uses of earnings by migrants on return to the source village indicated the very different motivations of migrating households. For example, one woman, whose husband had recently died, leaving her with two young children and a small piece of land mortgaged out against an outstanding loan, used savings of Rs.325 from migration in the *aman* harvest to repay most of that loan. Another very poor landless widow used her earnings to survive one and a half months of the subsequent lean season without deepening her indebtedness. In contrast, one landed household, organized as an extended family, deployed several members to migrate in the same season, returning with Rs.900, which was divided between new clothes, a goat and participation in the festivities at the biggest local *mela* of the year in mid-January.[13]

In some cases obligations to local employers hindered seasonal migration. Groups of labourers became beholden to groups of employers on the basis of the history of the settlement of both sets of ancestors. This was particularly acute when the employers concerned were not permitted to take part in manual labour on their own land according to caste rules. One neighbourhood in the Purulia locality was inhabited chiefly by labour selling households. They were implicitly obliged to provide the labour requirements of the main employer neighbourhood. In the *boro* (summer paddy) transplanting season migration took place from all labour selling neighbourhoods in the locality except that one. Employers expected to be able to call upon this labour for their own small amount of *boro* cultivation.[14]

The remuneration from different labour arrangements affected migration decisions as well. Less workers migrated during the transplanting of *aman* paddy (between late June and early August), when the daily earnings available for women in the Purulia locality were typically equivalent to 4.7 kg of hulled rice, which was well within the range of modal daily time rate earnings in both seasons in the Bardhaman locality.

One gang of Muslim labourers from Malda District encountered in the Bardhaman locality explained that they did not come at harvest because they had access to harvest share contracts in their own village. They were paid one-sixth of the crop they harvested. However, during transplanting they usually sought work outside.

Thus seasonal variations in earnings in source areas, together with obligations to local employers, influenced the pattern of migration, explaining why workers from particular districts were found to predominate in the Bardhaman locality in certain seasons.

Because the research on industrial migration has concentrated on the area of destination rather than of recruitment, we do not have similar information on the relation between the agrarian structure and migration. The data suggests, however, that, while some of those who migrate have little or no land, others own somewhat more. The migrants come from different economic strata, and these differences are often replicated in the town: people with better positions in the village also occupy better positions in the town. Also, motivations differed. In general people said that they migrated because of poverty or a shortage of land, but definitions varied considerably. Those with somewhat larger holdings also cited land shortage as a reason for migration.

Labour arrangements in manufacturing industry are of course very different from those in agriculture. In the first place the distance between workers and employers has been much larger: employers first were British and later Indian, but very often also not from Bengal and the distance between them and the workers is hardly smaller. In the recruitment process, a channel of intermediaries – clerks, labour recruiters – has existed. It has been argued that employers' strategies have been responsible for the absence of local labour. In other cases, employers have often tried actively to replace local labour by migrant labour (Breman 1990, p. 18; Chakravarty 1978, pp. 277ff). However, in the case of the jute industry, there is little or no evidence from which one can conclude that this was due to an active policy by employers.

In the explanation of the absence of local labour in the industry, many authors have referred to the role of the *sardar*,[15] the labour recruiter and foreman. In some of the accounts this *sardar* has obtained almost mythical proportions (see in particular Chakrabarty 1989, and Das Gupta 1976). There is no doubt that intermediaries played a central role in the recruitment of labour, even in formalized systems of labour recruitment like in the large-scale factories. But a closer look at the evidence on the role of the *sardar* shows that, also in the past, his role was not as important as often portrayed. From our interviews it appears that the most common pattern of migration and recruitment was through the contacts of family, husbands, neighbours or more generally people from the same village, although it may be that some of them were *sardars*. Old workers told that much of the recruiting happened at the railway station, where *sardars*, but also *babus* (clerks), asked the incoming migrant to come to work in their mill. Many of the migrants, as they had relatives in the town, did not need to pass through this channel.[16]

151

3.3 Social identities and social institutions

So far we have shown the importance of earnings differentials, agrarian structure and the industrial recruitment process in shaping the direction and pattern of migration. In this final section we describe the embeddedness of the migration in the social institutions of gender, caste and locality.

3.3.1 Gender. In the peak harvest season in the Purulia locality, unlike the lean seasons, there was no gender differential in daily earnings. However, women had less access to the higher earnings available through individual piece rate arrangements for binding and threshing paddy, and no access to the relatively highly paid work of bringing the cut paddy to the threshing yard by bullock cart. Half of the migrants from the Purulia locality were women. Most of them were *adivasi*, either Bhumij or Santal. Some 'untouchable' Bhuinya women also migrated, as did a few Muslims. There was a strong tradition of deploying women to wage labour common to all these groups. Only caste Hindu families did not hire out women or men, either locally or in migration.

There was no distinction in remuneration according to gender in the harvest season in the Bardhaman locality either. However, while women accounted for 43 per cent of the work days hired in from seasonal migrants by Bardhaman locality sample employers in the *aman* harvest, only 15 per cent of days hired in from local labour selling households in daily time rate arrangements were worked by women. Most of these were *adivasi* former seasonal migrants, who had settled within the last twenty years. Indigenous local labour selling households, belonging mainly to the 'untouchable' Bagdi *jati*, did not deploy women members to paid work. This gender bar on hiring out has been interpreted by others (e.g., Bardhan 1984) as reflecting a concern with maintaining or raising social status.

In the jute industry, women have been paid lower wages, and they have carried out specific tasks. Female labour in the past constituted 15 to 20 per cent of the labour force, and this has declined since legislation which made female labour costlier and less flexible was introduced. Before that, employers did not show a preference for male or female labour (Sen 1992). That there was no barrier to female migration is shown by the differences in patterns of migration. Although this has been predominantly male, some groups did migrate with whole families. The most significant difference encountered was between groups from North India (Bihar) and from the South: people from the South more often migrated as families. To some extent, this can be related to economic differences, since many of the migrants from the South did not have any possessions in their village. But this explanation is not sufficient, since many of the people from the North had few possessions, and, on the other hand, there were people from the South who did have a certain amount of land and did migrate with whole families. This leads to the conclusion that cultural factors, cultural restrictions on female migration, which are stricter in the North than in the South, are very important (see also Singh 1984, pp. 91–5).

The North-South divide is not the only factor relevant for the cultural embeddedness of female labour. First, the restriction on female labour is more important among Muslims than among Hindus. Secondly, there are important caste differences. The old reports indicate that lower caste women from the South migrated and took up work in factories. The restriction on female labour is mainly a higher-caste ideal. Finally, one observes important historical changes in the employment of women. Parallel to the decline in female labour, and the increase in wages for male workers, the idea that women should not work spread among larger sections of the population. Within a family it was considered normal that the older women had worked and that the younger generation should not.

3.3.2 Caste and locality. The *jati* of a labour selling household also affected the pattern of migration from the Purulia locality. The institutions of gender and caste work together. Thus while certain *jati*, particularly caste Hindus, were prevented from hiring out manual labour at all, others, such as the Bhumij and Bhuinya of the Purulia locality, developed a tradition of seasonal migration whereby women, other than widows, could only migrate if accompanied by their husbands or other close male kin. Santal women, on the other hand, can migrate as individuals in all-Santal labour gangs.

Locality and *para* (neighbourhood) with traditions of seasonal migration may increase the likelihood of that migration independently of *jati*, gender and agrarian structure. Indeed migrant gangs from the Purulia locality composed of men and women and combinations of two *jati* from the same *para* were not uncommon. The Santal migrants, originating from an exclusively Santal *para*, did not travel with workers of other *jati*. Santal gangs were organized as communitarian units composed of individual adult members from 10 to 15 households. One or two women were selected for preparing food at the end of each day in the destination area. Bhumij, Bhuinya and Muslim households often despatched more than one member, and especially where young children accompanied their parents, cooking was organized on a household by household basis within the gang.[17]

When migrants were recruited by employers visiting the villages of origin, caste and class barriers, which were maintained between employers and labourers *within* villages, diminished. Employers from outside the source district slept and ate in the homes of potential employees. During the *aman* transplanting in a locality adjacent to the study locality in Purulia District, Bardhaman employers recruiting in a labourer neighbourhood were physically threatened by local employers. In the destination villages, migrants were housed in the employers' neighbourhoods and did not have contact with local labourers. Caste Hindu employers in the Bardhaman locality did not enter the dwellings of local *adivasi* or Muslim labourers and never ate their food. These reversals indicate that self-interested maximization has a place in the explanation of the patterns of seasonal migration in West Bengal; the production requirements of employers override caste considerations, and both employers and labourers fail to act as classes-in-themselves.

The field research in the industrial area confirmed that ideas about unskilled manual labour were important to the local Bengali population. It was said that they considered it to be beneath their dignity, that they were not interested because it was hard and dirty work, that working in a jute mill would mean that they would lose respect (*saman*), and that people would not want jute mill workers as marriage partners. Living in the jute-mill lines was considered a problem as well: *Bhalo lok thakte chai na* (good people don't want to live here).

The division between local and migrant labour is not the only form of segmentation in the industrial town: one finds a myriad of groups of people with a common background who concentrate in certain living areas and within specific occupations (de Haan 1992). This background can have various, overlapping aspects. Regional background is one of the important factors here: for example, people from Orissa lived together and were concentrated in the unskilled departments; Telugu-speaking people from Andhra Pradesh lived in the *South lines* and concentrated in the spinning department of jute mills. Workers' identification with their place of birth was evident from their annual return home at *tana time*, the summer period lasting from April until the outbreak of the monsoon in June.[18] Religion is also an important factor, and although living very often is mixed, one does find concentrations of Muslims in certain areas, and relatively many Muslims work in the weaving department. Finally, caste is important, in the sense of trading activities being done by trading castes, and the *durwans* (guards) often being from higher castes.

The identification of a particular type of workers with particular operations has often been explained, in popular opinion and colonial reports, with reference to stereotypes: the Bengali was said to be unsuitable for factory work, or unwilling; whereas the Bihari migrant was suitable. *Adivasi* labour was not suitable for factory work and preferred to work in the open field. No doubt these stereotypes are inventions and often have racial overtones. But our field research shows that the stereotypes are relevant in the operation of the labour market. They often are not just stereotypes for the outsider, but they are shared by the people themselves. Workers of a particular district or caste frequently explain their concentration in a particular activity with reference to the stereotypes, to what *our people* are good at and what they have always done.

There is no mono-causal explanation for the diverse forms of segmentation. Very often we are not able to describe the historical origin of these patterns, but we note that once in existence, they tend to persist. From the workers' point of view, one needs contacts (a 'source') to get a job. The contacts may be of very different kinds, and the present shortage of labour has made the position of the middlemen, who now often appear in the person of local leaders, a profitable one. Because the contacts are of importance, the group to which people belong – which may be a combination of ethnicity, caste, language etc. – is an important factor in the segmentation of the labour market.

4. CONCLUSION

This paper has attempted to explain the leapfrogging of seasonal rural-rural migrants in West Bengal by Calcutta-bound migrants from Bihar. It has been suggested that although neither movement is new, in the context of a fast growing labour-intensive agriculture rural-rural mobility is currently the more marked.

The rural-rural migration is best explained by using the insights of both behaviouralist and structuralist approaches. Labourer households are motivated by reproduction requirements to respond to significant earnings differentials between source and destination areas. Caste Hindu employers break local caste taboos to increase their production and profit. Yet, the patterns of migration are embedded in the social institutions of gender, *jati* and locality; and poorer households are more likely to migrate than richer ones.

In the same vein, the leapfrogging migration needs to be explained by a combination of different factors. People from Bihar migrated because of economic conditions in their villages, and because the mills provided an option to stabilize their position. Status considerations are important in explaining both the absence of local labour and the low number of women working in the industry. Further, in working towards a fuller understanding of patterns of segmentation, one has to take account of regional, religious and caste identities.

MAP 1

SOURCE AND DESTINATION DISTRICTS FOR THE TWO MIGRATION STREAMS

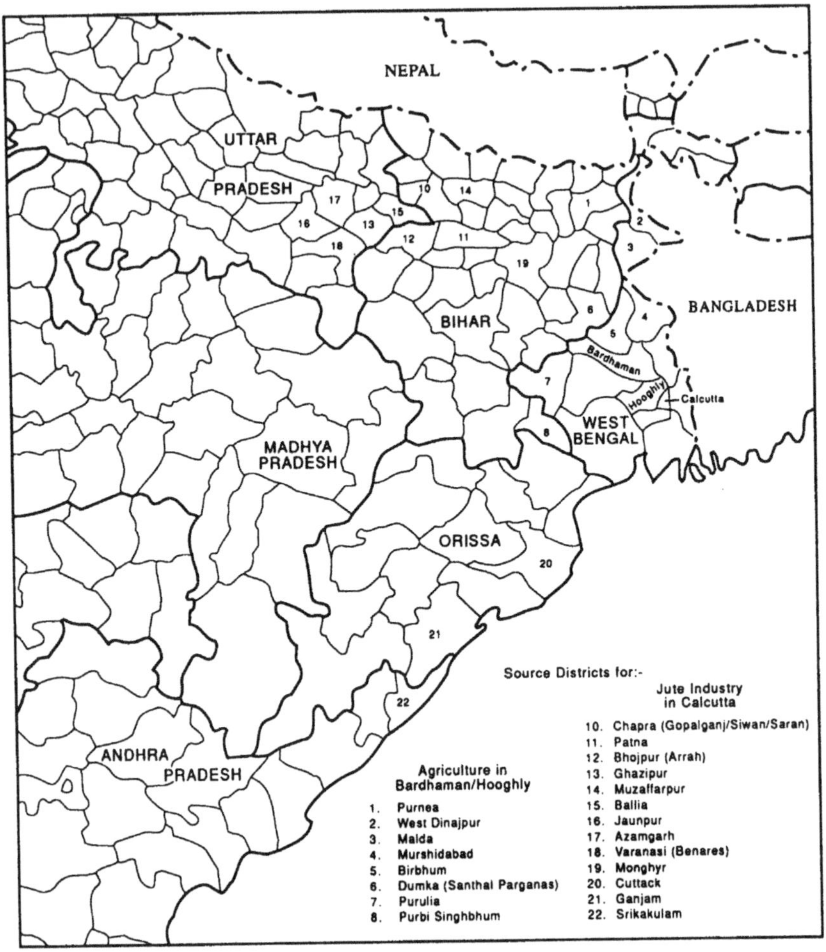

Source: the map is based on Joseph E. Schwartzberg, *A Historical Atlas of South Asia* (OUP, New York, 1992) and has been processed by Mrs. Catherine Lawrence, SOAS.

Note: the districts have changed during this century; therefore the present names and areas do not correspond exactly with those used in earlier reports (especially for the source districts of the jute industry).

NOTES

1. Respectively Amsterdam School for Social Science Research and International Development Centre, Queen Elizabeth House, Oxford University.
2. The paper draws on field work carried out in Purulia and Bardhaman Districts of West Bengal by Rogaly, and in an industrial area of Calcutta by de Haan. This paper is a first attempt to combine the studies of the two authors. The research was made possible by the Erasmus University Rotterdam and NWO, the Dutch foundation for scientific research (de Haan); and the Economic and Social Research Council (UK) (Rogaly). The authors are grateful to Paramita Bhattacharyya, Khushi Dasgupta, and Gautam Sanyal for assistance in data collection.
3. The argument of this paper does not consider the relationship between growth in agricultural employment and changes in rural non-agricultural employment. Many of these issues are tackled by Chandrasekhar (1993). We also omit the urban informal sector, focusing on registered factory employment.
4. *Aman* paddy is transplanted between late June and early August and harvested in late November and December. *Boro* paddy is transplanted in February and harvested in May.
5. The main exceptions are Chatterjee (1983 and 1991). Yet few students of agrarian labour in source or destination areas have been able to ignore the phenomenon (Rudra 1982, pp. 123–8; Chakrabarti 1986, pp. 131–2; Banerjee 1988; Roy 1992; Webster 1993). Evidence from other parts of the subcontinent suggest that despite its relative neglect in rural labour studies, seasonal migration is relatively widespread (e.g., Breman 1985, for Gujarat; Rahman and Das 1982 and Datta 1991 for Bangladesh; Oberai and Manmohan Singh 1980, for Punjab; Crooks and Ranbanda 1981, for Sri Lanka).
6. Debajyoti Chattopadhyay, personal communication. Chattopadhyay, the Bankura correspondent of the *Statesman* newspaper, estimated the figure of 70,000 by interviewing the conductors of bus services between the bus stand and labour hiring areas. For 15 days, 30 buses per day carried 150 migrants each.
7. The ostensible cause for this concern was the well-being of the labourers involved, though the real cause was thinly disguised self-interest. 'The overall domination of the privileged classes over the decentralized power structure ... remains at the district level in West Bengal' (Acharya 1993, p. 1080).
8. *Jati* was used to connote local social rankings on the basis of caste, religion or ethnicity.
9. Compared to 1971 the number of migrants in West Bengal had increased moderately: the number from Bangladesh increased by just over 200,000, while the number of people from within India increased by less than 200,000.
10. See especially Das Gupta (1976). In 1902, 22 per cent of the labourers in three jute mills were 'local'; in 1916 this was only 7 per cent.
11. Wood (1981), Chapman and Prothero (1985) and Chant and Radcliffe (1992) have all suggested a complementarity between structuralist and behaviouralist approaches to migration analysis.
12. The odds of a day of labour being hired out in Bardhaman or Hooghly districts rather than in the Purulia locality declined by a factor of 0.8 for each additional Rs 10,000 on the value of household assets, given the age and sex of the individual worker. Each dependant in the household decreased the odds by a factor of 0.5 (see Rogaly, forthcoming).
13. The timing of migration and return was influenced by the dates of festivals in the source village. For example, Santal migrants only migrated after the annual Vandhna *purab* in mid-November. Bhumij and Bhuinya migrants made sure that they returned to the locality in time for the mid-January *mela* mentioned above.
14. *Boro* paddy relies entirely on irrigation. Although Purulia District as a whole is characterized by rainfed agriculture, about 40 bighas (13 acres) of *boro* paddy were cultivated in the 1992 season, irrigated by the main village tank.
15. Note that the term *sardar* has a somewhat different meaning in the industrial context. In gangs migrating from the Purulia study locality, *sardar* were usually from the same neighbourhood (*para*) inside the village as the other members of the gang and worked alongside them.

16. See also de Haan 1993a, pp. 203–7 (and de Haan, forthcoming) on the role of the *sardar*.
17. This was explained by one migrant as necessary when dependants shared the kind portion of migrant earnings in the destination. If food provision was pooled, the per capita earnings accruing to households with dependants would be higher than to those without dependants.
18. This is not a period of major economic activity in the source villages. However, many marriages were held during *tana time*.

REFERENCES

Acharya, Poromesh, 1993. 'Panchayats and left politics in West Bengal', in *Economic and Political Weekly*, 29 May, pp. 1080–2.

Banerjee, Narayana, 1988. 'Women's work and family strategies: A case study from Bankura, West Bengal'. New Delhi, Centre for Women's Development Studies.

Banerjee, Nirmala, 1992. 'Poverty, work and gender in urban India'. Calcutta, Centre for Studies in Social Sciences.

Bardhan, Kalpana, 1984. 'Work patterns and social differentiation: Rural women of West Bengal', in Binswanger, Hans and Mark Rosenzweig (eds), *Contractual arrangements, employment and wages in rural labour markets in Asia*. London and Newhaven, Yale University Press.

Bhattacharya, N., A.K. Chatterjee, 1973. 'Some characteristics of jute industry workers in Greater Calcutta', in *Economic and Political Weekly*, February, pp. 297–308.

Bose, Sugata 1993. *Peasant labour and colonial capital: Rural Bengal since 1770 (The New Cambridge History of India*, vol.III.2). Cambridge, Cambridge University Press.

Breman, Jan, 1985. *Of peasants, migrants and paupers: Rural labour circulation and capitalist production in West India*. Oxford, Oxford University Press.

Breman, Jan, 1989. 'Particularism and scarcity: Urban labour markets and social classes', in Alavi, Hamza and John Harriss (eds), *South Asia. Sociology of 'Developing Societies'*. Hampshire/London, MacMillan.

Breman, Jan, 1990. *Labour migration and rural transformation in colonial Asia*, Comparative Asian Studies 5. Amsterdam, Free University Press.

Bureau of Applied Economics and Statistics, Government of West Bengal, 1990. *Statistical Abstract. West Bengal 1978 to 1989 (combined)*.

Chakrabarti, S., 1986. *Around the plough: Socio-cultural context of agricultural farming in an Indian village*. Calcutta, Anthropological Survey of India.

Chakrabarty, Dipesh, 1989. *Rethinking working-class History. Bengal 1890–1940*. Delhi, Oxford University Press.

Chakravarty, Lalita, 1978. 'Emergence of an industrial labour force in a dual economy – British India, 1880–1920', in *Indian Economic and Social History Review*, vol. 15, no. 3, July–Sept., pp. 249–327.

Chandrasekhar, C.P., 1993. 'Agrarian change and occupational diversification: Non-agricultural employment and rural development in West Bengal', in *Journal of Peasant Studies*, vol. 20, no. 2, pp. 205–70, January.

Chant, Sylvia and Sarah A. Radcliffe, 1992. 'Migration and development: The importance of gender', in Chant, Sylvia (ed), *Gender and migration in developing countries*. London and New York, Belhaven Press, pp. 1–29.

Chapman, Murray and R. Mansell Prothero, 1985. 'Themes on circulation in the Third World', in Mansell Prothero, R. and Murray Chapman (eds), *Circulation in Third World countries*. London, Boston, Melbourne and Henley, Routledge and Kegan Paul.

Chatterjee, S.N., 1983. 'Seasonal migration and rural development in Burdwan', in *Social Change*, vol. 13, no. 1.

Chatterjee, S.N., 1991. *Poverty, inequality and circulation of agricultural labour (a micro study of Birbhum, West Bengal)*. New Delhi, Mittal Publications.

Crooks, G.R. and H.A. Ranbanda, 1981. *The economics of seasonal labour migration in Sri Lanka*, Research Study Series No 46. Colombo, Agrarian Research and Training Institute.

Das Gupta, Ranajit, 1976. 'Factory labour in Eastern India: Sources of supply, 1855–1946. Some preliminary findings', in *Indian Economic and Social History Review*, vol. 13, no. 3.

Das Gupta, Ranajit, 1981. 'Structure of the labour market in colonial India', in *Economic and Political Weekly*, November, special number, pp. 1781–1806.

Datta, Anjan, 1991. 'Control, conflict and alliance: An analysis of land and labour Relations in two Bangladesh Villages', Ph.D. Dissertation. The Hague, Institute of Social Studies.

Economic and Political Weekly, 1993. 'Agricultural production: Bengal to the fore', 21 August.

Haan, Arjan de, 1992. 'Town and village: 100 years of circular migration to Calcutta', Paper for the 12th European Conference on Modern South Asian Studies, Berlin.

Haan, Arjan de, 1993a. 'Migrant labour in Calcutta jute mills: Class, instability and control', in Robb, Peter (ed), *Dalit movements, and the meanings of labour in India*. Delhi, Oxford University Press, pp. 186–224.

Haan, Arjan de, 1994. 'The jute industry and its workers: Changes in stratification in Eastern India', in Bandhyopadhyay, S., A. Dasgupta and W. van Schendel (eds), *Bengal. Development, communities and states*. Delhi, Manohar.

Haan, Arjan de, 1994. 'Unsettled settlers: Migrant workers and industrial capitalism in Calcutta', Ph.D. thesis, Erasmus University. Rotterdam, forthcoming.

Harris, J., and M.P. Todaro, 1970. 'Migration, unemployment and development: A two sector analysis', in *American Economic Review*, vol. 60, pp. 126–42.

Kabir, Ekhlasul, 1992. 'Wages and cost of living of the working classes of Bengal in the second half of the nineteenth century', in *Journal of Pakistani Historical Society*, vol. 11, January, pp. 21–31.

Lieten, G.K., 1992. *Continuity and change in rural West Bengal* New Delhi, Newbury Park and London, Sage.

Lubell, H., 1974. *Calcutta. Its urban development and employment prospects*. Geneva, ILO.

Meillassoux, Claude, 1981. *Maidens, meal and money*. Cambridge, Cambridge University Press.

Oberai, A.S. and H.K. Manmohan Singh, 1980. 'Migration flows in Punjab's agriculture', in *Economic and Political Weekly*, vol. 15, pp. A2–A12.

Rahman, H.Z. and S.P. Das, 1982. 'The rural labour market in Noakhali', Project Paper A.82.12. Copenhagen, Centre for Development Research.

Rogaly, Ben, 1993. 'Explaining diverse labour arrangements in rural India', in *Journal für Entwicklungspolitik (The Austrian Journal of Development Studies)*, vol. 9, no. 3, pp. 279–308.

Rogaly, Ben, forthcoming. *Rural labour arrangements in West Bengal, India*, D.Phil. thesis, Oxford University.

Roy, Debal K. Singha, 1992. *Women in peasant movements: Tebhaga, Naxalite and after*. New Delhi, Manohar.

Rudra, Ashok, 1982. 'Extraeconomic constraints on agricultural labour'. Bangkok, ILO-ARTEP.

Sen, Samita, 1992. *Women workers in the Bengal jute industry, 1890–1940: Migration, motherhood and militancy*, Ph.D. Thesis, University of Cambridge.

Singh, Andrea Menefee, 1984. 'Rural-to-urban migration of women in India: Patterns and implications', in Fawcett, J.T. et. al. (eds), *Women in the cities of Asia. Migration and urban adaption*. Boulder, Westview Press, pp. 81–107.

Shrestha, N.R., 1990. *Landlessness and migration in Nepal*. Colorado and Oxford, Westview Press.

Standing, Guy, 1985. 'Circulation and the labour process', in Standing, Guy (ed), *Labour circulation and the labour process*. London, Croom Helm, pp. 1–45.

Stark, Oded, 1991. *The migration of labour*. Cambridge, Mass., Harvard University Press.

Thadani, Veena N. and M.P. Todaro, 1984. 'Female migration: A conceptual framework', in Fawcett, J.T., et. al. (eds), *Women in the cities of Asia. Migration and urban adaption*, Boulder, Westview Press.

Todaro, M.P., 1969. 'A model of labor migration and urban unemployment in less developed countries', in *The American Economic Review*, vol. 59, pp. 138–49.

Todaro, M.P., 1976. *Internal migration in developing countries*. Geneva, ILO.

Todaro, M.P., 1980. 'Internal migration in developing countries: A survey', in Easterlin, R.A. (ed), *Population and economic change in developing countries*. Chicago, University of Chicago Press.

Van Schendel, Willem and Aminul Haque Faraizi, 1984. *Rural labourers in Bengal, 1880 to 1980,* CASP 12. Rotterdam.

Webster, Neil, 1993. 'The role of NGDOs in Indian rural development: Some lessons from West Bengal and Karnataka', Paper presented at the European Association of Development Institutes VIIth General Conference, Berlin, September.

Wood, Charles, 1981. 'Structural changes and household strategies: A conceptual framework for the study of rural migration', in *Human Organisation*, vol. 40, no. 4.

Yang, Anand, 1979. 'Peasants on the move: A study of internal migration in India', in *Journal of Interdisciplinary History*, vol. 10, no. 1, pp. 37–58.

7

Institutional Change in an Enterprise-based Society and its Impact on Labour: The Case of the People's Republic of China

JUTTA HEBEL[1]

The issue addressed in this paper is the current change in one of the basic social institutions in urban China, i.e. the socialist enterprise or work unit (*danwei*), and its impact on labour.

Since the 1950s, Chinese urban society has been based on work units. State enterprises have been conceived as all encompassing units, which were not confined to their economic targets. They had political, ideological, social and administrative obligations, e.g. they were expected to provide social security, housing and various facilities for their work force. Labour has been included into these units on a lifelong, non-contractual basis. Planning and administration were at the origin of a categorization of work units, jobs and workers. This gave rise to a differentiation and segmentation of the labour system. The work units produced a special type of labour inclusion for urbanites within the state socialist society.

Since China shifted the focus of its economic reforms to the implementation of the socialist market economy, state enterprises have been transformed. The boundaries between state and enterprise and between enterprise and work force were redrawn. State enterprises are now losing their monopoly role in employment and the distribution of social status. As market forces came into play, alternatives of employment within and outside the work units were opened up. Changes in the administratively given structure of the labour system are now under way.

1. THE CONCEPT OF AN ENTERPRISE-BASED SOCIETY

The term 'enterprise-based society', used in this paper, refers to the fact that the state-owned enterprises[2] were a fundamental social institution in urban Chinese society.[3] Since the 1950s state enterprises were not only the backbone of the Chinese economy, but, in addition to their economic obligations, these enterprises had numerous social, political, and administrative functions. Basic needs of workers were met by enterprises; social security and housing were provided, and facilities, such as schools, hospitals, dining halls, bath houses, day-care centres, grocery stores, recreation centres and hairdressers were supplied. Work units defined urban people's life and limited the set of choices for the individual. Political and ideological education of the work force were further major obligations of the firm. The Chinese labelled this type of institutional arrangement, which incorporated all these functions on the enterprise level and mediated the relationship between state and urban population, as work unit (*danwei*)[4] or as 'small society' (xiao shehui). Although not all the large and medium sized enterprises were communities which completely corresponded to the above, they all followed the *danwei* concept, deploring deficiencies when not able to provide these services to their work force.

The concept of this type of 'enterprise-based society' has its roots in the 1950s, when the Communist Party adopted the Soviet model of economic planning and tried to extend its authority to urban society.[5] The new order was established by a downward extension of the state's and party's organs to the enterprise level. Communist authorities

> had to gain direct control over urban society from the top down as soon as possible because of their drive to transform the society into one that could justify the ideological legitimacy of the new regime. The authorities therefore adopted a strategy of by-passing the upper structure of the urban economy to reach and mobilize directly the working masses whose support was indispensable to transform urban society. (Lu Feng 1993, p. 27).

To cope with the country's disastrous economic situation and the high rate of unemployment, the state developed a set of administrative principles in order to stabilize the urban work force. Administrative solutions were given priority over market solutions. Workers were appointed through an administrative act by state labour bureaux to their future work units. Assignments by labour bureaux covered the first entry of school-leavers into the labour force. Only people with an urban household registration (*hukou*) were entitled to an assignment by labour bureaux and to regular jobs within state-owned enterprises. This administrative act created non-contractual, lifelong employment for the regular work force, which stabilized the work force notably by means of the liabilities of enterprises towards the individual. The concept of work units resulted from the existing set of constraints and political decisions to give preferential treatment to the urban population. Under the conditions of a socialist planned economy the state's dominance over enterprises and, as

Kornai expressed it, the resulting soft budget constraints for enterprises[6], permitted access to that particular system of redistribution and provision for the majority of urban dwellers.[7]

The work unit produced a specific type of labour inclusion. Inclusion was not only a matter of employment, but also of security, participation, social status, and opportunities of the people. Regular members were integrated into their work units in an all encompassing way. On the one hand, no sharp boundary existed between work and privacy. This was not a question of a missing division between work and leisure, as is said to be the case in Japan. China has definite six days and eight hours working time regulations.[8] Work performance and private life were under the responsibility of managers and superiors. Superiors had to be concerned with the worker's private family affairs, mostly in order to avoid or to arbitrate in conflicts. The state and the party exercised political control over the urban labour force. On the other hand, being affiliated to a work unit meant not only control, but permanent employment and lifelong security in a material and a social sense.

Until the recent economic reforms[9] Chinese urban society was based on that particular type of work unit. It was confined to the urban population, excluding urban dwellers without an urban household registration[10] and also the rural majority.

2. THE CHINESE LABOUR SYSTEM

Before we describe the institutional changes further, we will give some more information on the basic institution of the *danwei* and, in particular, on its constituent role for the structure of the Chinese labour system. Both the unit and the labour system are the result of four decades of socialist policy and planning and, at least up to now, have proved to be highly effective stabilizing elements in the state socialist society.

When we use the term 'labour system' in this paper, it is thought of as a logical equivalent to the 'labour market', stressing the non-market mode of coordination.[11] This paper is based on empirical findings drawn from two research projects.[12]

2.1 Categories of work units, jobs and workers

The Chinese *danwei* and the labour system were both determined by a multifaceted administrative categorization, which subdivided the urban and rural population. Even today, people are not allowed to register with the officials of a chosen urban locality, but are confined to their 'inherited' household registration.[13] The combination of household registration with the distribution of food coupons for grain and oil (liangpiao) secured a stable population and prevented a substantial rural-urban migration. Urban and rural categories of households, with different channels and quantities of supply, were placed under state control, brought about by the work units and the rural communes respectively. The politically induced rural-urban divide resulted in two unrelated labour systems. In 1992, the rural work force numbered 438 million people, the urban work force consisted of 156 million employees, among them 148 million staff members and workers.[14]

In addition to the rural-urban divide, the urban part of the population was subdivided by various administrative criteria. A set of particular regulations of allocation, welfare and political participation, all based on the work unit, were applied to urbanites. The guidelines for the labour administration, for managers and for workers were dominated by the administrative distinctions between the different categories of work units, jobs and workers.

- Work units differ with respect to ownership (state-owned, collective, private and joint-venture), to size, to central, provincial or local administrative subordination, to branch, industry or age of the firm.
- Jobs can be stable or unstable, be part or not be part of the plan quota laid down by the authorities; they can be located in the first (manufacture), the second (e.g. unskilled production related work; transportation) or the third line (i.e. administration, service) of production; they belong either to the workers' or a cadres' section of employment.
- The (urban) work force is subdivided according to their urban or rural household registration and their different levels of training. The work force is strictly divided into the management-technical personnel (cadres) and shop floor workers. Workers may differ in their political activity and party membership, age, sex, health and marital status.

The differentiation of work units gave rise to unequal resource allocation, supply of material, skilled personnel or land use for construction, etc.; the assignment of workers by the labour bureau determined membership in more or less privileged units, and defined their social status and life chances. Allocation and reallocation as well as redistribution processes occurred within these definite categories of differentiation which made up the Chinese urban labour system. There was a strong connection between one's social status and the status of the unit.

> The worker's employment status is not an individual attribute, but follows from his or her place of employment.... Once a worker enters a particular workplace, that worker obtains an employment status that is determined by the nature of the workplace itself (either state-run or collective). This status, to a great extent, determines the worker's citizen rights from then on. (Lu 1993, p. 51f).

2.2 Segmentation and pre-reform segments within the Chinese urban labour system

The Chinese labour system can be labelled as segmented. Segmentation, as we understand it, is a process in which a combination of unequal job conditions and unequal chances of access results in a stable structure (see Sengenberger 1987, p. 60). A complex set of rules directs all further action within the labour process. Thus, a structure with its administratively given conditions of employment, living conditions, life opportunities and options can be characterized as 'segmented'.[15]

Differentiation along the above mentioned categories of work units, jobs and workers turned out to be more than a statistical classification. It directed all the participants in the labour process. Segmentation resulted out of abstract attributes of people and of planning criteria, and it was not related to the individual's performance or singular properties. The principles governing eligibility, selection, and rewards were purely administrative and impersonal, but they gave rise to different modes of allocation, contracting and rewarding. Until recently, individuals had little or no influence on access to work units or jobs, as well as on later career opportunities. No alternative existed for the urban population to employment in state-owned or collective units.

The global administrative categorization of work units, jobs and labour affected for example: entry into the state-owned enterprises, i.e. the core sector of the Chinese economy (see Lin and Bian 1991); status attainment of workers; social responsibility of enterprise managers for the regularly assigned members of the work units; bargaining processes between the enterprise management and the state administration; the sources of employee control over the job and over rewards; vacancy competition and career aspirations; the processes of internal reallocation and labour mobility; the employment relationship; the trilateral industrial relations formed by the state administration, the enterprise directors and the labour force.

Until the fresh impetus for enterprise and labour reforms in the 1980s, the Chinese urban labour system consisted of two distinct segments following the given administrative categorization and subdivision lines.

- The primary segment comprised the core of the Chinese economy, i.e. state-owned and large collective units under the supervision of the central or provincial governments. These units or *danwei* provided for stable and privileged employment and the full range of facilities, housing, subsidies and services to their regular members. Staff and workers were recruited from the urban school-leavers and were assigned by the labour bureaux. In many cases, school-leavers 'inherited' their jobs from their parents upon retirement (*dingti*). Assignments of workers did not necessarily meet vacancies in the enterprise nor were they effected upon request of either the worker or the firm. School-leavers were employed as staff members or as workers, for the most part upon their educational degree.[16] There were few or no direct possibilities of formal intervention in the administrative process of appointment, with the exception of personal relations (*guanxi*). Under Chinese conditions membership in these units meant a privileged social status for staff and workers. Rural school-leavers or peasants were not admitted to any regular assignment or jobs in state-run or even in collective units.

Although the state administration had intended to prevent rural-urban migration, state and collective firms found ways to hire labourers from the countryside. They were employed on the basis of simple and short term contracts.[17] The primary segment, with its privileged permanent staff and workers, also incorporated the most unfavourable types of urban employment, consisting mostly of the floating rural[18] and the older or disabled urban population. Although the aforementioned workers laboured in the same enterprise, they were denied all the *danwei*'s social benefits and facilities. Their jobs lacked stability and social security and their field of activity was made up of dirty, heavy and unhealthy work.[19]

• The secondary segment covered medium sized and small collective units under local administration or small street workshops run by street committees. These units provided permanent employment, despite the poor employment conditions. Nearly all facilities providing well-being were absent. The secondary segment was made up of mostly urban population, that was assigned by mischance to collective units. Only a medium or poor social status was allotted to workers in these units.

Jobs within one work unit did not differ decisively in monetary wages, but in work conditions, bonus and privileges. The positions of cadres were prominent in terms of prestige and connections, e.g. allowing access by personal connections to goods in short supply. Although there was a certain degree of differentiation within the units, the regular affiliation to a work unit (*danwei* membership) determined the social status and life chances of the individual. State administrative regulations produced and legitimized these unequal results of the job allocation and distribution processes, which were connected with the concept of an enterprise-based society.

3. RECENT REFORMS AFFECTING LABOUR INCLUSION

China is aiming at transforming its economy into a socialist market economy. Differentiation in political, economic and social affairs has been put on the reform agenda, notably the abandonment of the *danwei* concept which shaped urban society. Enterprises are supposed to become economic entities and should be freed from their social obligations. With the beginning of the reform process in 1978, various experiments have been carried out in order to remodel the basic relationship between society and economy. In particular, starting with the reforms of enterprises in 1984 and of the labour system in 1986, the mode of social integration of labour has been singled out as the root of the low economic efficiency of the state enterprises. In the political discussion, life-long employment and overall security for workers were made responsible for the bad performance of the enterprises. The critique has been made popular, first by using the well-known image of the 'iron rice bowl', which has to be smashed, and, since 1991, by blaming the 'three irons', i.e. in addition to the 'iron rice bowl', the cadres' 'iron armchair' and the 'iron wages'.

3.1 The enterprise reform

The enterprise reform, which had started earlier than the labour reforms, is now the core of the economic reform. Its main focus is the reconstruction of the relationship between government and enterprises and between manage-ment and labour.

After 1984, decentralization diminished the vertical line of control over enterprises and invigorated the function of management. Several types of contractual responsibility systems changed the relationship between state administration and enterprises,[20] and the Factory Director Responsibility System[21] enlarged the director's authority and responsibility. The opening up of an extra-plan sphere enlarged the firm's field of economic operation. At the same time, the emphasis on profitability weakened the political influence of the party on economic decision-making.

In 1988 an Enterprise Law further enhanced the autonomy of state-owned firms, in order to ensure market-oriented management.[22] In July 1992, new 'Regulations for a Change of the Enterprise Mechanism' were enacted in order to implement the Enterprise law.[23] State-owned enterprises now operate (more or less) independently and are responsible for their profits and losses. The regulations grant production and management decision-making powers to the enterprises, permit decisions on prices, investments, imports and exports, wages and bonuses, and personnel planning. With government approval, mergers and takeovers are allowed. The state's property rights over enterprise assets are separated from the management.[24] The state's role is defined as a coordinator of macroeconomic conditions.

Decision-making power in personnel planning is granted to the enterprise director. He is allowed to decide on the number of personnel to be hired, the qualifications and other circumstances of recruitment. High-school graduates allocated by the state may now be refused by enterprises. Personnel planning includes staff reductions, the internal reorganization of work, and decisions on wage and bonus payments.

The above mentioned reforms are intended to raise the profitability of state enterprises and to overcome their poor performance. In 1991, the total deficit of state-run enterprises reached its highest level ever. In June 1992, one third of these enterprises were still running at a loss.[25] Therefore, Chen Jinhua, the director of the State Commission for Restructuring the Economic System, said that the reform had to go beyond the reform of the 'three irons', and enterprises should be pushed towards the market and should concentrate their attention on production.[26]

Altering the *danwei* system and remodelling the prevalent type of labour inclusion into the work units seems to be a solution to the problem. Since the *danwei* system came into being forty years ago, it has stabilized Chinese society, but, at the same time, immobilized labour. It maintained stability under conditions of scarcity by implementing clear rules for matching workers with jobs and for status distribution. Stability in China was not only a result of direct control, political intervention and/or repression, but it was built into the accepted and legitimizing mechanism of status and income distribution. Seen from below, the Chinese state-run (and collective) enterprises were not just arenas of control, but also of stable life conditions, allowing bargaining and negotiation in order to improve the individual's family situation. The on-going changes rearrange the conditions of access to resources, enlarge the options of the individual, and alter the mode of labour inclusion into the work units. At the same time, insecurity for workers increases, the more so since housing, health care and old age pensions shall no longer be provided by the unit.

3.2 Labour contract system

The most important reform directly affecting labour inclusion was the introduction of the labour contract system (*laodong hetongzhi*) in 1986 (some experiments had been carried out earlier). For the first time, labour contracts were given to all workers on their first entry into state-run (or collective) units. The contracts were generally temporary, mostly between two to five years, and they specified the rights and obligations of both the workers and the firm.

The first introduction of this contract system resulted in two different categories of employment: permanent workers continued to enjoy full job security and were entitled to all provisions of the enterprise, whereas contract workers had only a rather short-term perspective. This division into two different employment conditions had consequences which counteracted the desired effects of the reform: (a) when work contracts had expired, managers were not able to lay off workers, even when bad conduct and performance were obvious; (b) to avoid conflicts, managers gave the same treatment to contract workers and the working conditions of contract workers approached those of permanent workers (*gudinghua*).

168

Since 1991, new efforts have been made to implement the labour reform. Firstly, the introduction of an All Staff Labour Contract System (*quanyuan laodong hetongzhi*) has been put on the agenda. The goal of this system was that all staff members and workers should sign a contract with an enterprise of their choice. At the beginning, these contracts should again be temporary and be either renewed or cancelled at the expiry date. Meanwhile, contracts must not be temporary any longer, but they can be cancelled. This new contract system was thought of as an instrument for managers to employ the right staff and workers in order to meet market conditions better. It was also said that workers should gain a greater choice in their jobs and enterprises. At the end of 1992, 25.4 million staff and workers, i.e. 17.2%, were reported to have signed a labour contract (*ZGTN* 1993, p. 117). Secondly, the reforms should not only reach the new employees, but were intended to also cover the previously employed permanent workers. The permanent work force was the object of a programme, called 'optimal labour combination programme'. This was started in 1987, and its aim was to reorganize the labour set-up in a more efficient way and to introduce more competitiveness into the appointment process. In 1992, around 10 million staff members and workers were involved in the optimal labour combination programme (*China News Analysis*, June 1, 1992, 1461, p. 3). Thirdly, by May 1992, a comprehensive reform of employment, salaries and social security (*sanxiang zhidu gaige*) was promoted and about 40,000 enterprises were reported as having adopted these reforms. They reached a total of 17 million staff members and workers, i.e. exceeding one tenth of the total (*ibid.*).

4. INSTITUTIONAL CHANGES AND THEIR IMPACT ON LABOUR

The process of reforming the state-owned enterprises and the labour system is slowly eroding the former institutional basis of the Chinese urban society. Within an existing set of constraints, a dual system of coordination is now emerging, which intertwines state planning and market regulation. On the one hand, there is a shift towards semi-state and private economic activities, and on the other hand, changes take place in the state-controlled sector, in particular in the state's controlling capacity, in economic decision-making in state-owned enterprises, and in labour management. The developing socialist market economy is not yet a real market economy nor is it any longer a centrally planned economy.

Recent statistics reveal that the economic reforms produced a shift in the control of economic resources from state-run units to collective and private firms.[27] A decade ago, state-owned enterprises accounted for 74.7% of China's industrial output, with collectives contributing 24.6% and the private sector and joint ventures 0.62%. In 1992, the contribution of state-owned units has decreased to 48%. In contrast, collective and private production has gone up to 38% and 14% respectively (*ZGTN* 1993, p. 414).

4.1 First results of the reform process

The current process of enterprise and labour reform embodies a number of inconsistent tendencies. On the one hand it is not yet quite clear to what extent economic decisions are really transferred to the enterprise level and are freed from political tutelage. Although decentralization does not always imply an increase of enterprise autonomy, a withdrawal of the state from decision-making and resource allocation is noticeable and greater scope is being given to the market mechanism. It is said that decentralization has often resulted in an increasing influence of the local administration on the units under their jurisdiction. The influence of the Party remains unclear. Political influence may be prevalent in some cases, because the firm director and party secretary are the same person.[28]

On the other hand, the market mechanism has been brought into play and has provided the people with numerous alternative options. We will present some of the available strategies in general terms.

New market options and the introduction of the All Staff Labour Contract System initiated substantial changes, even if it has not yet eroded the privileged employment conditions of permanent workers. Their favourable situation is only affected in as much as wages outside the state sector increased more rapidly.[29] The purchasing power gives access to products and services (even social security) previously supplied by the *danwei*. The permanency of employment in state-owned units is not yet questioned: both our empirical projects revealed that even workers with poor performance would not be laid off into open unemployment. Enterprises which run at a loss keep their work force, pay wages and even grant bonuses and subsidies.

Nevertheless, state-owned and collective units try to make use of their enlarged decision-making power in order to diversify with respect to labour. They expand into the market by opening up small business centres and/or labour service companies (*laodong fuwu gongsi*), mostly in the service sector. Redundant labour is transferred into these subunits, which are expected to function as profit centres.

Within the enterprises, managers try to 'optimize' the labour arrangement. Although dismissals are hardly ever possible, workers with bad performance may be kept on the pay-roll, maintaining their basic wages without any bonus, but they are pressured into applying for another post.

The new market chances induce changes among permanent workers in state-owned units. Some try to change their individual situation by taking a formal and unpaid release from the state or collective unit. These people want to succeed on the market as self-employed (*getihu*) or within a private business. Overstaffed enterprises are often in favour of these people taking leave, since they can reduce their wage bill. But, as independent social legislation has not yet been implemented, people still rely on the unit's medical and other welfare programmes, and the units tolerate it. An increasing number of staff members and workers are on long medical leave and receive a percentage of their wages as a convalescence allowance while they are moonlighting in a second job.

Staff members and workers of state-run and collective units have only recently been allowed to have a second job in order to raise their income, and the legal status of moonlighting and second jobs remains unclear. Professors, teachers, technicians and researchers are the leading cohorts among two-job holders.[30] In Shanghai, one half of the residents are reported to have second jobs (*China News Analysis*, March 1, 1993, 1480, p. 2). Moonlighting and second jobs are still the object of controversy: on the one hand, the success of the state enterprise reform is questioned. Enterprises which seek to improve their use of labour must cope with a labour force engaged in a second job, while having to pay for the medical bills and the pensions of these people.[31] The status of labour as a commodity is still under political discussion.[32]

The new market opportunities attract a large number of young people. School-leavers no longer necessarily apply for a post in state-owned enterprises. Joint ventures, private and rural enterprises, even urban collective units pay much higher wages. They compete with the state-owned enterprises to get the trained personnel and professionals. These enterprises offer less security, but the higher wages compensate. Young people take advantage of the better life opportunities offered to them there.

Today, individual or self-employed businesses are very common. Although widespread, their legal status is still ambivalent. At the end of 1992, 15.3 million self-employed businesses, with a total of 24.6 million workers, had started to engage in economic activities (*China aktuell*, Jan. 1993, p. 22). Meanwhile, the regular urban labour force of 147.9 million staff and workers breaks down into 108.9 million employed in state-owned units, 36.2 million in urban collective units and 2.8 million in units of 'other ownership' (i.e. joint ventures). In addition to the regular labour force, another 8.28 million people work as urban individual labourers (*ZGTN*, 1993, p. 97).

4.2 Impacts on labour

Recent enterprise and labour reforms are remodelling the former segmented structure of the labour system in different respects. The work unit will lose its key role in Chinese urban society. Labour allocation and redistribution processes have been affected by the reforms and labour inclusion within the work units has been reshaped.

In the past, the state was the main distributor of resources, and employment was its predominant resource to be distributed to the people. State distribution created inequality, and opportunities for redistribution were almost non-existent. Until the middle of the 1980s, no market functions corrected or eliminated the distributive monopoly of the state. Today, the above mentioned reforms undermine the state's monopoly of allocation and redistribution as they give greater scope to the market mechanism. As new opportunities are centred on the market, a redistribution of resources, power and privilege emerges. A net reduction of power and privilege for the state administration and its cadres occurs. As a result of this process, chances and risks for the individual increase.

Labour inclusion is changing dramatically. In general, labour is no longer administratively assigned and appointments are made by 'mutual choices' (*xianghu xuanze*). Labour in state-owned and collective units is currently pushed into more contractual employment relations. The introduction of labour contracts for all staff members and workers stresses the mutual rights and duties of the contracting parties. The employment relationship loses its administrative character and is beginning to be based on law.

Not only the above mentioned work contracts, but also new social legislation for handling social security and housing is under development. Work units no longer pay for the full range of social security (e.g. medical insurance, pensions). The recent implementation of a non-enterprise-based social security system helps enterprises to reduce their welfare funds[33] and to loosen their ties to employees. Units are still involved in housing, but they no longer offer free apartments to their members. A new system, separating the right of ownership from the use of the apartment, has been introduced, and employees have to pay a considerable amount for housing.[34] The construction and implementation of a social security system and the introduction of a market for real estate are two major preconditions for labour mobility.

Wages and bonuses of staff members and workers in state-owned work units are still rather low, and, as costs are rising and the market is offering a large range of consumer goods and food supply, they are considered to be insufficient. Personal and/or household monetary wages have become much more important than they were in the past. Money has taken on a new significance. People no longer depend on their unit's capacity to provide goods and services. Marketization and commodification made goods and services available to those who have purchasing power, and not only to particular unit members. The strong connection of one's status to the status of the unit is no longer valid.

A large number of new opportunities came into being as market activities were allowed. Both firms and individuals took advantage of these new opportunities. The new entrepreneurial climate is widespread, and a large number of people engage in private economic activities. These efforts have

172

been encouraged by the political leadership, and the slogan that 'some people should get rich first' has been promoted by Deng Xiaoping himself. Private economic activity is dependent upon the family and other personal connections. It currently results in the emergence of a stratum of rich people, demonstrating their new status by conspicuous consumption.

The moving away of the state from its roles as a redistributor of financial, material and human resources to units, and of jobs, wages and social security to the urban population, reduces its direct influence on status definition and social structuring. The state's withdrawal has downgraded the former obviously advantaged position of urban dwellers as a result of administrative redistribution. The primary segment of privileged employment within the core units is now undermined, firstly, by changes in the employment relationship and secondly, by the new market related chances.

The once sharp distinction between rural and urban China can no longer be sustained. Rural industry, rural towns and private farming display high rates of economic growth, at least in the more developed regions of the country.[35] Rural enterprises pay markedly higher salaries to their employees than do the state-owned and urban collective units. They still lack a net of social security and housing facilities as opposed to the state-owned firms. Provision of social security is often felt to be the only advantage of the latter. We were informed that while competing for employees with rural firms and joint ventures, state-owned enterprises increased their supply and subsidies. This was in order to maintain and to motivate their trained work force and to attract skilled workers, even if this contradicted their politics for better economic performance.

The state-imposed rural-urban mobility restrictions, upheld by the '*hukou*' and '*liangpiao*' systems, lost their importance during the last few years. Sixty to eighty million rural people are estimated in 1990 as being a floating population in the larger cities, an influx that increases the urban substratum. Solinger stated that these people make up 20 to 25 percent of the population in the areas of their relocation.[36] The arrival of this large number of migrants has dramatically changed the rural-urban divide. Rural labourers, as we were told during our interviews in Suzhou last March, were already permitted to hold regular jobs in the state-owned enterprises and an urban household registration was given to them in order to reward them for good performance.

5. CONCLUSION

The economic reform has, in the rather short period of ten years, induced a process of transition in the Chinese enterprise-based society. Economic and social changes transform China 'from a closed or semi-closed to an open society' and from a 'uniform to a varied society' (Group for Research 1994, pp. 72 and 73). The decentralization of decision-making and increased autonomy of the enterprises, combined with greater economic discipline and responsibility, are thought of as a step-by-step concept to transform the state-owned and the large collective units into firms fit to operate on the market. Principles of allocation and redistribution were redefined, as market coordination came into play. The state's influence on resource allocation decreased and new market opportunities emerged. The concept of an enterprise-based society has lost its function in urban Chinese society. The administrative guidelines and categories of work units, jobs and workers no longer serve as the basis of segmentation processes.

The institutional changes shaped the role of labour within and outside the existing state and collective enterprises. Although a real labour market is not yet in operation, and work units still keep the majority of staff and workers as a permanent work force, the urban sector is divided into many new economic entities. The division of labour has increased and transformed the occupational categories. As China has an average of over 10 million new entrants into the labour market every year,[37] the speed of change is considerable.

Although vested interests, in particular of state and party cadres losing their traditional influence, may again slow down the reforms, new social groups and interests have come into play. The social structure of China, including its structure of inequality, is now under transformation. A research group of the Chinese Academy of Social Sciences stressed that changes occurred in the type of work, as well as in life-styles, incomes, consumption, intellectual levels and interpersonal relationships (Group for Research 1994, p. 73). The processes of social and regional mobility remodel the prevalent social structure by downgrading the former privileged primary segment and by redefining the divide between the urban primary and secondary segments and between the urban and rural workforces.

NOTES

1. Georg-August-Universität Göttingen, Germany.
2. The term 'state-run enterprises' was changed to 'state-owned enterprises', following the Chinese Communist Party's XIVth National Congress in October 1992, in order to underline the separation of public ownership and management. 'The state-owned economy refers to the economic category in which the means of production are owned by the state ... This category includes enterprises run by central and local state organs at all levels, non-profit-making institutions and social organizations using state-owned assets to invest.' *Summary of World Broadcasts* (Jan. 14, 1993) B2/9. See also footnote 27.
3. The term underlines the units' basic role in urban society. It does not only apply to the economy: The famous economist Jiang Yiwei (1980, pp. 48–70) used the term 'enterprise-based economy', when he stressed that enterprises should become independent economic entities and should not be placed under administrative levels.

4. Work units are industrial and non-industrial organizations. Lu Feng (1993, p. 9) differentiates (a) administrative units (*xinzheng danwei*), (b) nonprofit business units (*shiye danwei*) and (c) enterprise units (*qiye danwei*), all in the state-run sector. 'Other entities often considered as units – rural people's communes, urban collective enterprises, and neighbourhood committees – are not units, strictly speaking.'

5. The origin of the *danwei* system is the object of a controversy. Li Hanlin (1991) and Lu Feng (1993, 1989) agree on the basic institutional character of the *danwei* system for urban China, but disagree on its roots. Li stresses the traditional features, in particular the former clan structure of China's past, whereas Lu demonstrates its political character in the development of state socialism.

6. Kornai (1980). See Lin Yimin (1992), p. 389, for arguments that cost-sensitivity is not necessarily a function of the budget constraints. Cost-sensitivity can be enhanced not only by the pressures of the survival of the enterprise, but also by the incentives of growth opportunities.

7. Public ownership guaranteed the firm's survival regardless of its performance and made it insensitive to cost and price considerations. Enterprises, operating under conditions of scarcity and resource constraints, and rewarded for expansion and physical output, developed particular strategies to overcome these handicaps. Labour was one of their main resources and they sought to hoard and hide the human resources. This type of enterprise behaviour corresponded with the ideology that socialist societies should not have any open unemployment.

8. A reduction of working time is under discussion (from 48 to 44 hours per week). The main argument is that people in overstaffed units work only 5.26 hours a day instead of 8 hours. *China aktuell* (June 1992), p. 252.

9. In 1984 economic reforms shifted from the rural to the urban areas, covering the reform of the state-run enterprises on a national level.

10. See section 2.1 below.

11. We use the term 'labour system' (*laodong zhidu*) in an abstract sense and not in the more common Chinese sense, in which the labour system (*laodong zhidu*) refers to (manual) workers' affairs and is opposed to the personal (i.e. staff, cadres) system (*renshi zhidu*).

12. Information for this paper comes from two studies, one conducted in 1988–1990 on the Chinese labour system, and subsequent research, in progress since 1992, on the Chinese work unit (*danwei*). In Jiangsu province (Nanjing, Suzhou), we had 19 interviews in enterprises of textile and machine-building industries, and in Beijing and Nanjing another 19 interviews in the Labour Ministry, the provincial labour administration, the labour union on central and provincial level, the Women's association, neighbourhood committee, etc. In the enterprises we had 3 to 6 hours interviews with the general manager and/or the personnel department manager. Personnel management was the topic in both studies, including labour administration, recruitment, personnel planning and training, labour contracts and dismissals, labour resistance, motivation and control, social security as well as wage and bonus policy. In addition to the study of the personnel management in state-owned units, the current research aims at elucidating the impact of reform on the work unit, in particular, on its strategy of enterprise organization and on the concepts of work organization and production processes. The results of the first study have been published in Hebel and Schucher (1992).

13. Over the last few years, household registration has lost its practical value. Today, it is planned to abolish it completely.

14. ZGTN (1993), p. 97. The category of 'staff members and workers' (*quanbu zhigong*) comprises the regular work force in state-owned and collective units and in different types of joint ventures.

15. In this paper we will not discuss the question of whether or not segmentation theories can be used to analyse state planned labour systems. In an earlier treatise (Hebel and Schucher 1992) this question has been addressed. Our main argument in favour of labour market segmentation theories is that, despite different coordinating devices, both market and planned economies have to solve the same fundamental problems of adaptation (i.e. matching persons and jobs) and (re)distribution (i.e., distribution of status, income, job security, career and life

chances). Both types of society have developed different institutional arrangements to solve these problems.

16. When a person has been hired by a state enterprise he or she will be given either cadre status or worker status. 'At state enterprise units, those employees who are college or technical secondary school graduates and those who have gone through *zhuangan* ('transformation into cadre') procedures are all given 'state cadres' status, regardless of the jobs they are assigned to or whether they are now acting in a leadership role or not.' (Kizaki 1990, p. 444).

17. These contracts and workers must not be confused with the new system of contract work (*laodong hetongzhi*). These workers (*linshigong, hetonggong, jijiegong*) are underprivileged in every respect. They are registered as rural population and therefore their rural home administration is thought to be responsible for them. After the termination of their contracts they are supposed to return to the countryside, and, in case of an accident, the rural commune had to take care of them.

18. An official definition of 'floating population' characterizes them as 'people engaged in partial temporary relocation whose legal residence registration remains in their original place of habitation.' (Solinger 1991, p. 10).

19. As is commonly distinguished, this type of subdivision of the primary segment could also be defined as 'internal' and 'external' labour system.

20. The contractual responsibility system displays a great variety. In all cases, the relationship between the enterprise director and the supervisory administration is governed by a formal contract with terms that range from two to five years. A certain (contracted) amount of revenue has to be remitted to the government. Given the contractual nature, it is required that the director be given authority to contract on behalf of the enterprise and to take the responsibility for enterprise performance. Contractual responsibility systems are opposed to income tax systems.

21. In 1986, the enterprise director was given the decisive role in the firm. The introduction of the Director Responsibility System (changzhang fuzezhi) separated the functions of the management and the party within the enterprise.

22. Law Governing State-Owned Industrial Enterprises. 13.4.1988. German translation in Münzel (1989), p. 53–73.

23. Regulations for a Change of the Enterprise Mechanism. 30.6.1992. German translation in *China aktuell* (Aug. 1992), pp. 559–576.

24. See footnote 2.

25. 31 billion yuan (state-run enterprises covered in the state budget). *China News Analysis* (June 1, 1992), 1461, p. 2; *China aktuell* (Dec. 1992), p. 874; *China aktuell* (Oct. 1992), p. 700.

26. Chen Jinhua in Wuhan, April 1992, *China News Analysis* (June 1, 1992), 1462, p. 5.

27. See footnote 2. 'The collective economy refers to the economic category in which the means of production are owned by citizens' collectives ... The private economy refers to an economic category in which the means of production are privately owned by citizens, and enterprises operate on the basis of wage labour ... The individual economy refers to an economic category in which the means of production are owned by individual labourers, enterprises operate on the basis of individual labour and the fruit of work is possessed and used by individual labourers.' *SWB* (1993) B2/9.

28. The party is still present on all levels of the enterprise. Although economic decisions should now be independent from political influence, directors told us in all our interviews in 1993 that there was good cooperation between management and party. The role of the party was said to be altered into one whose main goal was to motivate the work force for better economic performance.

29. The income situation is difficult to evaluate. There are variations according to regions and ownership of the enterprises. As an employee's total wage includes a basic wage and various subsidies, comparisons are often misleading. It is said that, as reported for Shanghai, 120 yuan in a state enterprise may be a better proposition than 500 yuan from a joint venture, which provides no accommodation while requiring hard work (*China News Analysis*, Nov. 1, 1993, 1496, p. 2).

30. The intellectuals number 25 million. Their income remains among the lowest in China, in particular because additional bonuses and subsidies are low. The monthly income of a senior

researcher does not exceed 500 yuan, and teachers' average monthly incomes amount to between 270 and 330 yuan. *China News Analysis* (Nov. 1, 1993), 1496, p. 5.

31. Moonlighting introduces a new distorting element in enterprise reform. Sometimes enterprises try to compensate by asking for part of the extra income to be delivered to them. *China News Analysis* (March 1, 1993), 1480, p. 8.

32. One position in the discussion says that labour is already a commodity, for instance all the non-resident workers in township enterprises. *China News Analysis* (March 1, 1993), 1480, p. 8.

33. This reduction will only be noticeable in the long run. At present, units have to pay for both the present pensions and the future pension system. These double costs were the rather short-sighted reason for many units deciding not to share in the financing of the security system.

34. The units which were investigated in March 1993 calculated about 50,000 yuan for an apartment of 60 square metres.

35. In 1992, there was a shortfall in the growth rate of the rural areas. The slower rural growth was caused by reduced output of grain, shortage of funds for purchasing farm produce and contributions levied on farmers. At the beginning of this year a rural uprising took place in Sichuan. The rural population opposed the bad conditions of life, incorrect taxation, and arbitrarily imposed fees by supervising bodies, i.e. '*tanpai*'.

36. Solinger (1991), p. 9f. Since 1984 rural people were allowed to enter the cities without changing their formal household registration, on the condition that they would raise their own funds, take care of their grain rations and find a place of abode. In other sources the floating population is estimated at 20 million people, more than one million in Beijing. See Group for Research (1994), p. 72.

37. Between 1986 and 1990. The demand for new labour declined during the same period. See Yuan Fang (1994), p. 28.

REFERENCES

China Monthly Statistics, 1993. China Statistics Information and Consultancy Service Centre. Beijing (Feb. 1993) Issue 11/12.

China News Analysis, 1992. 'State enterprises: no fool-proof reforms', June 1, No. 1461. Hongkong.

China News Analysis, 1993. 'The golden ghetto of individual businesses', Jan. 1, No. 1476, pp. 1–9. Hongkong.

China News Analysis, 1993. 'The two-job holders', March 1, No. 1480, pp. 1–9. Hongkong.

China News Analysis, 1993. 'Of wages and incomes', November 1, No. 1496, pp. 1–9. Hongkong.

Group for Research on Social Development, Sociology Institute of the Chinese Academy of Social Sciences, 1994. 'Changes marking the beginning of a period of transition in Chinese society', in *Social Sciences in China*, Spring, pp. 66–76.

Hebel, J., 1990. 'Der Betrieb als kleine Gesellschaft. Die Bedeutung des chinesischen Betriebstyps für den Prozeß der Reform des Arbeitssystems', in *Soziale Welt*, vol. 41, no. 2, pp. 222–242.

Hebel, J. and Schucher, G., 1992. *Zwischen Arbeitsplan und Arbeitsmarkt. Strukturen des Arbeitssystems in der VR China*. Mitteilungen des Instituts für Asienkunde, No. 204. Hamburg 1992.

Jefferson, G.H.; Th. G. Rawski and Yuxin Zheng, 1992. 'Growth, efficiency, and convergence in China's state and collective industry', in *Economic Development and Cultural Change*, vol. 40, no. 2, pp. 239–266.

Jiang Yiwei, 1980. 'The theory of an enterprise-based economy', in *Social Sciences in China*, vol. 1, pp. 48–70.

Kizaki, M., 1990. 'Changing state-enterprise management in China during its economic reform period', in *The Developing Economies*, vol.xxviii, no. 4, pp. 441–465.

Kornai, J., 1980. ''Hard' and 'soft' budget constraints', in *Acta Oeconomica*, vol. 25, nos. 3–4, pp. 231–246.

Li Hanlin, 1991. *Die Grundstruktur der chinesischen Gesellschaft. Vom traditionellen Klansystem zur modernen Danwei-Organisation.* Opladen, Westdeutscher Verlag.

Lin Nan and Bian Yanjie, 1991. 'Getting ahead in urban China', in *American Journal of Sociology*, vol. 97, no. 3, pp. 657–688.

Lin Nan and Xie Wen, 1988. 'Occupational prestige in urban China', in *American Journal of Sociology*, vol. 92, no. 4, pp. 793–832.

Lin Yimin, 1992. 'Between government and labor: Managerial decision-making in Chinese industry', in *Studies in Comparative Communism*, vol. xxv, no. 4, pp. 381–403.

Lu Feng, 1989. 'Dan Wei – A special form of social organization', in *Social Sciences in China*, vol. 3, pp. 100–122.

Lu Feng, 1993. 'The origins and formation of the Unit (Danwei) System', in *Chinese Sociology and Anthropology*, vol. 25, no. 3, pp. 7–91.

McMillan, J. and Naughton, B., 1992. 'How to reform a planned economy: Lessons from China', in *Oxford Review of Economic Policy*, vol. 8, no. 1, pp. 130–143.

Münzel, F., 1989. *Unternehmens- und Gesellschaftsrecht der VR China.* Mitteilungen des Instituts für Asienkunde, No. 176. Hamburg.

Nee, V. and Stark, D. (eds), 1989. *Remaking the economic institutions of socialism: China and Eastern Europe.* Stanford, Stanford University Press.

Sengenberger, W., 1987. *Struktur und Funktionweise von Arbeitsmärkten. Die Bundesrepublik Deutschland.* Frankfurt am Main, New York.

Solinger, D.J., 1991. *China's transients and the State: A form of civil society?* USC Seminar Series No. 1. Hongkong.

Summary of World Broadcasts (SWM), 1993. 'Categorization of economic entities revised', Jan. 14, FE/1586 B2/9f.

Yuan Fang, 1994. 'The employment problem and reform of the labor system in China', in *Social Sciences in China*, Spring, pp. 26–32.

Zhongguo tongji nianjian (ZGTN), 1993. Zhongguo tongji chubanshe, Beijing.

8

Chinese Labour in Transition 1978–92: A Case of Institutional Evolution

FLEMMING CHRISTIANSEN[1]

I. INTRODUCTION

The Chinese reforms have created a new situation in the Chinese labour 'market.' They are fundamental and change the ramifications of people's lives. They are most conspicuous in the Chinese villages, where rural enterprises have reshaped both the economy and the social structures. The cities have experienced the evolution of private, semi-private and non-planned enterprises. The labour structure in state-owned enterprises has been the target of reforms, until recently with little result, but at present with great impact. The civil service system is being slimmed down, and its fundamental structures are in the process of change. Privatization of state-owned enterprises makes great strides. Control mechanisms and social safety nets are gradually being replaced with a higher degree of 'market' regulation. These changes, which affect hundreds of millions of people, take place gradually, and – considering their scale – in a relatively orderly fashion.

The principal aim of this chapter is to explore the dynamics of this historic mass labour transition. It is interesting to examine how the specific realization of labour transfer is shaped by the dynamics of social change, prompted by the economic reforms.

I first intend to give a rough outline of the overall changes in the Chinese 'labour market' since 1978, discussing the complex economic characteristics of Chinese labour during the reforms. I will then proceed to analyse the social structures which determine how labour transfer manifests itself. They include (a) clientelism (*guanxi*); (b) family cycles, marriage patterns and property management; and (c) administrative and institutional barriers. The final part of the contribution will draw up the main conclusions of the discussion.

A SYSTEM IN FLUX: THE PROBLEMS OF LABOUR IN A
REFORMING SOCIALIST ECONOMY

Background

The pre-1978 labour situation was distinguished by an elaborate bureaucratic system for labour allocation, prevention of migration and population control. It had all the characteristics of a centrally planned economy. The putative advantage of a planned economy is that the available resources can be put to use in a rational way, far superior to the squandering of resources characterizing so many Third World countries, and with less detrimental social consequences for the livelihood of the great majority of the population. A socialist planned economy – for moral reasons and seeking to avoid capitalist exploitation – cannot let the market forces govern the pattern of development, so the choice of strategy for industrialization is precarious. The Chinese, between 1949 and 1962, devised a system aimed at promoting industrialization as the main element of development. The purpose of this system was to gain central control of the economy in order that the state could allocate industrial investment capital, labour, and raw materials in a rational way. In the absence of a free market mechanism, allocation was based on fictive prices, reflecting a bureaucratic cost calculation, and on state plans. The collectivization of the agricultural sector instituted a powerful instrument for appropriating capital resources for urban industrialization.

The price system, inspired by the Russian economist Preobrazhensky,[2] awarded the peasants a lower remuneration for their work than the urban workers: the prices for agricultural products were set 'below value' in the Marxist cost calculation, whereas industrial production factors for agriculture were set 'above value'; this phenomenon is called the 'scissors' gap' (*jiandaocha*) in Chinese debates. The resulting economic imbalance, however, did not come down hard on any specific group or class in rural China, since the organization of work and the systems for distributing food grain and cash incomes were largely egalitarian.[3] In this way the Chinese system *emulated the imbalance of a dual economy* (normally seen in a capitalistic environment) without allowing social stratification to emerge.

In order to manage the allocation of labour resources to the urban industry a firm and very successful ban on migration was introduced (the so-called household registration system). Labour bureaux were put in charge of planned allocation of workers to urban enterprises. In this way it was in principle possible to (a) avoid large scale migration to the cities; (b) avoid excessive staffing of urban enterprises with cheap labour; and (c) achieve more rapid advances towards technological improvement and high labour productivity. However, the system did not work in this way.

The migration ban was based on the household registration system, which divided people into 'agricultural' and 'urban resident.' The urban residents included state employees and their dependents. This status implied the entitlement to employment in state enterprises for their children when they came of age.[4] Instead of creating an instrument for planned labour transfer to the 'modern' sector, the labour system created *entitlement* to employment for adult urban residents, a group experiencing rapid growth in numbers.[5] The gate-keeper function of the labour bureaux, therefore, could not be sustained, and labour bureaux were increasingly in charge of overstaffing rather than staffing urban enterprises.[6]

While the 'scissors' gap' disguised the appropriation of funds from agriculture, it also deprived the planning authorities of control over the main capital flow from agriculture to urban industry. Capital transferred in this way was not available for targeted investment. Due to the low prices of raw materials and foodstuffs, it merely created a soft economic environment for the urban enterprises, favouring them irrespective of their efficiency, and negatively influencing the opportunity cost of technological modernization.[7] Both labour transfer and the scissors' gap thus contributed to the overall inefficiency and stagnation (low labour productivity, lack of technological innovation, low returns on invested capital).

The mock dual economy did not create sufficient growth, and its inherent problems impeded development, while at the same time delaying the problems of mass migration. The rigorous division of the economy in two bureaucratically defined sectors made it possible to guide development; the idea of achieving simultaneous development in agriculture and in industry was pursued vigorously, but the population increase limited the effects of this. Several points are of importance here:

(a) The countryside was regarded as a safety valve for pressures on the urban economy;[8] apart from overstaffing urban enterprises, the authorities also initiated campaigns for sending school leavers to the countryside instead of allocating them as workers to urban enterprises (this policy of '*xiaxiang, shangshan*' involved in excess of 17 million young people between 1965 and 1978).[9]

(b) The agricultural work force grew constantly due to China's demographic profile, while the available farmland resources declined. Hence, agricultural growth took place as a result of improved utilization of the land resources without regard for the cost of labour. While the net agricultural product value (NAPV) rose 270 per cent per unit of land, the NAPV only rose 50 per cent per rural labourer in agriculture in the period 1952–1987.[10] In the 1950s to the 1970s the time expenditure per agricultural worker increased (however with diminishing returns for each additional hour both in terms of income and productivity). In the same period intensive agricultural infrastructural development schemes (e.g. irrigation, roads, land reclamation etc.) were carried out in the slack season using conscripted rural labourers on low pay.[11] With the technological advances in this period, the underutilisation of agricultural labour grew (Aubert 1991, p. 520). The available surplus per agricultural labourer stagnated during the period. The feeling of development, therefore, was limited (however, thanks to the egalitarian distribution, the feeling of relative deprivation was limited).

(c) Agriculture did not merely supply capital investment for urban industry, but became the major source of revenue for subsidizing urban consumption.

Reforms

The stagnation of the Chinese economic system down through the 1960s and 1970s created a need for reforms. The main reforms started in 1978, and were initially mere macro-economic regulations of the exchange relations in the existing system. The terms of trade were changed by reducing the scissors' gap in favour of agriculture, the sending of school leavers to the countryside was stopped and the sent-down youths still in the countryside were gradually allowed back. The motivation for these measures was *political* rather than economic. The policy of sending school leavers to the countryside, for example, was resented by urban residents, among whom the new Deng leadership wanted to solicit support and legitimation. The change in the terms of trade with the countryside was motivated by a similar political urgency to avoid growing unrest and decline in production.

Labour in the urban economy

The immediate effect was that the urban sector could not any more use agriculture as a safety valve and source of revenue to the extent that it had done in the past. However, this did not solve the problems of the economy, since the urban sector itself was not reformed seriously. The lack of rural subsidies to the urban economy was turned into a deficit on the state budget,[12] and the problem of surplus labour in the cities was mainly solved by increased recruitment to the army, the universities and to already overstaffed enterprises.[13]

There were some minor structural changes at this stage: registration of individual households (*getihu*) in the cities, i.e. private entrepreneurs operating outside the state plan (Hershkovitz 1985; Rosen 1987–8), and the institution of so-called labour service enterprises (*laodong fuwu gongsi*) also outside the state plan.[14]

In this way a part of the urban surplus labour force could be funnelled into non-planned activities. The disparity between the economic conditions in the private and semi-private sector on the one hand and in the state sector on the other hand created a huge growth potential. Cashing in on the soft economic environment, scarcity of specific goods and services in the consumer market and distorted price relations in the state planned economy, the small scale private entrepreneurs and the non-plan enterprises could make a fast profit.

Although these new sectors remained volatile and very sensitive to changes in the economic environment, they absorbed an increasing part of the urban labour force.

The two new structures introduced were individual households (*getihu*) and labour service companies (*laodong fuwu gongsi*). They were different from each other in scale, perspective and purpose, but they shared the function of breaking up the planned economy in the cities. The individual households operated small private enterprises with maximally seven employees. They had to be registered with the Industry and Trade Offices and the Tax Authorities. Normally a licence would only be issued on the approval of the local government and other authorities. The licence would normally be given for operating a business in a specific trade.

The labour service companies were subsidiaries of urban enterprises set up specifically to solve the problem of unemployment. They were outside the state plan, and were allowed to develop in niches of the economy. Some of these were used for convenient purposes, like slimming down staff commitments. An enterprise could, for example, establish a labour service company to do the cleaning in the enterprise and farm this work task out to the new company. In this way, part of the staff would be placed outside the state plan, and the costs could be kept lower. The LSCs were technically collective enterprises with no fixed wages and only profit sharing.[15] Other LSCs were set up with large investment in highly competitive sectors, including transport, catering, the tourist industry, and even manufacturing. Operating outside the state plan and with less commitments to social overheads, LSCs were effective and contributed to the development of a 'market' outside the state plan.

Rural reforms

In the countryside an effort had been made as early as in 1970 to solve the problem of surplus labour, as well as to reduce the significance of urban appropriation of rural surpluses. The Northern Agricultural Conference in 1970 called for rural mechanization by which the people's communes should develop their own supply industries. These industries were combined with agricultural production so that their profits were united with the proceeds from agriculture, thus being reinvested or distributed as cash income within the brigade or the commune.

The egalitarian distribution principles and the integration of the rural enterprises in the commune- and brigade economy prevented them from becoming

183

an independent sector. However, the regime of distorted price relations under the scissors' gap made it advantageous for rural communes to establish cement, fertiliser, machine and other manufacturing enterprises for the purpose of 'import substitution'.

The advantage was not only in the exchange relations, but also in the relative bargaining power of the rural communities vis-à-vis the planning authorities with regard to the delivery of production factors. If less farm implements, artificial fertiliser or cement were demanded from the state, the state's squeeze on agricultural planning targets could be eased or manipulated somewhat.

The growth of rural enterprises from 1970 until the end of the 1970s was drastic, but there are few statistics to actually demonstrate this (see Wong 1988, pp. 4–5). Although they had a function in alleviating some of the tensions in the planned economy system (easing the effects of the scissors' gap and employing underutilized agricultural workers), they were in themselves not in a position to generate overall growth in the economy.

Reform, imbalances and growth: The impact on labour

By the end of the 1970s it was unrealistic to expect the existing economic system to 'take off' into sustained growth. However the pent-up tensions within the system (which were sustained by the elaborate institutional barriers), including the huge imbalance between the rural and the urban sectors, the potential imbalance between rural industry and urban industry and between rural industry and agriculture, as well as the likely imbalance between the planned and the private economy, created exactly the environment needed for sustained growth in the economy.

With hindsight, the Chinese economic reforms have been astonishingly prudent and shrewd. Whereas the radical and sudden changes in the Russian economy during the first years of the 1990s have created an intolerable situation for large parts of the population, the gradual and measured opening of the Chinese economy has created growth. The persistence of huge imbalances between rural and urban China generated growth. The migration ban on the rural population remained in force, and urban state-owned enterprises were protected from a sudden influx of cheap would-be workers from the countryside.

However, urban construction, which took an upswing after 1978, was almost exclusively based on rural labour, paid comparatively high nominal wages, but deprived of the much more expensive perks and freebies falling to the urbanites. Cheap rural labour was thus used for *expansion* of the urban economy. Lifting the restrictions on street markets in 1977 generated new income opportunities for the peasants, and they soon filled in the huge niches left in urban retailing of fresh food.

When the restrictions on rural 'individual enterprise' (*getihu*) were abandoned in early 1983[16] peasants in coastal regions and near large cities were in a position to supply flexible services to urban enterprises and residents. The distorted price relations in the state sector generated scarcity in the market, which could be filled in by private entrepreneurs. These first-day entrepreneurs often acquired their means of production at prices which reflected their opportunity cost in the ineffective rural collective economy where they had been underused.

In a shrewd move, the Chinese authorities thus took away the illusion that migration to the urban centres could provide better incomes. By maintaining a generally acceptable living standard in most of the countryside and by prompting rapid growth in some of the countryside, the population rush to the cities, predicted by Todaro (Todaro 1969 and 1977; Christiansen 1992), could by and large be avoided. An additional factor is that the policy choice of family farming in the *household responsibility system* as the main form of organization ensured sufficient flexibility to absorb temporary unemployment.[17]

The individual enterprise sector in the cities also profited from the distorted price relations in the urban economy, and with little investment people could generate relatively high incomes in the service sectors. In this way a relatively large part of the work force was attracted away from employment in state-owned enterprises. In many cases workers took (semi-illegal) leave from their work, only claiming basic salary and some of their perks from their work unit, to earn their main income as workers in individual enterprises.

The growth in the rural and urban private sectors created competition, and new market opportunities for urban state-owned enterprises. Some of them entered the new sectors by establishing non-plan subsidiaries with less rigid labour regulation, with cheaper labour expenses (e.g. no medical and social insurances, no free housing, no subsidies for consumption, education, etc.) and with greater access to set their own prices. Some saw an opportunity to sell used equipment to the new sectors, thereby partly financing their own technological improvement.

In the countryside, the abandoning of the people's commune system and the encouragement of individual enterprise brought about a new situation. The rural enterprises became independent. They remained the property of the local government, i. e. the village or the township, but they were divorced from agricultural production. The enterprises, whether collective or private, were in general more profitable than agricultural production, and therefore this sector experienced rapid growth in investment (Feder et al. 1992).

Rural non-agricultural enterprise helped solve a fundamental crisis which the urban industry was incapable of: from the beginning of the 1980s it has been able to absorb the major part of the new entries to the rural labour force.

Comparatively profitable alternatives for young people were available in the countryside or in small towns, thus diminishing the economic incentives to migrate.

While one would have expected that the introduction in China of a market economy would have unleashed a rush to the cities, and like in Russia would have caused serious economic instability, the Chinese economy has been remarkably stable. By gradually undoing various parts of the economy from their dependency on the planned economy, these sectors have been able to prosper rather than to become liabilities to the state. The persistence of irrational state intervention and distorted prices was highly conducive to growth in these sectors.

The next stage in the reform of the Chinese economy has already begun. The majority of the state-owned urban enterprises are to become private, and state institutions must slim down and must create a larger part of their revenue by selling their services on market conditions. This process of 'creating' what has since the Spring of 1992 been termed the 'Socialist Market Economy' (*shehuizhuyi shichang jingji*) is interesting in itself.

Some theoretical reflections

My presentation of the issues above has been based on three economic accounts, which are of general significance in explaining development: (a) the neo-classical account of growth induced by economic dualism; (b) the account of agricultural contributions to industrialization under socialism; (c) the account of the 'economy of shortage' under socialism and the emergence of parallel economies.[18] At this stage it is not my intention to test these theories in detail or to weigh their importance against each other. Their explanatory potential here is general and mutually supportive. Although they assume non-economic interference in the economic process, they do not examine its nature; they even imply a certain economic deterministic axiom.

While it can be said – and has been said – that the market forces with the import of a natural law prevailed over the socialist planned economy, this explanation is shallow and does not explain the fact that the planned economy was able to survive for almost 60 years in the Soviet Union and for between 30 and 35 years in China.

The idea that the market (or in neo-classical terms: the economy) rules as a fundamental law of nature may or may not be true as an axiom. What matters is which institutions a society establishes to solve its problems of development. In China, the planned economy through political intervention performed the tasks of economic development, and in so doing reflected fundamental economic regularities proscribed by neo-classical economics.

The imposition of a rural-urban dual system by means of institutional barriers and political control was intended to achieve what in developing capitalistic market economies would be accomplished by the dual economy. These institutional instruments and mechanisms, which can be summarized in terms of the agricultural contributions to industrialization, and the core point of which was the scissors' gap, were far from perfect. In practice, capacity problems emerged which could not be solved properly by the political system, prompting crises and policy measures which were regarded as repressive (especially the policy of sending school leavers to the countryside). The stagnation of the planned economy system became intractable, and reforms were started, which gradually changed the institutions so that new, non-plan, sectors in the economy were encouraged and grew strong. The main reason for the rapid growth of these new sectors was that the extant barriers in the economy only changed gradually and created an economic asymmetry favourable to them.

From this perspective, institutional change and its effects are of special significance here. In the following I shall discuss in more detail how the triangle, institutional change → social change → labour transition, interact during the reform process.

LABOUR AND THE SOCIAL FRAMEWORK

The role of guanxi

Guanxi in the economy. Guanxi is a term used to describe the Chinese version of patron-client relationships. Jean C. Oi, in her book *State and peasant in contemporary China* (Oi 1989), has convincingly argued that clientelism is an integral function of the Chinese economy of scarcity, and especially because the allocation of goods and services is in the hands of individuals. Clientelism, as discussed by Andrew G. Walder in his book *Communist neo-traditionalism. Work and authority in Chinese industry* (Walder 1986), to a large extent shapes the life of the Chinese workers. Clientelism is an inseparable part of the Chinese political economy. Let us take a look at the evolution of the concept in the Chinese labour 'market'.

How has the reform process impinged upon and changed clientelist relationships? How has clientelism shaped the reform process? Clientelism is an evasive and complex concept, and changes in its manifestation are difficult to discern.[19] However, it is possible to make some general statements that show a significant change over time.

The situation for rural labour has changed fundamentally. Oi describes how, under the people's commune system, rural cadres controlled the allocation of food grain and cash incomes, and how they were brokering between the state and the peasants in all aspects of life. The peasants, accordingly, depended upon their immediate leaders in firm patron-client relationships which were

187

sustained by the formal, economic structures of the people's communes. After the rural reforms started the firm grip of the cadres vanished, and the patron-client relationships changed. Due to the lack of experience of some peasants, they would seek the patronage of cadres to help them with market contacts. The limited allocation of production factors at differential prices generated yet other patronage bonds, while cadres also monopolized licensing of economic activities. There was, therefore very fertile ground for the evolution of *guanxi*.

There is a case for arguing that *guanxi* became increasingly important during the reforms. The reforms implied the co-existence of several price systems, i.e. fixed, subsidized prices for commodities on allocation quotas; official, variable, so-called 'negotiated' prices with fixed ceilings for goods delivered by state trading authorities outside plan quotas (however in reality sometimes as a part of plan quotas); free market prices and (in the case of restricted goods) black market prices. Buying and selling in this type of market, characterized by local and temporary shortages, speculation by officials, and few predictors of future changes, is very cumbersome and risky. One way of solving the problem for farmers and rural entrepreneurs would be to utilize their clientelist links to obtain preferential treatment, or to avoid paying bribes. For the great majority of the economically active in the countryside there was a direct and urgent need for asserting *guanxi* relationships.

Guanxi can help beat corruption in the sense that corruption reflects the appropriation by a power holder of the difference between the fixed price and the scarcity price for his or her own purposes in an impersonal market. *Guanxi* reflects a long-term relationship of mutual exchange; the transactions are based on the access to the power of allocation. The immediate object for exchange is not expressed or thought of in terms of money, but in terms of influence and power. The reciprocity and long-termism of *guanxi* means that the transfiguration of economic market exchange into power-based brokering could create stability. Since *guanxi*-based exchange is normally not calculated in exact amounts and does not necessarily imply immediate and direct recompense it is a more logical and useful way to exchange goods, favours, services than the market. Buying and selling large equipment, finding employment, obtaining licences, finding suitable workers, obtaining credit, getting hold of technical or market information, buying chemical fertiliser or other production factors came to be part of a larger *guanxi* exchange, rather than a straightforward market economy. The logic is that it is difficult, if not impossible to set the price of obtaining a job. Even if a bribe was required by a cadre, it was necessary to approach him or her through *guanxi* to achieve the goal. Purchase of large equipment, like lorries, was virtually impossible if one had not got *guanxi* relations who could help.[20]

The scarcity of specific goods that developed due to the dual or triple pricing systems led to great price hikes and uncertainty (for examples see

Sicular 1988; Christiansen 1992a, pp. 24–28). In this situation *guanxi* could stabilize the production environment for private enterprise and create a cohesiveness within the communities and across the communities. I will cite two examples. A peasant entrepreneur near Nanjing intended to buy a lorry in 1987. He used a family relation in a bank to raise credit, and approached the owner of the wanted lorry through a *guanxi* who acted as a middleman. In himself, he was a locally powerful person and he was certainly capable of 'paying back' in favours. For some permissions, however, he was either forced to pay bribes or to create a 'package deal' through middlemen, by which he could claim *guanxi* with the corrupt officials. Another case is the way in which non-local workers for rural industries in a township near Wuxi were hired. All had been introduced through *guanxi* or family relations.

To sum up, the existence of a market place and even a black market does not imply that it is governed by economic market forces. The market exists, many transactions are between total strangers or between people who would never contemplate *guanxi* relations with each other, but a very significant part of what superficially seem to be purely economic market transactions has an underlying structure of *guanxi* relationships.

Guanxi, rural labour and rural-urban migration. The consequences of this for the rural labour market are huge. When the people's communes were disbanded and replaced by townships, existing rural enterprises were made independent. While still collectively owned and formally governed by the villagers' committees and the township governments, they were autonomous in terms of remuneration and employment of labourers. The employment of new workers became a matter of bargaining with the enterprise director rather than influencing the overall distribution of work within the brigades and communes. The use of *guanxi* relationships became strongly manifest in employment in rural collective enterprises.

The private, so-called 'individual' enterprises that developed rapidly in the early 1980s had an employment structure that was bound together by *guanxi* considerations. Apart from the fact that many individual enterprises were pure family businesses, employment became a way of cementing *guanxi* relationships.[21] Especially individual enterprises in the transport sector and in other sectors that required access to resources in other villages, or even in other counties or provinces, recruited non-locals who could supply the proper links.

An important outlet for rural labour during the 1980s were the construction squads hired in by urban enterprises to undertake construction. The urban labour bureaux and the office of public security which were in charge of labour allocation and the management of the household registration were reluctant to allow a further expansion of the urban work force. The sudden demands for unskilled construction labour in the cities in the late 1970s and early 1980s were covered by temporary (*lingshigong*) or contract (*hetonggong*) workers, often referred to as 'peasant workers' (*nongmingong*). The urban state-owned enterprises would let a people's commune put together a squad with a foreman. Recruitment to such squads was based on *guanxi* links centred around the foreman. Other migrant workers would move even more freely to the cities. These included nannies and personnel in urban individual enterprises. Some would not be registered as migrant workers, but most would obtain a temporary permit to stay in the cities. Conversations with many such workers revealed that their long-distance migration was meant to be temporary, that it was based on introduction through contacts, and that the job in itself was seen as a valuable asset (apart from the income) because it created a resourceful *guanxi*-status of the worker vis-à-vis the members of his or her community of origin.

Rural-urban migration after 1978 increasingly reflects the economic disparity between the countryside and the cities. Higher incomes to be gained in the cities formed a significant incentive for peasants to migrate. In some sectors, especially among peasant traders and artisans, longer and shorter stays in the cities could be profitable, and they would operate in a market that did not base itself on *guanxi* networks. These types of rural-urban migration, however, did not reflect the hope of obtaining permanent, legal residence in the cities and access to the perks and benefits of urban workers. They were targeted at activities that by opportunity cost calculations (encompassing both money and *guanxi* aspects) would be profitable for the migrants, and many of them filled niches that could not structurally be covered within the formal frameworks of urban employment.

There do not exist any sufficient statistics on rural-urban migration. Estimates of a 'floating population' between 30 and 50 million have been made. On a registered urban population in 1987 of 212, 682,730 (non-agricultural population) or 261,114, 269 (total urban population) this is indeed a significant number. However, it should not lead us to hasty comparisons with Third World 'rush-to-the-city' phenomena. Migration in China is not mainly based on an *assumption* of a larger income potential in the cities, as suggested by Todaro. Most migrants are sure to be employed, through *guanxi* connections, on arrival in the cities, and they therefore belong to what would from Todaro's point of view be the workforce in the urban sector. The fact that they were not registered as such has to do with institutional barriers, not with their actual function. The persistence of these institutional barriers (household registration system, labour allocation system, etc.) at the same time as opportunities for rural-urban migration were opened up, made limited migration feasible, while upsetting existing urban structures as little as possible. The distorted economic relations arising from these barriers shaped the form of the migration to the effect that *guanxi* became a main regulating factor which modified the pure economic incentives to migrate. Todaro's observation about migration from the countryside to a saturated urban labour market was in principle correct in the case of China. However, the saturation of the urban labour market was identical to structural overstaffing of enterprises due to institutional barriers and distorted economic relations, while large niches of manufacturing, construction and service trades in the urban areas were not developed within the formal structures inherent to these institutional barriers. Therefore, there was in reality a large residual, unsaturated labour market in the cities.

On several occasions this pattern has been broken, and a considerable overcrowding of the urban 'unofficial' labour market occurred in some large cities. The main occasions were when state retrenchment campaigns suddenly led to the shedding of peasant construction workers in the cities, and during migration waves spurred by poor economic performance in the countryside. The latter is traditional and has occurred less frequently in the years after the reforms started. The former has consistently reflected a temporary capacity problem, solved by sending the workers back to the country and increasing the policing activities.

The incidents where small and large towns in Guangdong and Hainan were invaded by job seekers during the Chinese New Year holidays were more in line with Todaro's predictions. Guangdong's economy is more open than in the northern provinces and most of the institutional barriers have been abandoned.

Guanxi and urban labour. In the urban economy *guanxi* also performs a significant role. The workers in state-owned and collective urban enterprises have the security of life-long tenure. Their social life is centred around their work unit, and that means that their individual interest is mediated through *guanxi* relationships (Walder 1986; Hebel 1990; Hebel and Schucher 1991). The main concepts of this dependence of urban workers on their work unit are general knowledge, and will not be discussed here.

The new 'individual' urban sector, however, transformed the notion of *guanxi*. Like the rural individual sector, it depended on the existence of distorted price relations, deficient markets and the persistence of the command economy. Although those who registered as 'individual households' could not at the same time be employed in state or collective enterprises, they did hire employees from such enterprises. These would only use their work unit for basic wage income, social perks and benefits, housing and social environment, but would be fully active in the private sector. In this way society – in the form of state-owned enterprises – contributed with a large subsidy to this sector. Unskilled, very cheap labour could be imported from the country-side. While these rural workers would not enjoy social benefits in the city, they would enjoy formal rights in their place of origin.

The main lubricant in these urban markets was *guanxi*, helped by money. The distorted price relations of course generated speculation and corruption, but the mechanisms of *guanxi* seem to have limited their impact.

In conclusion, the question of how clientelism has shaped the reform process can probably best be answered with the answer that it has restrained the introduction of market forces. It has been of great importance for solving the problems of the persistence of irrational institutional structures. It has been possible to gradually shift from one type of allocation of goods and services to another without creating huge bottlenecks in the economy.

Marriage, family cycles and labour

From the point of view of individual people, choice and opportunity are precariously related. Labour opportunities are drastically different from generation to generation. In this section I will try to examine how the reforms have affected different families differently, and how transient social structures and norms affected the realization of the reform policies.[22]

I suggest that a mixture of (a) the cyclical evolution of families, and (b) gradual, long term shifts in the socio-economic significance of families both had a decisive influence on the course of the reforms. Families in Han Chinese communities in China are formed according to social norms and rules which only change gradually, and which seem to be broadly uniform. Although there may be differences among different social groups and regions, the fundamental conventions may for the sake of the argument be regarded as uniform. This uniformity in patterns (e.g. patrilocal marriage, boy preference, monogamy, female participation in labour outside the home, care for the elderly vested in the family, partial division of family property at the eldest son's marriage, marriage age, almost universal matrimony) causes infinite numbers of diverse forms of families to occur. This diversity is caused by the natural factors that influence family structures, e.g. death, birth, childlessness, lack of sons, as well as social and institutional circumstances and economic resources which influence the division of families.

An additional factor is that individual families change in income and composition over time. This means that the socio-economic changes of the post 1978 reforms, especially the labour transition, must be viewed in the context of the underlying dynamics of individual families. To put it differently, the opportunities, choices and reaction patterns of the individual during the reforms were determined by the dynamics of the family structures. In this way it is possible to explain why economic incentives may have a limited effect, and why seemingly irrational practices proliferate. It is also possible to explain

– at least in part – why the reforms led to social stratification in what had been a relatively egalitarian society.

This discussion will mainly focus on rural families. The major framework for the Chinese family pattern of today is based on the socialist policies of the 1950s, including the stipulations of the Marriage Law and the practices of the rural cooperativization and collectivization. The monogamic family with female participation in external labour, the family as a reproduction unit rather than a production unit, the patrilocal marriage pattern, the pronatalism, the son preference and the care for the elderly in the families are all directly attributable to the social systems created during the 1950s. The state and the Chinese Communist Party shaped the general parameters for family life. I shall not discuss all these aspects in detail, but refer to them in passing. Production was taken out of the control of the families during collectivization, and women were declared an important source of labour. The distribution systems imposed in the people's communes forced women to participate in labour. The distribution systems and the divorce of production and reproduction created incentives for bearing many children, i.e. the system was *pro-natal*. The household registration system made it impossible for a man to move from one village to another, even in the case of marriage. Hence, if the bride was not from the same village or commune, she would join the husband and his family; this patri-localism and the lack of sufficient and dignified social relief schemes placed the responsibility for the care of the elderly on their son(s). This again led to son preference and discrimination against daughters.

The ownership structures of teams, brigades and communes were based on collective work administration and collective distribution. When the commune system was abandoned in the period 1978–1983, collective work administration and distribution ceased to exist. The assets (land, equipment) were divided amongst the households, mainly to the labouring members of the community. Some types of production were transferred to *specialized households*, generally on favourable contracts. Large production lines in rural industries remained collective property, albeit as economically independent units. At the same time, members were encouraged to establish private (so-called *individual*) enterprises. The reforms, in other words, abruptly re-instituted the family as a productive unit. Apart from land and equipment, the most important asset of the family was its internal structure, which determined its ability to respond to the new situation.

The ability to acquire specialized household status depended on skills, and sufficient labourers in the family to enter a production contract. In agriculture and agriculture-related production fish ponds, vegetable fields, pig-farms, orchards and tea-fields were typical productions which were organized in specialized households on contract. Due to the price policies for grain, oilseed, cotton and similar products, a family would normally not be able to suffice with the basic allocation of land, and additional income had to be sought in other types of production. Specialized households had a higher profit margin and could gain higher incomes. However, only a small number of commune members were able to win these contracts. The distribution of contracts no doubt was based on local power relations. I have noticed in my own field studies that many successful specialized households were nominally run by the elderly parents of local cadres.[23]

The main criterion for a family's ability to respond to the new situation was the availability of persons able to take up non-agricultural pursuits either in rural collective enterprises, as individual entrepreneurs or as employees in individual enterprises. Below I give some typified descriptions of strategies that families could pursue.

(a) Some families had the combination of skills and available labourers (aged between 16 and 60), as well as *guanxi* to acquire large means of production. They could set up individual enterprises at a time when the assets were undervalued and the market rapidly expanding. Their profit margin was very high.

(b) Most families did not have the ability to set up individual enterprises. Normally, this was due to lack of sufficient savings or access to credit, combined with lack of specialized skills and/or lack of available labourers in the family. Their main strategy was to secure employment in collective enterprises for as many as possible of the family members, or alternatively in individual enterprises run by other families. Adolescents would start work at 15 or 16 years of age, but in some families the economic pressure was so great that even younger children were put to work. The patrilocal marriage pattern and the reliance on sons for the care of the elderly forced these families into a certain pattern of management. The main objective was to secure a good marriage for in the first instance the eldest son. In order to achieve this, they had to provide him with a house or a separate suite in the parental house, a large number of durable consumer goods and a wedding party. Failure to do so would mean that he could not marry, that he would marry late or marry a deficient woman (old, unattractive or lacking skills). Consequently, all family savings would go into construction and consumption expenditure rather than productive investment.[24] The incomes of younger brothers and of sisters would be used to this end.

This expenditure pattern created a market for construction and rural services and thereby labour opportunities in the countryside, especially in the private economy. Although most peasants would build their new houses themselves, they would need some professional help, transport, building materials and furnishings, most of which were supplied by individual entrepreneurs.

(c) Those who lacked the capacity to slot into the profitable parts of the rural economy, especially as entrepreneurs or wage-earners, were in a poor position. Lack of skills and/or an adverse age structure in the family could mean that the family experienced rapid decline.

These generalizations, of course, cannot reflect all individual cases, but can give an impressions of the dynamics at work in Chinese family structures. Families with two working parents in the 40s and a married son of 22–24, daughter-in-law of 20–22 and a daughter of above 16 in 1983 would in theory be able to react most successfully to the reforms, especially if the parents had a technical or administrative function in local leadership or a local enterprise, and their children had passed the lower middle school exam. All members of the family would be able to work, the parent's old age would be secured by the son's marriage, no funds would have to be set aside for marriage, the income of the daughter would be available for 4–5 years before her marriage, and during the first boom year the daughter-in-law would be able to work before having the first child.

Families with many dependents not of working age, or with a weak adult labourer, were poised for social decline in the early 1980s. Unmarried sons older than 11 or 12 years of age would be a liability for any family, since a considerable part of the family's savings would be set aside for their marriages. However, lack of sons to support parents in old age also created grim perspectives for families.

The house and durable consumer goods normally were for the exclusive use of the married couple. Since the practice in the reform era forced the value of these assets up, they would become a very substantial part of the average family property. The traditional role of the 'pater familias' as the one who controls assets, family expenditure and has the prime right to commandeer family members' incomes for common family purposes, was thus qualified by his limited access to the nuptial assets of his married sons (which is part of his 'contract' with his daughter-in-law's parents). The drastic increase in the relative value of nuptial assets during the reforms undermined the father's dominant role and gave the young generation increasing economic independence.[25]

Although the people's commune system had not been totally egalitarian, especially with regard to the individual's ability to command collective resources, it had created a basic safety net for all members. The reforms divided the communities arbitrarily and exacerbated the demographic and social differences between families.

The cyclical changes in family composition may, in the long perspective, give disfavoured families new advantages, and the fortune of families now well off may within a decade turn bad. However, the fundamental conditions changed in the 1980s, prompting a type of class division that had not existed for three decades. Sudden, new and extraordinary opportunities which were induced by the wider socio-economic framework between 1980 and 1985 gave some families disproportionate advantages, and the fundamental structures of the rural economy were altered so that a class division based on property rights emerged. The process of class division in rural China in the early 1980s was thus determined by a mixture of institutional, economic and social circumstances.

The distribution of assets and occupational opportunities did initially favour local elites, but demographic dynamics in the families had a great impact. While it may superficially seem that peasant choice became greater with the reforms, it is clear from my exposition above that choice was quite limited. Depending on the individual's situation and the demographic structure of his or her family there were only a few options open. The social environment would force most people into specific preferences. What has appeared to outside observers as extravagant, irresponsible squandering of capital on rural housing and purchase of durable consumer goods, is for the individual peasant family not a real choice between investment in luxury or production, or even between a reasonable standard of living and prudent saving or investment.

The social practice of house-building and purchase of durable consumer goods was aimed at attaining long-term stability for the family in a changing economic environment. Securing a spouse for the sons was a rational step, and the only way of doing so was to use family savings on houses and consumer goods. The 'price' of a son's marriage in the places I examined in 1987 was generally between 7,000 and 15,000 RMB, equivalent to between six and 12 times the total income a skilled male worker of 18 could expect to earn in rural industry during the whole of 1987. Young people were, in other words, forced by social circumstances to seek employment in rural enterprises, be it collective or private. Agriculture did not pose itself as a sufficient source of income. Migration seemed to be an option, but only in as far better conditions could be expected; parents would very likely oppose migration if they felt that their old age livelihood were endangered.

Which preliminary conclusions can be drawn from this? The distribution of incomes was changed due to the ownership shift introduced by the reforms. The surpluses of rural enterprises, which had earlier been ploughed back into agriculture and been part of the general distribution of incomes, became direct cash incomes for the workers in these enterprises. The expenditure patterns changed, so that rural service, transport and construction trades expanded their markets rapidly, and the market for durable consumer goods grew. The direct effects were (a) new opportunities for individual entrepreneurs to achieve very high turnover and large profits; (b) creation of new job opportunities in the countryside; (c) expansion of rural markets for urban products from the consumer goods sector. The emergence of 'new' inequalities and the evolution of specific social patterns are essential for explaining the sources of growth in the Chinese countryside. One can only guess that the development would have taken a different path if the Chinese peasants had had different value patterns with respect to marriage, old age and gender preference.

Institutional barriers and labour

One aspect that was not discussed above was the social impact of the household registration system. One of its salient features is the way it divides citizenship. Those with agricultural household registration have different rights from those who have urban resident household status. The macroeconomic significance has already been discussed: the household registration system was able to limit rural-urban migration.

The legal and institutional construction of the household registration system is:

(a) to allocate different ownership rights. The agricultural status gives the right to enjoy collective ownership of the means of production in a specific locality (defined as a team or a brigade until the 1980s and as a village since then). The urban status gives the right to employment in the state or urban collective sector and concomitant with this, pensions, cheap housing, subsidized food and fuel supplies, etc.

(b) to define place of residence. Household registration is only valid for a specific place of residence: in the countryside, a specific village; in the cities, a specific city. Change of residence can only be acquired with the permission of the Department of Public Security, either as temporary permits or permanent change. In the countryside only women who marry into a community are likely to acquire a permanent change of residence. The cities are more flexible for those who have an urban resident status; it is relatively easy to obtain change of permanent residence *downwards* along a preference continuum of cities. It is easy to leave Beijing or Shanghai for Lanzhou or Changchun, while the reverse is very difficult.

This system, of course, only functions as long as there are economic mechanisms to support it. The situation between 1957 and the mid-1980s was based on a rigid system of rationing of foodstuffs and other consumer goods, as well as the virtual state monopoly over urban employment.

As a consequence of the system, rural-urban migration was not a serious option for the individual with agricultural registration. Even temporary employment by the state only yielded marginally higher incomes, but no change in status, and thereby no urban rights. When the reforms gradually abandoned the rationing system (through the introduction of parallel markets for foodstuffs), migration became viable, and some peasants found occupation in expanding urban sectors outside the state plan. However, migration remained unattractive for most peasants; they would lose their title to collective assets at home, or would have to pay a 'labour fee' to their home township government; the comparative advantage of staying at home in an expanding economy was to be preferred above the uncertainties of migration.

However some peasants became urban residents. After several years of service, so-called peasant workers could acquire the urban status. The same applied to leaders of the people's communes, as well as to certain types of rural schoolmasters during the school reform in the 1980s. This did normally not bestow any rights on their dependents. The household registration in terms of agricultural or urban status was only inheritable in the maternal line to minor children (under 16). Most of the peasants given urban status were men. The registration, in terms of locality, however, was inheritable in the paternal line.

Some areas near large cities where urban development took place, were characterized by gradual transfer of the population from peasant to urban status. Whenever land was requisitioned by the state for development, an appropriate number of peasants would be transferred and given occupation by the state; 'peasant workers' would gradually be given urban status; various exemptions would be made from the system. These 'peri-urban communities' constituted special cases of development, and their labour force would be in a transient position. Most would have given up farming, would rely on collective and private enterprises for incomes, and would be oriented towards the city. Migrants from poorer areas would take over farming tasks on their fields. In these areas the distinction between household statuses would become socially negligible, only impinging on (a) which school children could attend; (b) choice of spouse; and (c) economically insignificant perks.

During the reforms the household status has lost much of its importance as a dividing factor. In peri-urban communities the distinction between people with agricultural and urban status is dying out, and in Shanghai, Guangdong and other rich places, this distinction has been abandoned in practical administration. What remains is the local aspect of the household registration. Migrant workers from North Jiangsu working in Wuxi or Shanghai do not have the communal rights of local residents; they obtain temporary permits and their social, educational and other aspects are governed by local regulations and/or contract stipulations.

The conclusion of this is that the limitations imposed by the household registration system forced rural labourers to seek occupation in the country-side; this promoted the development of rural non-agricultural enterprises, both those collectively owned and those privately owned. Urban enterprises wanting to expand production were not given permission to recruit new workers and were under strict town planning rules. However, some enterprises were able to retain a large investible surplus, which they invested in the countryside. They would provide machines, know-how and market outlets, while villages or townships would provide land, buildings and workers.

This type of development was only possible due to the existence of the institutional divisions. Due to the lower overhead costs (there were no expenses for pensions, medical care, and consumption subsidies in rural enter-prises), rural subsidiaries of urban enterprises were very profitable.

The gradual abandoning of the division of agricultural and urban household status can only take place because of the local aspect of the registration. The main cleavage that will persist for a long time is based on regional inequality. For this reason it is likely that the household registration system will be upheld with regard to the place of residence. The registration of the population based on residence began in the mid-1980s and many have had their identity cards issued.

CONCLUSIONS

China seems to be an exception to general assumptions regarding labour transfer. This paper has tried to demonstrate how the socialist institutions for economic development adopted in China sought to emulate the mechanisms of the (proto-)capitalistic dual economy. Labour transfer between the 'traditional' and 'modern' sectors, therefore, was based on administrative systems which were not able to react to scarcity and plenty. The institutions therefore came to reflect vested rights, and the only correctives possible were political decisions which ultimately caused popular resentment and had to be revoked for reasons of the legitimacy of the leadership.

The assumption, however, that economic growth and successful labour transfer in China during the reforms is attributable to market forces *per se* is refuted, and the point is made that only the persistence of imbalances in the economy, based on institutional boundaries, created the environment in which growth and labour transfer could take place. The mechanisms for growth in the countryside were closely linked with the family structures and institutional barriers. The 'market' element in the opening economy was that of a mechanism which reflected local scarcity and unleashed corruption, not that of market competition and realistic prices. The countervailing force which balanced this out was the changed forms of clientelism.

The implication of this is that development and especially inter-sectoral labour transfers cannot be viewed in purely economic terms. The institutional system and the social structures of the population form the framework from within which we can analyse development issues. Similarly, features that at the first glance look similar to those in other countries should not be taken out of their context. The Chinese floating population is an example of this. This concept is used vaguely by Chinese sociologists as a measure of people staying away from home, with or without temporary residence permits in the place they visit and without regard for the purpose of their stay. The criterion is their formal household registration – if someone stays in Beijing without a Beijing household registration, she or he belongs to the floating population. At the same time as there is a large floating population, there is general overstaffing of state-owned enterprises (in Chinese bureaucratic argot 'unemployment in the factory' – *changnei shiye*) and (according to official statistics) two per cent 'awaiting job allocation' (*daiye*). A careful analysis, however, should reveal that China does not fulfil the predictions by Todaro, not to speak of Lewis. Only in those cases where institutional controls are given up, like in Guangdong and Hainan, will Todaro-like phenomena occur.

The recent decisions in China to make enterprises independent, do away with central price controls, open stock markets and facilitate both domestic and foreign investment, will indeed lead to further changes in the Chinese labour system. Guangdong Province has abandoned state labour allocation, and every school leaver is supposed to find a job on his or her own. The state only supplies a backstop and some aid. In other Chinese provinces, job allocation is so much out of tune with young persons' own ambitions that they seek all possibilities to shape their own future. However, we must watch these developments cautiously and not hastily conclude that China has developed a capitalistic labour market.

NOTES

1. Government Department, The Manchester University. This chapter was published earlier in *Economy and Society*, vol. 22, no. 4 (November 1993), pp. 411–436, under the title 'The legacy of the mock dual economy: Chinese labour in transition 1978–1992'. It is reprinted here with permission, with minor modifications. The author is grateful to participants in the EADI workshop in Göttingen, 19–21 November 1992, and anonymous readers for comments on earlier versions of this work.
2. See Preobrazhensky (1965) and Saith (1985) for descriptions and analyses of accumulation for industrialization in socialist countries.
3. See Saith (1985, p. 38) who acknowledges the existence of a basic needs floor in rural China. However, the point made is not that there was no poverty in the Chinese countryside, only that the system of surplus extraction did not rely on the emergence of an exploitative rural upper class which was instrumental for the accumulation process.
4. For detailed descriptions of the household registration system, see Zhang Qingwu (1988), Christiansen (1990), and Potter (1983). Davis-Friedmann (1985) outlines the *entitlement* of urban residents to be employed by the state.

5. Chen (1972), Chan and Xu (1985, p. 597), Zhongguo Shehui Kexueyuan Renkou Yanjiu Zhongxin (1986, p. 814) all give different tabulations of the rise of the urban resident population. These statistics do not reveal the pressure on the system from young urbanites coming of age, claiming work allocation, and it is impossible to make reliable estimates of their number. In addition to the problem of entitlement, a number of menial tasks were considered unsuitable for urban residents so that large numbers of peasants were recruited for urban jobs (Chan 1987, p. 108; Taylor 1988).

6. Conservative estimates indicate that between 15 and 30 million workers in urban state-owned enterprises were superfluous in the mid 1980s (Schucher 1989, p. 328). An analysis of unemployment-underemployment is found in Jefferson and Rawski (1992).

7. According to a comparison between industrial investments in India and China, the proportion used on machines was significantly smaller in China than in India, indicating a more labour-intensive strategy. See Boillot and Lemoine (1992, pp. 74–75). It is interesting to note that low, preferential energy costs to heavy industry and higher, discriminatory energy costs to small scale and light industry enterprises (cited by Jefferson and Rawski (1992, pp. 54–55)) does *not* constitute a bias *against* labour-intensive industry, but *favours and encourages* it. Low energy costs in industries using heavy factory equipment mean that the incentive to investment in energy-saving less labour-consuming modern equipment is low. Conversely, high energy costs in labour-intensive, under-mechanized industries mean that the incentive to invest in modern, labour-saving equipment is low.

8. It is interesting to note that contrary to Saith's (1985, p. 38) description, according to which Chinese agriculture was *socialized*, the Chinese practice of surplus accumulation for industrialization was ambiguous. The state treated rural areas as an external resource base (this was possible due to the difference in ownership, by which industry was linked to the state economy, while rural production was organized in collectives); this practice resembles Preobrazhensky's (1965, p. 84) characterization of 'primitive socialist accumulation.' Socialization of Chinese agriculture, therefore, was a necessary step to create the basis for 'primitive socialist accumulation.'

9. See Chen (1972). The numbers are basically confirmed by Guojia Tongji Ju Shehui Tongji Si (1987, pp. 110–111). Apart from these 17 million there were cadres and workers sent to the countryside (Chan 1987, p. 108), as well as the transferral of cadres to 7 May cadre schools which meant a transferral of household registration to non-urban localities.

10. Guowuyuan Yanjiushe Nongcun Jingjizu (1990, p. 5). The gross agricultural product value (GAPV) per unit of land increased 314 per cent, while the GAPV per agricultural labourer grew 102 per cent.

11. This amounted to between 10 and 20 days annually per agricultural labourer in the 1960s and 1970s according to an estimate by Aubert (1991, p. 524).

12. The budget deficit in 1979 reached 17,060,000,000,000 yuan, partly due to the change in the terms of trade between the rural and urban sectors decided on by the Chinese Communist Party Central Committee in December 1978 (Zhongguo Tongji Ju 1983, p. 445).

13. See for example Zhongguo Tongji Ju (1987, p. 110).

14. See Chen Gang (1990), Zhongguo Baike Nianjian bianji bu (1981, p. 537), and Laodongbu Zhengce Fagui Si (1990, pp. 393–417). There is a brief introduction in Hebel and Schucher (1992, pp. 190–194).

15. Urban collective enterprises had existed since private enterprise was forced to amalgamate into larger collective enterprises in the mid-1950s. Large collective enterprises (so called '*jiti qiye*') were under the state plan and differed from them mainly in that the workers received a share of the profit rather than fixed salaries. From the early 1970s, however, neighbourhood industrial enterprises had become widespread, providing some outlets for urban unemployed. These enterprises were operating outside the state plan, and formed a structural precursor for labour service enterprises, and also established the background for other non-plan economic activities.

16. With the promulgation of Central Document 1 that year; see Christiansen (1989).

17. A similar point is made by Chang (1992, p. 439).

18. Theories on agriculture's contribution to industrialization on socialist economies: Merl (1990); Ellman (1975); Saith (1985); Preobrazhensky (1965). Dualism: Ranis and Fei (1961);

Putterman (1992). Economy of shortage: Kornai (1980). Comprehensive analyses of Chinese rural industrialization, incorporating some of these aspects: Guowuyuan Yanjiushe Nongcunjingjizu (1990).

19. For general descriptions of *guanxi*, see also Yang (1989) and King (1991).
20. Compare this with Oi's (1986) analysis of corrupt practices and abuse of power.
21. Bruun (1988) gives an analysis of urban individual households; see also Christiansen (1992).
22. For recent analyses of Chinese family cycles and their link to property management, see Lavely and Ren (1992) and Cohen (1992).
23. This observation is also supported by Croll (1987, p. 119).
24. See Feder et al. (1992) for a very interesting analysis of rural investment priorities. They make the point that 'relatives and friends are more inclined to lend money for purposes of housing construction and special social events (e.g. weddings) which are perceived as basic needs deserving assistance' (p. 10).
25. The practice of dividing family property *(fenjia)* normally includes the nuptial assets. However, the author's observations in households in southern Jiangsu indicate that the exclusive use of nuptial assets was guarded jealously by the married couples, and that the understanding was that these assets would ultimately become the property of the couple at the *fenjia* settlement. In many cases the division of property was already provided for in the way new housing was built, so that provision was made for accommodating younger, unmarried brothers.

REFERENCES

Aubert, Claude, 1991. 'Investissement-travail et infrastructures agricoles: Bilan et actualité des corvées en Chine', in *Revue Tiers Monde*, vol. xxxii, no. 127, pp. 512–532.

Boillot, Jean-Joseph and Françoise Lemoine, 1992. 'Le financement de l'industrialisation. Investissement, épargne, croissance' (Financing industrialization. Investment, savings, growth). In *Economie Prospective International*, no. 50, pp. 67–98.

Bruun, Ole, 'The reappearance of the family as an economic unit: A sample survey of individual households in workshop production and crafts, Chengdu, Sichuan Province, China', *Copenhagen Discussion Papers*, no. 1.

Chan, Kam Wing, 1987. 'Further information about China's urban population statistics: Old and new', in *China Quarterly*, no. 109, pp. 104–109.

Chan, Kam Wing and Xueqiang Xu, 1985. 'Urban population growth and urbanization in China since 1949: Reconstructing a baseline', in *China Quarterly*, no. 104, pp. 583–613.

Chang, Kyung-Sup, 1992. 'China's rural reform: The state and peasantry in constructing a macro-rationality', in *Economy and Society*, vol. 21, no. 4, pp. 430–452.

Chen Gang (ed.), 1990. *Zhongguo laodong fuwu gongsi*. Beijing, Nongye Chubanshe.

Chen Pi-chiao, 1972. 'Overurbanization, rustication of urban-educated youths, and politics of rural transformation', in *Comparative Politics*, April, pp. 361–386.

Christiansen, Flemming, 1989. 'The justification and legalization of private enterprises in China, 1983–1988', in *China Information*, vol. iv, no. 2, pp. 78–91.

Christiansen, Flemming, 1990. 'Social divisions and peasant mobility in Mainland China: The implications of the Hu-k'ou system', in *Issues and Studies*, vol. 26, no. 4, pp. 23–42.

Christiansen, Flemming, 1990a. *The de-rustication of the Chinese peasant? Peasant household reactions to the rural reforms in China since 1978.* Proefschrift ter verkrijging van de graad van Doctor aan de Rijsuniversiteit te Leiden. [Doctoral Thesis, Leiden].

Christiansen, Flemming, 1992. ''Market transition' in China. The case of the Jiangsu labour market', in *Modern China*, vol. 18, no. 1, pp. 72–93.

Christiansen, Flemming, 1992a. 'Stability first! Chinese rural policy issues, 1987–1990', in Eduard B. Vermeer, *From peasant to entrepreneur: Growth and change in rural China.* Papers originating from the second European Conference on agriculture and rural development in China. Wageningen, Pudoc, pp. 21–40.

Cohen, Myron L., 1992. 'Family management and family division in contemporary rural China', in *The China Quarterly*, no. 130, pp. 357–377.

Croll, Elisabeth, 1987. 'Some implications of the rural economic reforms for the Chinese peasant household', in Ashwani Saith (ed.), *The re-emergence of the Chinese peasantry. Aspects of rural decollectivisation*. London, Croom Helm, pp. 105–136.

Davis-Friedmann, Deborah, 1985. 'Inter-generational inequalities and the Chinese revolution', in *Modern China*, vol. xi, no. 2, pp. 177–201.

Ellman, M, 1975. 'Did agricultural surplus provide the resources for the increase in investment in the USSR during the first Five Year Plan?', in *The Economic Journal*.

Feder, Gershon; Lawrence J. Lau, Justin Y. Lin and Xiaopeng Luo, 1992. 'The determinants of farm investment and residential construction in post-reform China', in *Economic Development and Cultural Change*, vol. 41, no. 1, pp. 1–26.

Guowuyuan Yanjiushi Nongcun Jingjizu, 1990. 'Zhongguo xiangzhen qiye fazhan ji qi yu guomin jingji de hongguan xietiao (shang)' (The development of Chinese rural enterprise and its macroscopic coordination within the national economy (first part)), in *Zhongguo Nongcun Jingji*, no. 5, pp. 3–14.

Guowuyuan Yanjiushi Nongcunjingjizu, 1990. *Biewu Xuanze – Xiangzhen qiye yu guomin jingji de xietiao fazhan* (There is no alternative – The coordinated development of township and town enterprises and the national economy). Beijing, Gaige Chubanshe.

Hebel, Jutta, 1990. 'Der Betrieb als kleine Gesellschaft. Die Bedeutung des chinesischen Betriebstyps im Prozeß der Reform', in *Soziale Welt. Zeitschrift für sozialwissenschaftliche Forschung und Praxis*, vol. 41, no. 2, pp. 222–242.

Hebel, Jutta and Günther Schucher, 1991. 'From unit to enterprise? The Chinese *Tan-wei* in the process of reform', in *Issues and Studies*, vol. 27, no. 4, pp. 24–43.

Hebel, Jutta and Günther Schucher, 1992. *Zwischen Arbeitsplan und Arbeitsmarkt. Strukturen des Arbeitssystems in der VR China*. Hamburg, Institut für Asienkunde.

Hershkovitz, Linda, 1985. 'The fruits of ambivalence: China's individual economy', in *Pacific Affairs*, vol. liix, no. 3, pp. 430–439.

Jefferson, Gary H. and Thomas G. Rawski, 1992. 'Unemployment, underemployment, and employment policy in China's cities', in *Modern China*, vol. 18, no. 1, pp. 42–71.

King, Ambrose Yeo-chi, 1991. 'Kuan-hsi and network building: A sociological interpretation', in *Dædalus. Journal of the American Academy of Arts and Sciences*, vol. 120, no. 2, pp. 63–84.

Kornai, János, 1980. *Economics of shortage*, vols. A and B. Amsterdam, North Holland.

Laodongbu Zhengce Fagui Si, 1990. *Zhonghua Renmin Gongheguo laodong zhengce fagui quanshu*, vol. i. Changchun, Jilin Kexue Jishu Chubanshe.

Lavely, William and Xinhua Ren, 1992. 'Patrilocality and early marital co-residence in rural China, 1955–85', in *The China Quarterly*, no. 130, pp. 378–391.

Merl, Stephan, 1990. 'The role of agriculture in Soviet industrialization', in Karl-Eugen Wädekin, *Communist agriculture. Farming in the Soviet Union and Eastern Europe*. London, Routledge, pp. 3–22.

Oi, Jean C., 1986. 'Peasant households between plan and market', in *Modern China*, vol. xii, no. 2, pp. 230–251.

Oi, Jean C., 1989. *State and peasant in contemporary China. The political economy of village government*. Berkeley, University of California Press

Potter, Sulamith Heins, 1983. 'The position of peasants in modern China's social order', in *Modern China*, vol. 9, no. 4, pp. 465–499.

Preobrazhensky, E., 1965. *The new economics*. Oxford, Clarendon Press.

Putterman, Louis, 1992. 'Dualism and reform in China', in *Economic Development and Cultural Change*, vol. 40, no. 3, pp. 467–493.

Ranis, Gustav and John C. H. Fei, 1961. 'A theory of economic development', in *American Economic Review*, vol. 51, pp. 533–565.

Rosen, Stanley (ed.) 1987–88. *The private economy*, vols. i and ii. Armonk, M.E. Sharpe.

Saith, Ashwani, 1985. 'Primitive accumulation, agrarian reform and socialist transition: An argument', in Ashwani Saith (ed.), *The agrarian question in socialist transitions*. London, Frank Cass, pp. 1–48.

Schucher, Günther, 1989. 'Überschüssig – Aussortiert – Arbeitslos? Zur Reform der Arbeitsorganisation in der VR China' (Redundant – Singled out – Unemployed? On the reform of the labour organization in China), in *Internationales Asienforum*, vol. 20, no. 4–4, pp. 325–347.

Sicular, Terry, 1988. 'Agricultural planning and pricing in the post-Mao period', in *The China Quarterly*, no. 116, pp. 671–705.

Taylor, Jeffrey R., 1988. 'Rural employment trends and the legacy of surplus labour, 1978–86', in *China Quarterly*, no. 116, pp. 736–766.

Todaro, Michael P., 1969. 'A model of labour migration and urban development in less developed countries', in *American Economic Review*, vol. lix, pp. 138–148.

Todaro, Michael P., 1977. *Economic development in the Third World*. New York and London, The Longman Group Ltd.

Walder, Andrew G., 1986. *Communist neo-traditionalism. Work and authority in Chinese industry*. Berkeley, University of California Press.

Wong, Christine P. W., 1988. 'Interpreting rural industrial growth in the post-Mao period', in *Modern China*, vol. 14, no. 1, pp. 3–30.

Yang, Mayfair Mei-hui, 1989. 'The gift economy and state power in China', in *Comparative Studies in Society and History*, vol. 31, pp. 25–54.

Zhang Qingwu, 1988. *Basic facts on the household registration system*. Translated and edited by Michael Dutton. In *Chinese Economic Studies*, vol. 22, no. 1.

Zhongguo Baike Nianjian bianji bu, 1981. *Zhongguo Baike Nianjian 1981*. Beijing, Shanghai, Zhongguo Dabaike Quanshu Chubanshe.

Zhongguo Shehui Kexueyuan Renkou Yanjiu Zhongxin, 1986. *Zongguo Renkou Nianjian (1985)*. Beijing, Zhongguo Shehui Kexue Chubanshe.

Zongguo Tongji Ju, 1983. *Zhongguo Tongji Nianjian 1983* (Statistical Yearbook of China 1983). Beijing, Tongji Chubanshe.

Zhongguo Tongji Ju, 1987. *Zhongguo laodong gongzi tongji ziliao 1949–1985*. Beijing, Zhongguo Tongji Chubanshe.

9

Transitions from the Public to the Private: Different Strategies for the Labour Market in the Transforming Chinese and Hungarian Economies

FLEMMING CHRISTIANSEN and KLÁRÁ FÓTI[1]

What happens to the labour market when the transforming socialist economy heads in the direction of privatization? While there is clear evidence from Central and Eastern Europe that unemployment, a feeling of relative deprivation and social instability may emerge, a general assumption to this effect is not suitable. The question can only be faced adequately with a proper political economy analysis of the institutions of change.[2]

The institutions of different socialist economies may in name and professed function have shared similarities (which countries in the 'communist bloc' did not have planning commissions, public ownership and almost identical state-controlled foreign exchange mechanisms?), but the vast differences in the economic performance and the political economy of these countries cause aggregate statements to be of limited value. Policy options and policy choices have been infinitely diverse, so generalizations and straightforward comparisons seem helplessly doomed. The trajectories from the socialist command economy to the market economy hardly bear any resemblance to one another. Even if the 'capitalist' or 'market economy' are supposed (by some) to be governed by converging and equilibrating forces which iron out institutional differences, the institutions bequeathed by the communist *anciens régimes* have diverging outcomes in the various economies. This especially holds true where the size, endowments, historical and cultural heritage, and other features show distinct differences. By comparing China and Hungary, we are, therefore, able to present a particularly accentuated example of structural diversity, which would presumably not be as obvious if we were to compare two countries from Eastern Europe with each other.

Our endeavour here, then, is to explore the institutional diversity within which transforming socialist states seek to disengage themselves from the role of 'commanders' in the economy, looking at the unique labour market structures which emerge in the two countries – China and Hungary – we are studying. China, with its reforms starting in 1978, has attempted to emulate the Hungarian pattern of reform which had been introduced ten years earlier, in 1968.[3] However, apart from the obvious differences in size, population, endowments, history and culture, *the institutional diversities* between them have caused important differences to arise in the courses and results of the reforms in the two countries. Their positioning in relation to and the fundamental changes in the international economic and political environment are also major factors in explaining domestic developments, and thereby the differences between Hungary and China. International factors influenced the Hungarian reforms more immediately and obviously.

While China's reforms have progressed in a relatively orderly fashion, the Hungarian reform process suffered set-backs caused by economic and political constraints, partly emanating from Hungary's international commitments as an integral member of COMECON and the Warsaw Pact. Although the Chinese Communist Party is firmly in the driving seat, the country has embraced a 'socialist market economy', which some would describe as proto-capitalist. China has virtually disbanded central state planning, and is presently making its state-owned enterprises autonomous; in this respect the Chinese achievements resemble the main aims of the Hungarian reform in 1968. In 1968, the Hungarian reformers presumed that central planning could be abolished and enterprises could be independent without a fundamental transformation of the economy into a market economy. Now, following the collapse of the communist system, Hungary has, together with its Eastern European neighbours, openly embarked on the transition to a Western type market economy – unlike the Chinese case, not qualified by the adjective 'socialist'.

SOME REFLECTIONS ON PRIVATIZATION AND LABOUR

In both countries transition from a planned to a market economy implies privatization on a massive scale. The term privatization can only be understood in the concrete political economic environment to which it refers. Privatization in Western Europe may seem simple to describe, basically as selling part or all of the shares of an enterprise on the stock market (like British Telecom in Great Britain) or selling the assets of an enterprise to an individual or a legal person (like most of the former GDR enterprises handled by the Treuhandanstalt in Germany). These types of procedures presume (a) the existence of established enterprise forms, financial markets and legal frameworks which can absorb yet another private enterprise; and (b) sufficiently complex social and labour policy environments (redundancy procedures, unemployment benefits, social security, public health institutions,

pension schemes etc.) in order to function. A workable concept of privatization, therefore, does not merely encompass the transfer of juridical ownership,
but incorporates its political and economic environment.

Socialist economies did not normally include financial markets, did not
have an extant sea of private enterprises into which new ones could be
floated, and did not have social policy frameworks. The absence of the latter
has had important consequences, particularly in the Chinese case, as will be
evident from the discussion below.

Privatization in the context of reforming socialist economies has a different
significance. In general terms, the reforming socialist economies did not have
institutions and frameworks like stock markets, or legal structures for protect-
ing and recognizing private ownership or for allowing private management.
Neither did there exist suitable social security and labour market institutions.
While socialist states, in general, did supply job security, social insurance and
public health services, in China the very way in which these were organized
constituted a major obstacle to enterprise privatization.

The above considerations indicate our broad use of the term privatization in
this contribution. We find it necessary to examine the whole process of private
sector expansion, and so include not only the sale of state assets, but also the
legal and economic circumstances and prerequisites which govern individuals'
investments. What really matters, and this is our focus, is the development of
economic activities which are not directly controlled by the state authorities.
From within this conceptual framework it should be possible to capture the
main processes in economies as diverse as China and Hungary.

Similar problems arise with respect to the measurement of the labour
market. The parameters used to understand and monitor the functioning of the
system are part and parcel of the system. Even the existence or non-existence
of open unemployment is closely linked to the specific way a nation's
economy is organized. In this sense, unemployment can be regarded as an
essentially political notion. Therefore, a straightforward, quantitative comparison of the Chinese and Hungarian labour markets (e.g. the unemployment
rate) is out of the question.

The Chinese do have a rate of 'people awaiting work allocation' (*daiye
renshi*), which is about two per cent of the urban work force. However, this
figure does not represent unemployment as such, it only represents the
number of people whose files (*dang'an*) are temporarily placed with the
labour bureaux. School leavers with an entitlement to job allocation will
normally have to wait for placement. When they are given a job, their file is
passed on to the receiving work unit.[4] If they are discharged from the labour
system because they obtain private employment or start an individual enterprise, their file is taken out of circulation and is not counted. Since there is no
national provision for unemployment benefit, official unemployment rates are

not available. The ways in which redundancies are handled also mean that people are not normally sacked from their work, but that there is so called 'unemployment in the factory' (*changnei shiye*), i.e. a high level of over-staffing in enterprises, even to the extent that people are asked not to turn up at work, but receive their basic salary and minimal entitlements from their employer. About half of the workforce in non-agricultural pursuits are in rural enterprises and are not state employees. The (potential) unemployment of this group is not recorded; since the workers belong to the rural workforce, they are by default 'cultivators' (*zhongdi* or *zhongtian*), and as such can never be officially considered unemployed whatever their real situation may be.

In Hungary, job allocation existed only in the early years of the communist era (mainly in the 1950s), and the state did not interfere directly in the labour market later. However, overstaffing (termed 'unemployment within the factory gates') was a well-known phenomenon throughout the period of communist rule, and in this way full employment was attained. At the same time acute labour shortages characterized the economy.

It is remarkable that although presently hidden unemployment is replaced by open joblessness, overstaffing persists in Hungary, much as in the case of China. Some industries, faced with drastic falls in orders, let employees work part-time or force them onto temporary leave.

A glance at this situation should be enough to satisfy us that there is no point in wanting to establish universal definitions of unemployment for the purpose of comparison, let alone to use superficially similar statistics to draw conclusions. The only reliable procedure is to examine the trajectory of institution-building in the labour system or market during the reform process, to highlight the dynamics.

While the above observations may seem self-evident to the degree of being banal, the actual studies of China's and Hungary's institutional develop-ment during the reform processes may yield some useful comparisons and conclusions.

THE CASES: CHINA AND HUNGARY

Hungary: The reform in 1968 and its effects. Concept and reality

The 1968 reform in Hungary, called the New Economic Mechanism, was followed by a series of set-backs. The main question which we want to address in this contribution is to what extent the original concept could be realized: What did the abolition of central planning and the rise of independent enter-prises mean in practice?

The declared main objective of the 1968 reform was to decentralize decision making, transferring it from central authorities to firms. Once independent, they could become more responsive to demand, and their performance would be clearly measured by their profit. However, since market entry and exit still remained very limited, firms were not under pressure to adapt to changing market requirements. New competitors did not emerge, and firms had no fear of bankruptcy. As a consequence, the whole highly monopolistic industrial structure did not basically change. Although tight, direct control in the form of plan directives had been abolished, the positive implications of market relations, such as competition, were not re-established. Central bureaucracy (in its basic structure) and monopolistic giant public firms remained in place, and without a proper market selection mechanism the former's intervening function of resource allocation was also left virtually unchallenged despite the original intention of the reform concept. However, as decision-making was transferred to firms, a wide scope for bilateral bargaining between the centre and the enterprises was enabled, substituting for both plan and market coordination, as well as discipline. This bargaining process was facilitated by patronage relationships between managers and high-ranking party officials.

These features indicate why this type of control resulting from the reforms came to be considered as *market simulation*. The very inconsistency of the market relations that were introduced came to be identified as the main reason for the reform's eventual failure.

The reformers in Hungary, however, were cautious because they anticipated that drastic strides towards a market economy would probably entail massive unemployment. Some estimates made at the time suggested that about 500,000 people could lose their jobs, equivalent to an unemployment rate of about ten per cent. Full employment being one of the main pillars of the socialist system, unemployment would have been politically unacceptable.

Despite flaws in the reform concept and later set-backs, the introduction of the New Economic Mechanism and the publicity given to the concept itself undoubtedly contributed to the introduction of some market elements within the economy, not least in the expansion of a 'Second Economy'[5] which is of major significance for the evolution of the labour market. The non-state sector not only took root in the economy, but also greatly influenced the labour market and the attitude of labourers in the 'First Economy'.

Hungary: Characteristics of the Second Economy

From the reform of 1968 until the collapse of communist rule the Hungarian economy was characterized by an expanding second economy. Its expansion reflects the ambivalence of all reform attempts towards the market during the period of communist rule.

Although central planning was abolished, bureaucratic coordination in the 'socialist sector' (i.e. the first economy) was not totally lifted. This sector fought a permanent struggle with inherent production problems, including lack of supplies, low performance and loose labour discipline. The more liberal atmosphere created by the reforms caused the second economy to flourish, easing some of the problems of the first economy. It, among other things, filled the niches where the 'socialist sector' was unable to be present.

During the periods of set-backs, especially in the early 1970s, the state authorities sought to impose some restrictions on the second economy. But in the wake of the two oil price explosions, which adversely affected the Hungarian economy,[6] the export commitments inevitably increased, heralding further shortages in the domestic market. By the early 1980s, Hungary's external position had further deteriorated (besides trade problems, foreign indebtedness had also grown). At the same time, the budget deficit had expanded, partly as a result of massive subsidies to several highly inefficient giant state enterprises. Under these pressures another major reform was launched – a decentralization campaign aimed at devolving the 'socialist sector' to make it more efficient.[7] At this time, the authorities eventually acknowledged that the second sector was indispensable. There were even high expectations attached to it. According to the original ideas held by economic decision-makers, the second economy would be capable of easing supply bottlenecks due to its small scale, its flexibility of organization and its complementary nature, which meant that it could provide a background industry to the giant state firms. In addition, living standards had started declining after a rise during the 1970s, real wages fell, and the economy stagnated. The non-state sector was expected not only to boost the economy, but also to provide (at least) supplementary income to people, which could off-set the fall in real wages.

The authorities tried to encourage the second economy by permitting the founding of small private enterprises, lifting existing restrictions, and legalizing activities of the second economy which had been illegal.[8] Thus the legislation enacted in 1982 created the possibility of setting up various 'new entrepreneurial forms', including entrepreneurial work teams (VGMKs) within socialist enterprises. The VGMKs were private partnerships consisting of workers of an enterprise, who subcontracted particular jobs. The work (which was either the worker's regular job or production of something different) was overtime work and paid at a much higher rate than in regular working hours.[9] The fact that the central wage regulations did not apply to these partnerships made the higher remuneration possible.[10] Numerous case studies have documented that the work organization of the VGMKs was much more efficient than during regular hours, obviously partly due to the incentives. As the case studies (e. g. Kóvári and Sziráczki 1985; Stark 1989) indicate, only the best workers were selected to become members of VGMKs, and the bureaucratic rules of the first economy did not apply to them, so instead of the rigid hierarchy, close cooperation characterized the relationship between the workers.

With the help of the VGMKs, the socialist enterprises were enabled to deploy their capacities more efficiently than before. Therefore, by setting up VGMKs they could overcome their most pressing problem, which was the acute shortage of labour.[11] Before the legislation made it possible to establish VGMKs, the tasks had often been awarded to outside contractors who had carried out the work at much higher prices (the outside contractors were in a 'monopolistic' position because the Hungarian background industry was underdeveloped) and they were obviously more inflexible than in-house work teams.[12]

Due to the fact that even the socialist enterprise became increasingly cost-sensitive[13] during the 1980s, from the point of view of the enterprise management it was often profit-maximization which was the main motive for setting up VGMKs.

It is therefore not surprising that these teams were by far the most popular of the new 'entrepreneurial forms'. In the early 1980s they, together with similar specialist teams operating in the cooperatives, employed 79 per cent of all staff in the new 'entrepreneurial forms'.[14]

Despite the fact that VGMKs totally relied on labour, equipment and machinery of the given socialist firm, they could not be regarded as an integral part of the enterprise. Neither could they be regarded as autonomous private enterprises. They were rather semi-autonomous units *within* the state firms. Accordingly, their participants did not fulfil the criteria of an entre-preneur, but remained employees.

In contrast, the other, less popular new 'entrepreneurial forms' like the 'business work partnerships' (GMKs), which were set up in the 1980s, remained autonomous, even though the majority subcontracted to state enter-prises. Most of them, however, were under pressure to rely on subcontracting due to lack of their own capital and lack of access to credit (this is why only small enterprises with small investment requirements emerged), and because they had virtually no independent access to machinery, equipment and raw materials. Leasing arrangements did not exist due to lack of proper institu-tions. Laky (1984) has claimed that labour was the only factor to which these small enterprises had an equal access. This seems to be true, although the small enterprises could not compete with the state firms in granting social pro-visions, a point which is offset by the much higher wages, as high as those paid by VGMKs.

The main reason why the second economy as a whole paid higher wages was the fact that central wage regulations were not enforced there. The effect of this on the state sector was negative. While higher incentives made people work harder in the non-state sector, labour discipline continued to plummet in the first economy. What could be termed a 'labour market segmentation' between the participants and the non-participants in the second economy emerged[15] and created tensions.

Despite the much higher remuneration in the non-state sector, most people kept their full-time job in the first economy and worked part time in the second sector. When some of the second economy activities were illegal, this was understandable, but why did this attitude persist *after* the introduction of liberal measures in the early 1980s? People felt more secure in their first economy job. They maintained a small, but guaranteed income, whereas the second economy was riddled with uncertainties. Some social provisions, including child care and recreational and health facilities, were only linked to the first economy job. This situation bears, as we shall discuss below, some similarity to the dilemmas facing Chinese families.

The initial expectations towards the second economy were only partly fulfilled. Although in many cases it proved able to ease shortages in goods and services, it has never provided a background industry (let alone a network of suppliers) to the socialist sector. The reason to some extent resembles the origin of the failure of the 1968 reform. Market entry remained restricted, and in the case of the state-owned enterprises exit was out of the question. The second economy was by no means sufficient to 'release the brakes'[16] in the existing monopolistic, highly centralized industrial structure, which was basically structured as a planned economy. Its failure to accumulate capital especially bears witness to this.

Gábor and Galasi (1985) are right in saying that the principles under which the two sectors operated separated the state and the economy and brought about duality in the economy. This caused a conflicting relationship between them throughout the period of communist rule. An example of this is the wage differential between the two sectors, which Kornai (1989) characterizes as a 'hidden cost of bureaucratic regulation'. This formulation can be extended in the sense that the wage differential, due to the encouragement of the second economy in 1982, became the hidden cost of economic duality.

Hungary: The second economy in transition. Does it have a raison d'être?

It was widely expected by both politicians and prominent economists in Hungary that the transition would be easier than in other countries in the region, where the reforms had difficulty in taking root, due to the fact that Hungary had gained more market experience. However, Hungary at the moment faces difficulties similar to those in other Eastern European countries, especially the other 'early starters', the Czech Republic and Poland, and does not appear to have progressed further than these countries.

There are several reasons for this. The successive reform attempts aimed at introducing more and more market relations into the economy. However, *the basic structure of the economy has not changed.* The existence of the second economy (its early spontaneous development and its limited expansion following the official acceptance and encouragement in 1982) supports this view since the duality which it caused to emerge in the economy underscored the inherent contradictions within the socialist sector.[17] Although the 1982 measures no doubt had some positive effects, they exacerbated the existing duality and made it more visible. The constraints on the second economy, however, prevented the dominance of the first economy from being challenged right up till the collapse of the communist regime.

A present, when the state sector is being dismantled and privatization is under way, duality is poised to disappear. The transition from the planned to the fully-fledged market economy has caused the second economy (in its capacity as a quasi-market sector co-existing with the socialist sector) to lose ground. Among the factors indicating this is that the VGMKs – the most important institution of the second economy – were dissolved in conformity with legislation passed in 1989.

The fate of the small companies (including the GMKs) points in the same direction. According to recent case studies and surveys, subcontractors were the first to be abandoned by state firms when the international and domestic market for their products started to contract. The formal status of the GMKs, especially those with weak links to the state enterprises, has either remained the same (unlike the VGMKs, the GMKs were not dissolved), or has been changed into limited liability companies or other private enterprise forms. It remains to be seen whether the majority of small enterprises can survive when their former contractors collapse or undergo radical transformation. The current macro-economic environment[18] does not indicate progress for small enterprises in spite of the efforts of the government.

The expectations of the participants in the second economy, regarding them as the bearers of the needed entrepreneurial spirit and skills and as the proto-type of the new entrepreneurs, could prove to be an illusion in spite of the sporadic examples[19] which support this common view. Although empirical evidence is not yet available and there is not yet a basis for drawing con-clusions, it is reasonable to assume that just as the most valuable assets of state enterprises have already been privatized, so the most precious sector of the human resources (mainly the former workers in VGMKs) has also 'gone private'. This would mean that they are already engaged in private enterprises, the most skilled and qualified presumably employed in foreign owned com-panies. Alternatively, following massive lay-offs in state enterprises, the majority of those who remained in employment were presumably former VGMK members. However, numerous former VGMK members, who were working in state enterprises which produced for the COMECON market and went bankrupt subsequent to the events in 1989, became unemployed, especially the unskilled and those with very specialized skills.

Some of the GMKs are likely not to have been transformed into legal private enterprises, opting to become part of the informal economy, either keeping or changing their original scope of activity; this is due to the high tax burdens imposed on enterprises. That this may be the case is visible from the fact that the share of the informal economy is estimated to have increased from 26 per cent of GDP in 1988 to more than 30 per cent by the early 1990s.[20] Gábor (1992) also maintains that the 'spill-over effect' of the contracting labour market in the state sector constitutes a new kind of duality. The small enterprise sector would rely on cheap labour (released by the giant state firms) and insecure conditions of employment. Features following from this are low capital intensity and attempts to avoid proportionate tax sharing within the small enterprise sector. Wage statistics and other surveys (e.g. the Household Panel) seem to corroborate this. Wage differentials between the state and the private sector, including the small enterprises, are – contrary to commonly held views – smaller than before. However, the significance of these trends still merits further examination, especially due to the problems of gauging private sector activity satisfactorily in terms of statistics.

In order to give a clearer picture of the extent of decreasing employment in the state sector, we will in the following section review the causes of unemployment.

Hungary: The emergence of unemployment

Towards the end of the communist era during the 1980s, when the pressure of the macroeconomic imbalances and the external difficulties mounted, more and more emphasis was placed on the necessity of 'efficient employment', with the aim to abolish overstaffing.[21] It was said that it was the responsibility of the state to ensure full employment, while firms can dismiss people for the sake of their efficiency. This view can be considered as one of the first moves to prepare people for massive lay-offs, mainly from the large numbers of ailing enterprises, from which the state withdrew its subsidies during the late 1980s. Although bankruptcy in a socialist economy was unheard of up till then, several large enterprises were on the verge of collapse.

The emphasis on the state's *responsibility* explains why labour market policy measures were introduced relatively early, before massive joblessness appeared.

One year after the free elections, in 1991, there was, for the first time, a considerable increase in unemployment. The number of unemployed tripled, from 100,526 in January to 380,000 in December, the unemployment rate increasing from 2.1 per cent to seven per cent by the end of the year. The main reason for the decline in employment was the collapse of the COMECON, and especially the Soviet market. At one stroke, Hungary (and with it other former COMECON countries) lost the huge market it had supplied for decades. Although Hungary's reliance on COMECON relations had been reduced since the late 1980s,[22] reflecting a general decay in the COMECON in general, the rapid breakdown in 1991 affected the economy unexpectedly. The fall in employment reflects this. Between January 1991 and January 1992 the number of employees fell by about nine per cent.[23] It is also seen in the decline in the number of employees in traditionally COMECON-oriented industries. For example, in metallurgy and machine building the decline in employment was higher than the average within industry. These branches were two pillars of the heavy industry which had been overdeveloped for military reasons during the period of 'socialist forced industrialization' in the 1950s. Despite their heavy burden on the whole economy, they had not been dismantled due to their 'strategic importance' and COMECON orientation.

Apart from the COMECON collapse and monetary restrictions, there is one other cause of the rising unemployment: the fast and very radical import liberalization, with virtually no protection measures. By 1992 between 94 and 95 per cent of all import restrictions had been liberalized, a move which led to the sudden exposure of the whole Hungarian industry to the competition of the much more advanced Western producers. Despite increasing trade orientation towards the West during the 1980s, Hungarian industry had remained relatively insulated from the world market (which is why many products were unsaleable). It is a question whether such drastic and sudden steps were necessary. According to some views they should have been implemented on a more gradual basis (presumably combined with some protectionist measures) in order to provide the opportunity for the more viable industries to survive. There is no general consensus on the extent to which import liberalization contributed to the decline in employment.

The collapse of the COMECON severely affected the giant state enterprises since most of their production went to the COMECON (Soviet) market. Their production was based on economies of scale, and with the collapse of their huge market they were unable to direct their products to other markets. Among the reasons were the COMECON technical specifications and standards, the lack of an adequate infrastructure (including transport facilities to other markets), and the specific organization of the input-output system created by specialization within the COMECON.

Their internal organizational structure also prevented the large state enterprises from switching to other lines of production.

The transformation process, with all its implications, obviously affects employment. Privatization inevitably results in enterprise restructuring, which in many cases also causes lay-offs. It is still not clear to what extent privatization contributes to changes in the level of employment.[24]

A growing number of small enterprises is generating employment, many of them belonging to the second economy. According to some estimates, their role is increasing to the effect that they engage between 15 and 18 per cent of the labour force, and they have been able to absorb nearly half of the labour released from the 'socialist sector' (Tímár 1992). It is however uncertain whether their capacity to absorb labour is sustainable, given the unfavourable environment in which they operate, including high interest rates, inexperience of the banking sector in financing small enterprise, and poor coordination between small enterprise development agencies.

However, while the output of the Hungarian economy has fallen drastically, employment has not fallen at the same rate.[25] This reflects a decrease in productivity, making the prospects of a recovery within the short run rather gloomy.

The role of foreign capital in the privatization process of East European countries is obviously of great importance due to the scarcity of domestic capital. In the case of Hungary it has already had a significant impact on the transformation process, with foreign capital inflow here the highest within the region to date. This can partly be attributed to the early (1988) introduction of liberal regulations on foreign direct investment, which have since become increasingly generous and, in comparison to other countries in the region, exceptionally liberal. An additional explanation is that the reforms have brought about comparatively advanced market relations in the Hungarian economy.

Liberal regulations brought with them high expectations, including with respect to the potential employment-generating effect of foreign capital. This, however, proved to be an illusion. Not only has less foreign capital come than expected, but its capacity to absorb labour from the 'socialist industry' has proven very limited. Its demand pattern differs greatly from the emerging labour supply.

In some cases foreign capital has been able to contribute to maintaining employment. This especially applies to those joint ventures where the Hungarian firm (for example a former unit of a transformed state enterprise) acts as a sub-contractor, supplying its foreign parent company. It remains to be seen, however, how long this type of cooperation can last. A subcontracting relationship alone, without any other form of cooperation (e.g. research and development), makes the Hungarian part extremely vulnerable to market changes. In this sense such deals create a potential source of further increases in unemployment in the future.

Relating to the collapse of the COMECON and to the growing role of foreign capital, a certain polarization of the labour market can be observed. As a consequence of the former, the ratio of manual to all workers employed in industry is rapidly falling -implying their marginalization – whereas as a consequence of the latter the importance and value of highly qualified specialists (e.g. in electronics) has increased. Demand for this type of worker has increased from the newly established joint ventures. This polarization calls attention to the new educational requirements for a changed labour market.

For the reasons discussed above, the levels of unemployment reached, and in some cases even exceeded, those in the industrialized market countries, especially since 1992. Demographic factors also contributed to the rise in unemployment. The relatively high birth rates at the beginning of the 1970s caused the number of new entrants to the labour market in the early 1990s to exceed those of the preceding years.

Hungary: Labour market policy measures and their financing

Unlike most other East European countries, Hungary introduced labour market measures well in advance of the emergence of mass unemployment, the first being a retraining allowance. This allowance was introduced in 1983 (at a time of full employment) in the wake of a rationalization drive launched by the government. Initially it had only marginal scope and effect, but as unemployment rose it gained ever-growing importance (Hárs, Kóvári and Nagy 1991; Fóti and Illés 1992).

Other measures followed, including job creation subsidies and incentives for employing university graduates; assistance for organizing public works; subsidies for early retirement; assistance to regions facing the highest unemployment; and start-up loans (to promote self-employment). The unemployment benefit system was introduced in 1989.[26] For the administration and implementation of the measures a nationwide labour market institutional network has been set up in the late 1980s.

It is evident that the measures basically followed the models applied in industrialized countries. The main question is not their relevance (as suggested by some; see ILO 1992), but how to adapt them to the specific needs of a society which has not lived with unemployment over the previous four decades. Thus, despite the early introduction of some measures, labour market policy has to face some serious challenges. They include not only psychological factors (implying a high exposure to social tension), but at least three others: (a) the institutional dimension; (b) the time horizon; and (c) financing. The nationwide network of labour centres which has been set up was established within a very brief period under the increasing pressure of rapidly growing unemployment. This entails many problems of coordination between the centre and local labour institutions. However, the most pressing problem seems to be financial, since rapidly growing need is constantly confronted with very limited financial means.

Until the emergence of mass unemployment, financing for the measures was provided by the state budget (before 1988 directly, and from 1988 through the Employment Fund established for this purpose). However, with the rapidly rising numbers out of work, the state budget could no longer sustain the increasing financial burden. In 1991, therefore, under the Employment Act adopted in Parliament, the 'Solidarity Fund' was established in addition to the existing employment fund. It is specifically designed to cover costs of unemployment compensation and has contributors other than the state, with employers and employees also sharing the growing burden.

China: Jumping into the sea

In 1992 and 1993 new expressions have entered the Chinese language, which in a slightly jocular fashion reflect new phenomena in the labour market. One expression is 'jumping into the sea' (*xiahai*), meaning to leave the firm and life-long tenure in the work unit in order to take up a private occupation. 'Jumping into the sea' is a serious matter, for the worker leaves her or his work unit for good, loses the certainty of a basic wage income, forfeits all entitlements to work unit-based social security, housing, subsidies and status. The replacement value of the 'iron rice bowl', in fact, is very high:

basic salary + work related + bonus + perks + status + psychological
allowances well-being

For workers in relatively unattractive jobs in poor work units which have only few perks to offer there is a great incentive to leave. The wage income and the aggregate material and immaterial advantages of the 'iron rice bowl' cannot measure up to the potential high incomes in the 'market economy'. School leavers with high expectations who are allotted lousy jobs are especially likely to seek their fortune in the private sector. These cases are called 'voluntarily jumping into the sea' (*ziji tiao xiahai*). A case like this which is known to the authors is that of a senior middle school graduate who failed the university entrance exam, and was put on the waiting list for job allocation for six months, after which he was assigned work to rent out video tapes on a relatively insecure contract, at a low salary, and with few perks; he registered as an individual entrepreneur renting video tapes, earning a better income. In many recent cases, people in relatively good positions in good work units have been made 'internally redundant', meaning that their post is not any more relevant. These people may be transferred to other work, receive cuts in their bonus and allowances (i.e. the main part of their pay), lose relative status, and come into a poor position in the perks queue. Although they do not lose their job, their basic salary or their basic entitlements, their position in the work unit becomes untenable and unattractive. In these cases, they are 'pushed into the sea' (*beitui xiahai*). One such case is known to the authors, where a man in charge of procurement of production materials in a petro-chemical concern was transferred to other work because the relevant production materials were taken out of the state plan; not willing to take the loss of status and disinclined to move to Shenzhen (while his family was in Beijing), he resigned and started a one-man company brokering trade in production materials, earning a high profit. Some work units in charge of public services are called upon to generate incomes to cover their operating expenses, and are allocated less or no state budget funds (*guojia bokuan*). Such work units are 'jumping into the sea in a boat' (*zuochuan xiahai*).

One thing is obvious from the above: 'jumping into the sea' is dangerous. Families are therefore presently adopting the strategy of 'one family, two systems' (*yijia, liangzhi*),[27] where one spouse works under socialism and the other is engaged in a capitalist endeavour. In this way, basic social security, living space (at preferential rates) and other assets identified with the 'iron rice bowl' form a safety net, while higher 'market' incomes ensure a high living standard. In the cases referred to above, the 'jump into the sea' was only possible because the family could provide a safety net within the state-owned enterprises. The production materials dealer was only able to quit his job because his wife was entitled to suitable accommodation in her work unit, a ministry. The young lad was only able to set up his own video hire shop because he lives with his parents who are pensioners entitled to cheap accommodation and large consumption subsidies. However, in both cases, it is highly probable that the future development will make the advantages of the 'socialist' partner in retaining state employment negligible. These cases give at least anecdotal testimony of fundamental changes in the Chinese labour situation, which we will analyse in more detail below.

China: The rise of the mixed economy

The hard-nosed Chicago School observers of and self-imposed advisors to the Chinese economy believe that China is in a mess caused by the 'mixed economy', and that the only salvation is 'open markets and rational prices to guide resources', which will 'spontaneously generate order'.[28] Due to its mixed nature, the Chinese economy is likely to go 'pfut', 'like the Soviet one before it', 'unless spontaneous forces from below become strong and resolute enough to take over the half reform from the discredited and economically irresolute party and guide it to its only effective and viable modernizing conclusion in a full market system' (Prybyla 1990, 122). Such reveries of Adam Smith's paradise on earth ignore that the ostensible Soviet misery was incurred by imprudent and hasty abandonment of state-controlled institutions before new frameworks had emerged to take their place. The visible hand of the state plan therefore gave way, not to the invisible hand of the market, but to the *manus nigra* of the rackets and mafiosi. Exactly the cure that the unsophisticated followers of Milton Friedman have ordained for

China would have been likely to cause chaos, and certainly not 'spontaneous order'.

The Chinese reforms since 1978 have had the *dual goal* of creating market regulation of the exchange of goods and services *and* of achieving growth. All reform measures should be appraised from these two perspectives. The development of a private economy, hence, was never and is not a goal in itself, but is a measure taken to solve certain long term, strategic problems in the Chinese economy which hindered growth at par with the demographic increase. The mixed economy of the Chinese reforms is the outcome of a state-led and politically controlled transformation of the economy. The targeted, discriminatory manipulation of specific sectors and fields stimulated growth and allowed private and semi-private sections of the economy to emerge and take root.

In the following discussion we will examine the above hypothesis with regard to the most crucial part of the economy, namely the labour 'market'. The pontification of the Chicago school to the effect that the private economy and the market emerged in spite of the state, has its own dynamic opposed to the state, and will fail if the state does not withdraw its interference, does not merit further consideration.

China: Labour policy since 1978

Chinese labour policy, as it developed around the rise to power of Deng Xiaoping in 1978, has mainly been directed at (a) solving an instant capacity crisis in urban industry; (b) increasing productivity per worker; and (c) optimizing the distribution and utilization of labour in production. As all students of command economies know, the Achilles heel of such systems is the irrational use of labour. The methods adopted by the Chinese state did not allow the emergence of an independent labour market, characterized by workers' unions and industrial negotiation structures. Spontaneous attempts in 1980–1981 and later in 1989 to establish a nation-wide independent workers' union were foiled, and no organization similar to Solidarity in Jaruzelski's Poland has emerged.

The methods adopted in China were

(a) the 'employment policy of 'three combinations,' which integrated job introduction by the labour authorities, the voluntary creation of occupation and self-employment under the overall planning and guidance of the state' (Zhu Jiazhen 1992, p. 1);

(b) the policy of 'breaking the iron rice bowl,' i.e. changing the system of life-long tenure into a fixed-term labour contract system and introducing bankruptcy as a way of dealing with enterprises operating at a deficit;

(c) the introduction of independent social, medical, and pension insurance schemes, and the separation of responsibility for social care from enterprise management; and

(d) the autonomization of state-owned enterprises, freeing them from direct state planning.

China: The three combinations

The main, tangible crisis in the labour system that faced the leadership of Deng Xiaoping in 1978 was that the 'rusticated youths' (*xiaxiang shangshan qingnian*) or 'young intellectuals' (*zhishi qingnian*) were to return from the countryside,[29] at the same time as still larger cohorts of urban school leavers were entitled to job allocation in the cities. The state, thus, had the option of (a) expanding urban employment by allocating more workers to the work units; (b) allowing the number of unemployed to grow;[30] (c) funnelling larger numbers through higher education and military service; or (d) finding new types of employment.

Job creation within the urban state sector would be the traditional way of handling the problem. The state would meet its obligation to employ school leavers by adding them to the existing work force. The state had, throughout the 1960s and 1970s, expanded urban employment in response both to the pressure of need for *unskilled* labour, to be recruited in the countryside; and the pressure of urban school leavers[31] and returning sent-down youths with job entitlements.[32] The 'sending down' of school leavers had served as a convenient buffer for the labour allocation system. The absence of this policy led to an increased pressure on the labour bureaus. While the cohorts of new urban school leavers became larger and all school leavers would have to be accommodated in the cities, four million sent-down youths had by 1980 already returned to the cities, and were waiting for jobs, and another one million were entitled to return (*Zhongguo Baike Nianjian* 1981, p. 537). An estimate from 1980 predicted that there would be a need for 37 million new urban jobs in the period 1980–1985 (Ling Hu'an and Sun Zhen 1992, p. 135).

However, the economic wisdom behind the Chinese reforms indicated that the urban enterprises showed low productivity and were riddled with bottlenecks. While the salaries were low (but higher than rural incomes), the investment required to create new jobs in the urban sector was considered to be very high – according to a report reflecting the situation in 1979–1980, 12,000 yuan per worker in heavy industry and 6,200 yuan per worker in light industry (Hua Yinchang 1981, p. 536). Due to the low productivity in the state sector, the returns on the investment (for the state's coffers) were negligible if not negative. A substantial part of the investment was not in productive assets, but in social infrastructure, housing, etc., thus implying a subsidy to urban consumption.

The state was not able to pay for the needed expansion of occupational opportunities and had to turn to different means. It was important to create structures with high productivity, to facilitate investment outside the state budget (and thereby the state plan), and to encourage mass employment outside the orbit of the state plan. The creation of urban job opportunities were realized within the framework of the 'three combinations', decided upon at the National Employment Conference (Quanguo Jiuye Huiyi) in August 1980 (see Zhongguo Baike Nianjian 1981, p. 537, and Ling Hu'an and Sun Zhen 1992, p. 135–139).

China: The individual entrepreneurs

The most thriving and dynamic sector in the urban economy resulting from the 'three combinations' policy was the small-scale private sector, driven by the 'individual entrepreneurs' *(getihu)*. This sector was characterized by (a) low investment; (b) high degree of labour intensity; (c) high turnover, but small profit margins; and (d) complementarity with other sectors, mainly taking up niches. In 1978 there were in all of China 150,000 persons registered as urban individual entrepreneurs, a number which rose to 6.71 millions in 1990 (Ling Hu'an and Sun Zhen 1992, p. 3) and 8.38 millions in 1992 (Statistical Bureau 1993, p. 17). The statistics probably underestimate the size of the individual enterprise sector. It is generally assumed that many *de facto* individual entrepreneurs never take out a licence and are therefore not counted in the statistics. It is evident from interviews that during the 1980s a large number of state employees stopped turning up on their regular job and took employment in the individual sector (losing their bonus, but retaining their basic salary and perks).

While the sector started reluctantly in 1978, basing itself on a residual, neglected urban undergrowth of petty services, and was strongly acclaimed by the National Employment Conference in 1980, it was not until 7 July 1981 that it was publicly regulated in a policy statement by the State Council (Herschkovitz 1985; *Zhongguo Jingji Nianjian* 1982, III, pp. 91–92), juridically affirming it.[33] An important feature was that urban state-owned or collective enterprises could lease, rent or contract specific activities to private entrepreneurs.

The state instructed all relevant trade organs to supply goods and raw materials to the individual sector. The main rule was that goods purchased by individual entrepreneurs on restricted conditions (fixed factory prices and quotas) could only be retailed at prices set by the local price commission. However, all goods that underwent some form of processing could be sold at prices negotiated by the individual entrepreneur and the customer, and goods obtained without quota restrictions could be sold without price restrictions (*ibid.*, p. 91).

In a joint circular, several ministries indicated how small businesses could be given space for shops and workshops etc. The main method was to allow state and collective enterprises to let rooms to them, allowing them to calculate a rent, based on maintenance costs, administration fees, depreciation, taxes and interest (*ibid.*, pp. 90–91).

The interaction between state enterprises and individual entrepreneurs is the crucial point. While one impression has been that jealous bureaucrats and state-owned enterprises, loath to see small enterprises run at a profit, plotted to gag the new sector, a more plausible assumption is that state-owned and the urban collective enterprises saw the individual enterprises as a way to pursue their own interests. The state and urban collective enterprises were – as a part of the reforms – allowed to produce goods outside the state plan, they could retain profits (the profit transfers of the pre-reform command economy had been replaced with enterprise taxation), and they were enabled to invest in and trade with the unplanned economy. While still being tied in with the state plan quotas, and still directing much attention to bureaucratic bargaining for funds, quotas, and production factor allocations, their administrative behaviour changed under the pressure of (using a formulation due to Byrd 1991, pp. 112–119) 'market penetration at enterprise level', pursuing profit maximizing objectives. The profit maximizing behaviour of state enterprises was made possible by the opportunities for investments and earnings outside the state plan. State enterprises would aim at achieving higher incomes from non-plan activities in order to finance the most urgent needs they faced. These needs included improvements in workers' residence conditions and various social benefits to workers, improvements that were long overdue and could not possibly be realized under the state plan regime, the absence of which increasingly caused disciplinary problems and worker protest to arise. Earnings outside the state plan would also be invested in activities *outside* the plan, in order to increase the scope for additional income. Conversely, these non-plan incomes would not be invested in plan fulfilment, and enterprises would cover the need for investment funds to meet plan targets by obtaining bank credits, to which they were entitled under the plan. In as far as meeting the plan targets did not create financial constraints on the profit maximizing objective, the objective of plan fulfilment remained compatible with profit maximization (Byrd 1991, p. 117).

This change in urban enterprise behaviour was only possible in symbiosis with an expanding private sector. On the one hand it was a *conditio sine qua non* that the retailing of extra-plan products, and a large number of similar labour-intensive tasks, could be handed over to flexible management in the private sector. Assets that would otherwise be unused or used irrationally could be hired out. A very interesting suggestion in the regulation on supply of work space for individual enterprises (*Zhongguo Jingji Nianjian* 1982, III, p. 90) was that ground floor space in residential buildings could be purpose-built for hiring out to individual entrepreneurs, and that unused workshops, equipment, etc., could be hired out to create an income. In an environment where the value of an unused or underused asset cannot be established because of the constraints in the planned economy, prices and rents are likely to be fixed below the levels at which they can be set in an expanding market. This gave an enormous boost to the individual enterprises in the initial phase.

The rapid growth of the small scale private economy, therefore, was induced by the growing profit-maximizing behaviour within the state sector. The existence of a dual price structure left a sufficient margin for individual entrepreneurs to operate, and apart from filling niches in the urban service sector, they also supplied a source of profit maximization for state enterprises. Enjoying some preferential treatment from the tax authorities (the regulation issued in 1981 opened the possibility of targeted tax exemptions by local tax authorities), and often being able to profit from provisions of state-owned enterprises through family relations, individual entrepreneurs often fared well.

China: The labour service companies

The labour service companies (*laodong fuwu gongsi*) were introduced in the policy document of the National Employment Conference in 1980 as 'various types of cooperatives which are responsible for their own gains and losses'. Young people awaiting job allocation had spontaneously begun to set up such groups and cooperatives based on their own investment and

> last year [1979] quite a number of state enterprises ... adopted the form of 'collectives run by [companies under the ownership of] the whole people' in order to solve the employment problem of employees' children.[34]

These enterprises were to be treated as 'small urban collective enterprises',[35] and were later termed 'labour service companies' (Ling Hu'an and Sun Zhen 1992, pp. 136–137, 145–147). The Central Committee gave its full support to these measures and even introduced strong preferential treatment to them, including easy access to bank credits, permitting 'mother companies' to extend loans, allow deferred payments, etc. In addition, tax exemptions were introduced for collective enterprises having more than 60 per cent returned sent-down youths among their staff.

The advantages awarded to these labour service companies were, in short, innumerable. Again, the profit-maximizing behaviour of state-owned enterprises which emerged during the first years of the reforms was central to their success. The labour service companies were the very embodiment of extra-plan economic activities within the ambit of the state-owned enterprises. The first profit-maximizing objective was their employment generation: the burden of new entries on the regular payroll could be avoided, and so could the obligation to supply a vast array of services to the staff. The returns from their use of abandoned or underused assets was a gratis income. They could create new market outlets, and were an interesting target for investment in tax-exempted activities. While the 'mother company' skimmed off the cream in the form of rents, depreciation and charges, many labour service companies were able to pay out high wages (equitable shares in the profit), higher than those to be earned in the state sector.

The overall success of the individual sector and the labour service companies in terms of employment can be summarized as follows. While only 1.5 million (or 28 per cent) of the 5.4 million new entrants on the job 'market' in 1978 went to the cooperative and individual sectors, the numbers increased to an average of 2.93 million each year in the period 1980–1985 (Social Statistics Office 1987, p. 110), an average of 2.75 million each year during 1986–1990 (Statistical Bureau 1991, p. 191) and an average of 3.18 million in 1991–1992 (Statistical Bureau 1993, p. 19). For the state this meant that large investments were initiated outside the state budget, and that a substantial burden was taken from the labour administration.

China: Breaking the iron rice bowl

The state cautiously began to change the system of permanent tenure in the state industry in 1981. It was then decided that a work contract system should be set up in experimental areas all over the country before the end of 1983. In 1986, a comprehensive national legislation was introduced, making the contract system compulsory for all new recruits. The contracts could be long-term (more than five years), short term (one to five years) or fixed term. At this time, the whole recruitment system was broken open, and for the first time, enterprises were asked to be active in the recruitment process, appraising the skills of applicants; before, they had received the allocated workers from the labour bureau. A separate regulation introduced procedures for dismissing workers, and rules were introduced for declaring enterprises running in deficit bankrupt. However the labour contract system

> only developed slowly and the proportion of labour contract workers on the total number of employees remained modest. At present [1988/1989] it only constitutes about ten per cent of the employees in Chinese state enterprises. There are at least three causes for this slow development: This system is only applied to newly appointed workers; the enterprises resist it for reasons of costs and prefer short term labourers, or they try

to avoid new appointments because there are already too many workers (Schucher 1989, p. 334).

The main impression at the time was that the introduction of these trappings of autocratic labour management was like building castles in the air. Apart from the odd anecdotal cases of dismissals and enterprise bankruptcies, the legislation seemed to be bypassed. Even dismissals on disciplinary grounds were hardly ever effected. People who did not turn up for work could *de facto* not be fired, and bankruptcies were largely avoided. The main sanction against indolent workers was that the wage system was gradually reformed towards performance-related pay, the centre devolving the responsibility for industrial and commercial enterprises' pay schemes to the companies. This meant that enterprises were able to set inactive workers at a nominal basic wage, a pay which continued to dwindle due to inflation. The state governed this process indirectly by manipulating the quotas for numbers of workers, restricting the total size of the salaries, imposing rules on relating bonus pay to overall enterprise performance, and introducing a bonus tax, which penalized enterprises which paid out too large sums in bonuses. Performance related pay, therefore, made a slow entry into the Chinese firms where the ample supply of labour and the low pressures for achievement frustrated attempts at change. Even the objective of profit maximization was, under such circumstances, *not* directed towards the increase of the workers' individual productivity. Only with the introduction of 'optimized labour groups' (*youhua laodong zuhe*), with which enterprises were encouraged to define work tasks and labour input clearly, was a managerial instrument introduced which had the potential of focusing on individual performance in more than a crude sense, as well as formally creating internal lay-offs. The next step was, in 1992, to introduce enterprise autonomy, by which enterprises were put in a position to decide themselves on the size of their work force. This, for the first time, brought the objective of profit maximization in line with the supervision of the individual worker's performance. It remains unknown what the effects are on the use of labour.

The state was apparently unsuccessful in applying the thumb screw of hard budget constraints to enterprises. Poor enterprises running with a deficit were not normally closed down, but were administratively reformed. The negative employment effect of bankruptcy explains this. The state intervened heavily to reform badly run enterprises, sometimes merging them with other enterprises.

In conclusion, it is possible to discern a substantial effort to increase the productivity of individual workers by introducing managerial measures for reward and punishment. These, however, remained largely ineffective because individual productivity remained irrelevant to the enterprises' profit-maximizing objectives. However, new appointments were on contracts, the wage systems were transformed and the administrative procedures were put in place for a more radical transformation of the labour relations.

China: The establishment of labour and social insurance

The establishment of a social insurance system was aimed at solving the problem that social security was mainly the responsibility of the individual enterprises, which were obliged to budget for pension funds, health funds, etc. Under the system of central planning this system functioned quite well, but the reforms made it helplessly inadequate. The government made it clear that a social insurance system outside the enterprises was essential. The autonomy of enterprises meant that the burden of social care would have to be taken away from production. A level playing field of competition should not be obstructed by unequal obligations. Of specific importance was the fact that state-owned enterprises had comprehensive social security schemes, while individual entrepreneurs and rural small-scale enterprises did not have such expenses, while different rules applied to urban collectives. In order to give the employees maximum confidence, it was also considered important that such a system could guard against the consequences of bankruptcy.

China in 1986 introduced a regulation on unemployment insurance.[36] The premium was one per cent of the total wage bill of the enterprise, and the size of the benefit would vary, depending on the seniority and the length of unemployment, ranging between 50 and 75 per cent of the average standard wage during the preceding two years. The duration was restricted to 24 months. The standard wage (*biaozhun gongzi*) is normally only a minor part of the salary, since bonuses and allowances normally constitute more than 50 per cent. During the first years of operation, 380,000 enterprises with a total of 65 million employees participated, and between 1986 and 1990 200,000 persons received unemployment and sickness benefit. In addition to this, the labour administration established 750 training centres and 430 self-aid production centres in order to facilitate reemployment. More than 140,000 unemployed persons were subsequently reemployed.

Similar schemes for medical insurance and pensions are operating locally, and the People's Insurance Company of China also extends policies to cover social and medical emergencies.

These social security schemes have not yet had to stand the test. However, they are not aimed at full cover for the loss of occupation, but are only geared to avert fundamental hardship. Within the Chinese culture there is a greater tendency to rely on relatives for bridging over periods of difficulty and in old age, and so the low rates of benefits should be seen as a supplement to a traditional solidarity. The restructuring of the economy and the transformation of the labour system, therefore, is also based on recourse to people's own savings.

China: Enterprise autonomization

The Fourteenth National Congress of the Chinese Communist Party, convening in October 1992, announced the introduction of enterprise autonomy. State-owned enterprises were made independent of all plan restrictions, and were given the autonomy to decide over work force and salaries, sign contracts with foreign companies, etc. This enterprise autonomy has had a certain impact on the labour market situation.

In order to allow for more flexible ways of collecting capital for investment, various forms of share holding were also instituted in 1992, based on tested structures which had been introduced in the 1980s. These also included sale of shares in enterprises to workers and the general public.

State enterprise autonomization can take place in an environment where a large part of the working population has already sought employment outside the frameworks of the state enterprises, and where the private and the collective sectors were given preferential treatment and were directly supported by the economic behaviour of the state enterprises during a period of almost a decade.

We can, behind the maze of complex developments, discern some fundamental patterns:

(a) The state initiated the process of reform by manipulating existing institutional barriers in the economy; the main one was the introduction of a dual distribution of goods (plan and non-plan) for actors positioned differently in the economic system;

(b) Privatization of the economy did not take place as a rapid transfer of authority over state assets to new owners, but was characterized by giving opportunities to individuals to use assets outside the plan, so as to gradually develop a private economy. The autonomization of state enterprises was preceded by comprehensive reform efforts, by which they were internally strengthened and given administrative structures that would facilitate profit-oriented behaviour in a market economy. One could say that the lagging behind of state-owned enterprise favoured the individual and collective economy, which made the market outgrow the plan. The state enterprises were given the opportunity to share in this market after a long, protracted reform.

CONCLUSIONS

It is possible to identify a set of very dissimilar outcomes of superficially comparable policy measures. Complex variables like Hungary's strong exposure to COMECON and the West and China's demographic profile have to a large extent framed the policies. Both Hungary and China encouraged the emergence of small enterprises, but the motives differed. In Hungary the early VGMKs responded to a problem of low productivity, while the Chinese *getihus* and the labour service enterprises were mainly aimed at creating employment. In Hungary, excess labour supply was only occasionally a concern and did not generally influence nation-wide policies.

In a wider sense, one could say that Hungary, like most other Eastern European countries, suffered from *labour shortage*, i.e. insufficient supply of workers for the socialist firms' 'perpetual hunger for resources', the rationales for which were the soft budget constraints and the political rewards to enterprise management for expansion. Limited availability of investment resources caused a labour-intensive strategy to be chosen. The lack of comprehensive industrial infrastructure may be an additional reason for this situation. The lack of or the insufficient development of a background industry caused the socialist firms to seek vertical integration in order to make up for the lack of the background industry *internally*.

In China, the situation was dissimilar. There was a surplus of labour and a substantial overstaffing of state enterprises. This led to a preference for labour-intensive expansion, and like in Hungary state-owned industry tended to be 'large and comprehensive' (*da er quan*).

These inadequacies of the existing state sectors in Hungary and China set the parameters for the development of small enterprises in these countries.

The fact that small enterprises could operate as labour-intensive or capital-intensive additions to urban enterprise under the totally segmented labour market conditions in China helped them to gain a foothold. While, on the one hand, they were subjected to hard – very hard – budget constraints, they were on the other hand given a competitive advantage, strongly supported by their complementarity to state enterprises.

In Hungary, the VGMKs were mainly structured *within* the socialist firms in order to solve the productivity problem. While small enterprises also emerged and took root, they depended strongly on the state sector, and have, generally, suffered strong competition from them.

Similarly, the autonomization of Chinese enterprises is taking place at a slower pace, seconded by the building up of a rudimentary labour insurance system with relatively low benefit levels, and the institution of internal measures for individual labour productivity. This is likely to cause an increasing unemployment rate, but at a much slower pace than in Hungary where the shock therapy resulted from the sudden withdrawal of a major market and the abrupt exposure to a technologically superior and more cost-effective western economy.

In contrast to China, Hungary initiated a social and labour policy relatively early, which was sufficiently complex for the introduction of a market economy. The labour market policy gradually took root in the 1980s, and it expanded when unemployment emerged at the end of the 1980s.

The lack of a coherent labour *market* policy in China is contrasted with the fact that the Chinese authorities seem to have moved gradually towards a situation where the unavoidable unemployment is minimized. The main factors are the presence of an active, self-investing private sector that has the capacity to absorb a large work force, and the placing of the financial load of unemployment benefit on enterprises – who pay a small percentage of the total basic salary sum as a premium – and on families – who have to shoulder short-falls of (depending on local conditions) between 50 and 90 per cent of the income of a redundant family member, or the total lack of income from unemployed school leavers. The pull factor of non-state enterprise has gained in importance during the 1980s for those directly exposed to unemployment. Price inflation has also hit workers in state-owned enterprises, adding to the pull of non-state enterprises where higher incomes can be expected.

With enterprise autonomization and the gradual inclusion of individual productivity in the profit maximizing objectives of enterprises, the push factor out of state enterprises is likely to be intensified. In Hungary, the process was much faster and more radical, not giving adequate time for reorganization of enterprises. The push-factor out of the 'socialist sector' was therefore strong, while at the same time the 'second economy' sector faced difficulties. The situation in Hungary, therefore, necessitated a more rapid expansion of the public provisions of an unemployment benefit system, adopting a structure similar to that in Western Europe.

Such structural similarities and differences between these two 'economies in transition' give a striking picture of the diverging conditions of development in the former command economies.

The wider question that can be asked is whether the economy can be trans-formed into a real market economy under a one-party system. It is not possible to address this question here in a meaningful way. It bears noting that the Chinese reforms have been successful in solving or reducing some of the problems which faced China at the outset of the reforms; this success can partly be credited to the fact that the Chinese Communist Party was in control of the process. So far, however, there has not emerged a fully fledged market economy in China. Hungary, having abandoned communism altogether, has chosen a different route towards the market economy and is presently exposed to difficulties of unemployment and declining external trade due partly to exogenous factors. The nature of transition from the public to the private in these two nations is dissimilar and has different effects.

The systemic dissimilarity of the two countries, and their difference rather than their comparability, are evident at the empirical level. However, the *insti-tutions of change* which we set out to examine at the more abstract level give us substantial new insights when looked at through the prism of empirical comparison of the two countries. A problem hardly addressed in the theory of labour institutions (see for example Gerry Rodgers' contribution to this volume) is how fundamental, rapid changes in the political and economic environment trigger new roles for existing labour institutions. During the last few decades, and with particular intensity since 1989, the massive upheaval in the former socialist world has created new scenarios for labour.

In stable institutional systems, change is gradual and the causation of change is *internal* to the institutional system, which mediates outside pressures. The role of institutions in facilitating the operation of the economy and minimizing transaction costs is analytically helpful in contexts where the economic system is assumed to have achieved a high degree of stability. Neo-classical explanatory models are not adequate for understanding the situation in reform economies, and applying them only yields partial and skewed inter-pretations. Veblen's view of an 'open-ended process of cumulative causation in institutional change' (using Gerry Rodgers' formulation in Chapter 1) offers a more credible perspective from which we may view the institutions of change, which also captures the processes in transforming socialist economies.

The dominant role of the state, which through regulatory means and manipulations of divisions in the economy alters fundamental economic insti-tutions (ownership system, management structures, price structures, distribu-tion of production factors, etc.), continues and is gradually seconded by various new formal and informal structures governing the use of labour. The simultaneous existence of 'old' and 'new' forms of ownership/management during transition sparks off a complex re-segmentation of the labour market, which is highly volatile and responds rapidly and directly to external factors. This dualism generates economic expansion, e.g. the VGMKs in Hungary and the individual enterprises in China which epitomized the cleavage between state and private economy. The expansion of a successful private sector in turn erodes the foundation of the state sector and introduces a new profit maximization objective into the state enterprises' calculus, which provokes further state regulation.

The main difference between China's and Hungary's labour situation is that the COMECON market fell away for Hungary, while China (starting from economic autarky) gradually widened international economic cooperation. The external shock to the Hungarian economy caused the effects on the labour market in terms of unemployment to emerge more rapidly and with more force than in China. The similarity between the two systems is that reform of the economy was state-led and depended on direct intervention. Privatization emerged as an outcome of institutional change and became a part of it.

The perspectives for the future are perplexing. The most important aspects are concerned with (a) social and labour market insurance and (b) workers' safety, dignity and welfare, which will become increasingly important as the structures of the labour market evolve. Some pertinent trends can be mentioned: the Hungarian labour market is likely be increasingly inspired by structures in the European Union, while the Chinese labour market insurance and other such structures will for a long time to come be selective, optional, and informed by the state's reluctance to commit large funds to unemployment benefits. The Chinese trade unions, as they exist, are insufficient to represent worker interests, and the new sectors of the Chinese labour market do not fall within their remit. Workers' safety and dignity is at stake in many new private enterprises, which function under what some observers have termed 'slave-like conditions', dirty, dangerous sweat-shops with migrant workers working in overlong shifts, for minimal wages and without spare time. It is an open question how the Chinese state will cope with these aspects of transition, and how the workers in such enterprises will be able to organize themselves. Independent trade unions are politically unacceptable to the leadership, and the private enterprises are *de facto* outside the regulatory reach of the government. These problems do not exist in Hungary to such an extent, but even here, the future evolution of trade unions and their function in the labour market must be closely watched.

NOTES

1. Respectively Government Department, The Manchester University and Institute for World Economics, The Hungarian Academy of Sciences, Budapest.
2. The term 'institution' in this paper signifies any regulatory mechanisms, measures, structures, procedures and physical entities established or utilized in order to influence or dominate the economic activities of the nation.
3. The reformers in China discussed the use of the Hungarian model during the early years of the reform, but found that it could not be used as a blueprint. However, approaches and ideas in the Chinese reform process are coloured by inspiration from the Hungarian model.
4. The term 'work unit' (*gongzuo danwei*) signifies any work place, e. g. factory, school, ministry or other administratively circumscribed entity. Work units may be subdivided in workshops, offices, departments etc, and are subordinated to *xitongs* (literally: systems, signifying ministries or other nationwide organizational structures); *danweis* may be shared by several *xitongs*. The term is mainly use to describe entities belonging to the state and the collective sectors. The work unit includes employees' housing, their social and political organization, as well as a wider range of services for the employees. See Hebel (1990), Lu Feng (1993), and Walder (1988) for comprehensive analyses.
5. We use the terms 'first' and 'second economy' to denote the state-dominated public owner-ship sector and the emerging private and semi-private sectors in Hungary. As D. Stark said, defining the second economy, 'legality as such is not a dimension' (for detailed explanation, see Stark 1989, 137–138).
6. The terms of trade deteriorated, especially vis-à-vis the western markets; this necessitated increased commitments to export to these markets, both in terms of volume and increased demands for quality improvements.
7. This effort failed, basically because decentralization was imposed on an unchanged

industrial structure. The newly independent units – big trusts and large enterprises – were cut off from their earlier vitally important cooperation links, and so became unviable.

8. Despite this, even the legalized second economy had some functions of an illegal nature, stemming from the dominance and more favourable position of the state sector (see details in Gábor and Galasi 1985).

9. In his empirical study Stark (1989) found that hourly earnings in the partnerships were usually two to two and a half times higher than earnings during regular hours, but it was not unusual to find participants who made four times the average of industrial hourly wage rates.

10. The enterprise paid an entrepreneurial fee to the VGMK which was not charged against the wage fund, but was regarded as a cost like that paid to any other unit of the economy for goods or services. This point is important since payments from wage funds were burdened by tax levies in order to prevent wage inflation.

11. In this respect, VGMKs could be regarded as an extension of working hours.

12. Stark (1989) has indicated that this was the case.

13. Under the pressure of mounting external imbalances and foreign exchange shortages, especially since the second half of the 1980s, the central authorities gradually withdrew subsidies for exports to COMECON countries, while they used soft loans to encourage enterprises to export to western markets.

14. See Laky (1984). The popularity of VGMKs is also evident from estimates (Sziráczki 1989) that one in ten of all manual workers in the industry were involved in VGMKs in 1985, and that 60 per cent of all industrial enterprises has such subcontracting arrangements.

15. Estimates (Gábor 1989) indicate that by the late 1980s approximately 75 per cent of households were involved in the second economy.

16. There existed a view among reform economists and party officials that the second economy would suffice to reform the economy.

17. The small internal market, and the lack of significant energy reserves and of industrial raw materials caused Hungary to be, from the outset, conspicuously inappropriate for the Soviet model of industrialization.

18. The most adverse features of which are: high tax burdens, drastic import liberalization measures, high interest rates, high inflation, contracting domestic and foreign demand, the collapse of the COMECON, and economic recession in all trading partner countries.

19. One example is that one of the most successful and renowned entrepreneurs, previously a member of a GMK, became the president of the National Federation of Entrepreneurs.

20. Lackó (1992) has substantiated this with an analysis based on cash outflow.

21. This implicitly raised the issue of potential lay-offs, but at the time the possibility of unemployment was never discussed openly.

22. Trade figures show this. While, for example in 1989, the COMECON share in the total trade turnover of Bulgaria, Czechoslovakia and the German Democratic Republic exceeded 60 per cent, this figure was only around 50 per cent for Hungary (*UN Monthly Bulletin of Statistics*, July 1990, pp. 238–239).

23. According to preliminary estimates, between January 1992 and January 1993, employment declined by approximately seven per cent (government data, Central Statistical Office, 1992).

24. In many cases massive lay-offs precede privatization. This fact certainly adds to the problems of measuring the employment effects of privatization.

25. Figures from industry give a particularly clear indication of this: For example, between 1989 and 1990, output fell by 9.2 per cent, while employment only sank by 5.5 per cent (government data).

26. The unemployment benefit system superseded earlier compensation measures, which were not termed unemployment aid because the existence of unemployment was not admitted. See details in Hárs, Kóvári and Nagy (1991).

27. A pun on the People's Republic's Taiwan policy, stating that China is 'one country, two systems' (*yiguo liangzhi*), i.e. that socialism and capitalism can co-exist in one nation state.

28. See 'Editor's Preface' to Dorn and Wang (1990, xiii).

29. At the Third Plenum of the Eleventh Central Committee of the CCP in December 1978 it was decided that the rusticated youths should be allowed to return to the cities. Sending young school leavers to the countryside had been a policy from the early 1960s, which reduced the

pressure on urban employment. This policy had been regarded with much resentment among peasants and urbanites, caused widespread misery in families, and became associated with the wrongs of the Cultural Revolution. According to official statistics, about 15 million people had been involved in the scheme from its inception in 1962 until 1978.

30. The unemployed would be those people entitled to job allocation through the labour bureaux, whose file was not passed on to an employing work unit. This notion is referred to as 'persons/youths awaiting job allocation' (*daiye renshi/qingnian*).

31. The policy of sending school leavers to the countryside did not apply to children whose elder sibling was in army service, or children of revolutionary martyrs or of families in hardship.

32. About ten million sent-down youths returned gradually in the years before 1978 and were normally entitled to job allocation on return.

33. The 1978 Constitution allowed the small scale private enterprises to exist, but they had not been formally regulated. As a response to the legalization in 1978, the number of registered individual entrepreneurs increased from 150,000 to 320,000 (Ling Hu'an and Sun Zhen 1992, p. 138).

34. As one of the measures to solve the pressure on the labour administration, in 1978 the labour bureau made state-owned enterprises responsible for solving the employment problems of the sons and daughters of their employees, at the same time as allowing 'inheritance' of employment (*dingti*), if the parent took early retirement (*dingti* was abolished in 1983).

35. Small urban collectives (*xiao jiti qiye*) formed a residual type of small scale enterprise, mainly run by neighbourhood committees. In contrast to 'large collective enterprises' (*da jiti qiye*), they were not governed by the state plan, and normally only performed community-based services. Allowing this category to be used, the Central Committee indicated that the new small enterprises should be addressed with much flexibility and were not subject to the state plan.

36. The term used was '*daiye baoxian*', literally meaning an insurance against 'waiting for assignment of employment'. The Chinese do not accept the term 'unemployment' to describe the lack of employment in China.

REFERENCES

Byrd, William A., 1991. *The market mechanism and economic reforms in China*. Armonk, M. E. Sharpe.

Dorn, James A. and Wang Xi (eds.), 1990. *Economic reform in China. Problems and prospects*. Chicago, The University of Chicago Press.

Fóti, János and Sandor Illés, 1992. *A munkanélküliség demográfiai vonatkozásai* (Demographic aspects of unemployment), in *A Népességtudomanyi Kutató Intézet kutatási jelentései 43. sz.* (Research Report Series No. 43, Demographic Research Institute). Budapest.

Fóti, Klara, 1993. *Lessons for industrial restructuring: Experiences of some Hungarian enterprises*, Institute of Development Studies, Discussion Paper No. 322. Brighton, University of Sussex.

Gábor R., István, 1986. 'Reformok, második gazdaság 'allamesocializmus'' (Reforms, second economy, 'state socialism'). Budapest, Valóság, 7.

Gábor R., István, 1989. 'Main issues and major trends of government employment and wage policy', in Sziráczki, Gy. and T. Hórvath (eds.), *Flexibility and rigidity in the labour market in Hungary*. Research Series No. 90. Geneva, International Institute for Labour Studies.

Gábor R., István, 1992. 'A második gazdaság ma – az átalakulás kérdôjelei' (The second economy today – question-marks of the transformation). Budapest, Körgazdasági Szemle, 10.

Gábor R., István and Péter Galasi, 1985. 'Második gazdaság: Lehetôségek és korlátok – Tésisek' (The second economy: Possibilities and limits – Thesis). Budapest, Mozgó Világ, 1.

Hárs, Ágnes, György Kóvári and Gyula Nagy, 1991. 'Hungary faces unemployment', *International Labour Review*, vol. 130.

Hebel, Jutta, 1990. 'Der Betrieb als kleine Gesellschaft. Die Bedeutung des chinesischen Betriebstyps im Prozeß der Reform', (The enterprise as a small society. The significance of the Chinese type of enterprise in the reform process). In *Soziale Welt*, No. 2, pp. 222–242.

Hua Yinchang, 1981. 'Jiuye jiegou' (The employment system). In Ma Hong and Sun Shangqing, *Zhongguo jingji jiegou wenti yanjiu* (Studies of issues in the Chinese economic system). Beijing, Renmin Chubanshe, vol. 2, pp. 526–542.

ILO, 1992. *Economic transformation and employment in Hungary. Report of a study mission, December 1991*. Geneva, International Labour Office.

Kornai, János, 1989. 'The Hungarian reform process: Visions, hopes, reality', in Nee, Victor and David Stark (eds.), *Remaking the economic institutions of socialism – China and Eastern Europe*. Stanford, Calif., Stanford University Press.

Kornai, János, 1992. 'Még egyszer a piaci szocializmusról' (Once again on market socialism). Budapest, Körgazdasági Szemle, 9.

Kôvári, György and György Sziráczki, 1985. 'Túlmunka – vállalkozásban' (Overtime – in enterprises). Budapest, Mozgó Világ, 1.

Lackó, Mária, 1992. 'Az illegális gazdaság aránya 1970 és 1989 között (Share of the informal economy between 1970 and 1989). Budapest, Közgazdasági Szemle, September.

Laky, Teréz, 1984. 'Mítoszok és valóság' (Myths and reality). Budapest, Valóság, 1.

Ling Hu'an and Sun Zhen (eds.), 1992. *Laodong gongzi tizhi gaige juan* (Labour and wage system reform volume), in the series Ma Hong et al. (eds.), *Zhongguo Gaige Quanshu, 1978–1991* (Thesaurus of Chinese reforms, 1978–1991). Dalian, Dalian Chubanshe.

Lu Feng, 1993. 'The origins and formation of the Unit (Danwei) System', in *Chinese Sociology and Anthropology*, vol. 25, no. 3.

Munkaerópiaci helyzetkép (Munkaerópiaci Információk, havi jelentés) 1992 április, július, szeptember, novemner. Országos Munkaügi Központ (Labour market situation, monthly report, published by the National Labour Centre).

Munkaerófelmérés, 1992 elsó negyedév KSH. Budapest (Labour Force Survey, first quarter of 1992, Central Statistical Office, Budapest).

Prybyla, Jan S, 1990. 'Economic reform of socialism: The Dengist course in China', in *The Annals of the American Academy of Political and Social Science*, vol. 507, January.

Schucher, Günther, 1989. 'Überschüssig – Aussortiert – Arbeitslos? Zur Reform der Arbeitsorganisation in der VR China' (Redundant – singled out – unemployed? On the reform of the labour organization in the PRC), in *Internationales Asienforum*, vol. 20, no. 3–4, pp. 325–347.

Social Statistics Office, State Statistical Bureau, 1987. *Zhongguo laodong gongzi tongji ziliao, 1949–1985* (Statistical material on Chinese labour and wages, 1949–1985). Beijing, Zhongguo Tongji Chubanshe.

Standing, Guy, 1993. *Labour market developments in Eastern and Central Europe*, Policy Papers No. 1. Budapest, ILO Central and Eastern European Team.

Stark, David, 1989. 'Coexisting organizational forms in Hungary's emerging mixed economy', in Nee, Victor and David Stark (eds.), *Remaking the economic institutions of socialism – China and Eastern Europe*. Stanford, Calif., Stanford University Press.

Stark, David and Victor Nee, 1989. 'Toward an institutional analysis of state socialism', in Nee, Victor and David Stark (eds.), *Remaking the economic institutions of socialism – China and Eastern Europe*. Stanford, Calif., Stanford University Press.

Statistical Bureau, 1991. '*Qiwu' shiqi guomin jingji he shehui fazhan gaikuang* (Outline of the development of the national economy and society in the seventh Five Year Plan period). Beijing, Zhongguo Tongji Chubanshe.

Statistical Bureau, 1993. *Zhongguo tongji zhaiyao* (A statistical survey of China). Beijing, Zhongguo Tongji Chubanshe.

Sziráczki, György, 1989. 'Changes in the labour market and employment policy (1973–1987)', in *Flexibility and rigidity in the labour market in Hungary*, Research Series No. 90. Geneva, International Institute for Labour Studies.

Tímár, János, 1992. 'Munkanélküliseg, foglalkoztatáspolitika' (Unemployment, employment policy). In *A világgazdaság és a magyar gazdaság kilátásai 1992 szen. Knjunktúrajelentés, 1992/3*. (Prospects of the world economy and the Hungarian economy – Report on market conditions 1992/3). Kopint-Datorg.

Walder, Andrew G, 1988. *Communist neo-traditionalism. Work and authority in Chinese industry*. Berkeley, University of California Press.

Zhongguo Baike Nianjian 1981. Beijing, Shanghai, Zhongguo Dabaike Quanshu Chubanshe.
Zhongguo Jingji Nianjian 1982. Beijing, Jingji Guanli Zazhi She.
Zhu Jiazhen, 1992. 'Jiwang kailai shenhua gaige' (Continue the great cause, forging ahead into the future, while deepening the reform) in Ling Hu'an and Sun Zhen (1992), pp. 1–17.

EADI is 20 years old

The European Association of Development Research and Training Institutes (EADI) started its activities in 1975.

In fact, the decision to create the Association was taken in Ghent, and a founding conference took place in 1974 for this purpose; but the constitution was adopted only a year later, in Linz. The theme of the first general conference was *A New International Order: Economic, Social and Political Implications.* From then on, conferences were held every three years, in Milan, Budapest, Madrid, Amsterdam, Oslo and Berlin.

Quite a number of these venues, as well as the years the meetings took place and the themes chosen, symbolically characterise the vicissitudes of very recent European history and the changing orientations of development co-operation. As early as 1981 in Budapest, reflection was made on the nascent opening of Eastern Europe. Later, in 1987 in Amsterdam, participants dealt with the initial evolution towards globalisation and the problems that it created for the welfare of people: the theme was *Managing the World Economy or Reshaping World Society?*

In those years, much attention was dedicated to the theme of environmental degradation, and because of this the relation between development and environment was thoroughly discussed during the Oslo conference in 1990. The theme of the conference also concerned *Changes in Europe* as the Berlin Wall had just come down. But this major event and its consequences were thoroughly examined three years later, in 1993, at the Berlin conference. It was also at that time that Eastern European colleagues substantially increased their participation in EADI and that attention started shifting slightly from the problems of the South to those of the East. In relation to the profound changes taking place the world over, the next conference, which will be held in Vienna in 1996, will focus on *Globalisation, Competitiveness and Human Security.*

Entering its 21st year, EADI has now come of age, and has proved that it was indeed the missing link between development researches, decision-makers, and aid agencies in Europe, as well as international organisations, NGOs and colleagues in the South. With 220 institutional members and more than 150 individual members, EADI's prestige and reputation is increasing every year. EADI was the missing link 20 years ago; it is now an essential link in development studies and training.

EADI BOOK SERIES

For Product Safety Concerns and Information please contact our EU
representative GPSR@taylorandfrancis.com
Taylor & Francis Verlag GmbH, Kaufingerstraße 24, 80331 München, Germany

www.ingramcontent.com/pod-product-compliance
Ingram Content Group UK Ltd.
Pitfield, Milton Keynes, MK11 3LW, UK
UKHW042201240425
457818UK00011B/329